POISONED IVY

POISONED IVY

Lesbian and Gay Academics
Confronting Homophobia

TONI A. H. McNARON

TEMPLE UNIVERSITY PRESS
PHILADELPHIA

Temple University Press, Philadelphia 19122

Published 1997

Printed in the United States of America

⊗ The paper used in this publication meets the requirements of the
American National Standard for Information Sciences—Permanence of
Paper for Printed Library Materials, ANSI Z39.48-1984

Text design by Cheryl Carrington

Library of Congress Cataloging-in-Publication Data
McNaron, Toni A. H.
    Poisoned ivy : lesbian and gay academics confronting homophobia
    / Toni A. McNaron.
        p. cm.
    Includes bibliographical references (p.   ) and index.
    ISBN 1-56639-487-2 (cloth : alk. paper). — ISBN 1-56639-488-0
(paper : alk. paper)
        1. Homophobia in higher education—United States—History—20th
century.   2. Gay college teachers—United States—Attitudes.
3. Lesbian college teachers—United States—Attitudes.
4. Educational surveys—United States.   I. Title.
LC212.862.M35 1997
378.1'2'08'664—dc20   96-35334

For Susan
with special love and gratitude

Contents

Preface

When I began discussing plans for my sabbatical research project, a colleague and friend of many years suggested that I write what no one else could: the story of my 30 years working as a lesbian at the University of Minnesota. At first this seemed outlandish, since I was planning to compete for a coveted salary augmentation that makes sabbaticals possible. But the more I thought about her suggestion, the more excited I became. And I had to admit, my initial reluctance came from deeply ingrained homophobic habits which I have consciously abandoned but may never completely escape.

The solipcism of the design, however, prompted me to think more broadly about the project. Why not tap into the countless "unique" stories that I knew belonged to other lesbian and gay academics? I decided to distribute a questionnaire as widely as possible, focusing on people with at least 15 years experience in the profession. The long time frame was necessary because I wanted to focus on the presence or absence of change in faculty and institutions. I would canvas gay men as well as lesbians, because in a workplace context it would be worthwhile to find out if gender made any difference in how we saw ourselves or how we were seen by colleagues and superiors. Once the results were in, I would look for similarities and differences among us and design a book that would tell our composite story.

Goodwill for this project was immediately forthcoming. In the early stages, a colleague and philosophy scholar replied to my query for likely participants by sending two single-spaced pages filled with names and addresses. People I did not know wrote via e-mail to challenge my omission of bisexuals or to ponder the problem of approaching closeted colleagues without disclosing identities that were kept carefully insulated from public scrutiny. Faculty at Canadian universities wondered if I might want an international component in the study.

Some faculty just beginning careers were disappointed that they were excluded from the study; a few volunteered help even though they themselves were not qualified to complete a questionnaire. One such person, who received my request for names of faculty who might qualify, said he realized that by not being out as an undergraduate at a prestigious eastern university, he was disconnected from potentially helpful faculty. Thinking about my request had forced him to recognize just how homophobic that campus had been during his illustrious student career.

A colleague who read an early segment of the manuscript asked whether I saw my book as a report of what I had learned from the slightly more than 300 questionnaires or as a narrative of my own experience enhanced by what I had found out. My inability to answer neatly suggests that I see my work as being both a report and a narrative. Sometimes I am speaking from my own story and sometimes from the stories of respondents. Always I am aware of accounts that are not here because their authors cannot offer them.

Key Terms Defined

Before launching into the body of this study, I want to define two key terms that figure throughout my argument: *homophobia* and *heterosexism*. By *homophobia,* I mean an individual response of fear or hatred toward lesbian or gay people based on personal insecurities and cultural conditioning. These feelings exist most often in an unexplored emotional vacuum, buttressed my minimal personal knowledge of or contact with lesbian and gay history, culture, or daily life. *Heterosexism* refers to an entrenched system of moral or religious beliefs, social attitudes, and legal and economic politics that offer privileges to heterosexuality over all other forms of sexual expression or reality. One of the clearest discussions of heterosexism is in Adrienne Rich's germinal essay, "Compulsory Heterosexuality and Lesbian Existence," first published in 1980 (Rich, 1980). Distinguishing between the heterosexual practice and the institution of heterosexuality, she argues that our culture views everyone as heterosexual or "single," a failed version of heterosexual. Furthermore, because all major social and cultural institutions are similarly myopic, otherwise intelligent and sensitive people remain ignorant of the amazing range and variety of human behavior while criticizing and often persecuting the men and women in their midst who claim alternative sexual identities.

Overcoming homophobia is possible when an individual decides to change his or her automatic responses to lesbians or gays. Heterosexism, because it is institutionalized, is much less amenable to change, requiring concerted effort on the part of leaders in virtually every arena of politics, religion, and culture.

A Study Preview

Between my arrival at the University of Minnesota in 1964 and 1992, when the English Department hired a gay man with impeccable credentials who lobbied the chair to find a way to hire his partner (with equally impeccable credentials), the picture at the University of Minnesota was dismal and frightening. No other lesbians joined me in the department. Two "single" men, who seemed to my heterosexual friends and me to be gay, are now dead. One, hired the same year I was, drove off into a late November snowstorm after having secured his first driver's license only weeks before and over strenuous objections from friends. Somewhere between Minneapolis and Chicago, he lost control of his car, slammed into a culvert, and was killed on the spot. The other man, a severely inward person, was found after having lain dead for several days on his apartment floor from "mysterious causes." When he did not report for classes, the department sent someone over to his building, since he was too frightened of being "found out" even to list a telephone number with the secretary.

As I listen in 1995 as colleagues sing the praises of and vote overwhelmingly to grant tenure to the two openly partnered gay men, I often think of those two early colleagues. In each case, I had tried in my own coded and halting fashion to befriend them. One or two lunches with the man hired with me were punctuated by long pauses during which we failed to say the most important things. A single invitation to the other man to come by for a drink yielded an awkward hour that neither of us had any desire to repeat.

In sharp contrast, the newly hired gay couple joyously hosted my partner and me for a homemade Indian meal where all of us were openly affectionate and where the truth of our lives was in the foreground of the evening. I felt indelible change during a tour of the couple's charming new home. We were ushered into one of two second-floor bedrooms, and our host said matter-of-factly, "This is our room," not even accenting "our." Suddenly I was in my first apartment in Minneapolis where my partner and I maintained two fully furnished bedrooms, only one of which was slept in until our relationship began to disintegrate. The few times we opened our door to guests, my partner proclaimed stiffly, "This is Toni's room, and this is mine." No one was fooled by our lie, but the charade pushed us ever further into our already dangerously deep closet.

Much has been gained by individual gay and lesbian academics, but much remains to be accomplished at an institutional level before more of us are able to bring our intimate lives into the workplace. Meanwhile, a profound ambiguity lies at the heart of trying to teach and conduct research as women and men whose sexual identities fall outside the academy's parameters of acceptability. I can only hope that what follows will give energy and encouragement to those determined to enlarge such parameters or perhaps even to redraw the map of the territory.

Acknowledgments

This book would not exist without the generosity of the 304 lesbian and gay faculty across the country who completed questionnaires and provided telephone and electronic mail follow-up narratives for inclusion in its pages. I thank them individually and as a group. Another pivotal person in this book's timely completion is Carolyn Law, my research assistant. Her expertise with the Internet, coupled with her superb organizational skills and calm encouragement, contributed greatly to my work.

I thank the Graduate School of the University of Minnesota for a Grant-in-Aid-of-Research, which allowed me to employ a research assistant and to complete the several mailings involved in this project. In the research process, I received essential help from Elisabeth Palmer at the University of Minnesota's Center for Urban and Regional Affairs. She taught my research assistant to enter data on our respondents and answered SOS calls months after providing the initial instruction, assuring us that such help was not extraordinary. I know otherwise.

My friend and colleague in the Law School at the University of Minnesota, Mary Louise Fellows, volunteered to read the first draft of the first two chapters at a stage when I very much needed an outside eye. Her trenchant questions about my own position sharpened my perspective considerably. My friend and colleague Carol Miller gave me lively encouragement after reading an early chapter and throughout the writing process. Once a draft of the entire manuscript existed, I asked several colleagues to critique my work. John Watkins and Andrew Elfenbein not only read it immediately but also offered enthusiastic and pointed suggestions for pruning and expanding my arguments. I especially thank my colleague and friend, Valerie Miner, who read with a blue pencil and a creative writer's sensibilities all 360 pages of an early version of the book. Additionally, she met with me to discuss her broad responses to the book and to suggest possible editors.

As always, I benefitted from the intellectual and emotional support of Shirley Nelson Garner, my oldest Minnesota friend. She listened carefully over many lunches as I read aloud from the manuscript, offering her acute psychological perceptions of internalized homophobia and institutional neglect. More than her specific responses, however, she constantly reassured me that I could finish the project and that it would be a significant contribution to our growing understanding about workplace issues for lesbians and gay men.

My editor at Temple University Press, Janet Francendese, could not have been more helpful. Her attentive concern for my well-being at every stage of the project, together with her expert work on the manuscript itself, have significantly enhanced the quality of the book.

Finally, I want to thank my life partner, Susan M. Cygnet, for her unflagging support of me during the many months of writing and revising this work. As the closest and most demanding of my readers, she pored over the initial chapter, making invaluable stylistic observations that I carried with me throughout the composition phase. When my resolve waivered, she would remind me of one of our favorite moments in Dickens by repeating "Prop me up, Judy," a phrase guaranteed to shake me out of my torpor. After hearing the first draft of the conclusion, Susan nudged me to make more explicit my own views about such central ideas as being closeted or out as a faculty member and about refusing to be overly grateful to institutions which take years to grant crumbs. Most important of all, when I was thrown into sadness by yet another story of repression and its destructive consequences, Susan understood from her own life experiences and extended confirmation that such stories must be told and retold if things are ever to change. I can never fully articulate the love I have been given—I can only attest to my reliance upon it in this and all other writing projects.

POISONED IVY

CHAPTER 1

"Who and Where Are We?"

My Own Story

In 1964, when I began work at the University of Minnesota, there simply were no publicly defined lesbian or gay faculty. Perhaps faculty were able to declare their sexual orientation on a few campuses in California or New York City. In the overwhelming majority of cases, however, such faculty were silent, reluctant to risk credibility and jobs by announcing their sexual identities. This self-monitoring, based on homophobic displays at the national and local levels, as in the political efforts of Senator Joseph McCarthy and the House Un-American Activities Committee and in the routine raiding of gay bars, allowed universities and colleges to avoid even thinking about the needs or concerns of lesbian and gay faculty.

At the time of my arrival, the English department employed two unmarried women and one unmarried man. Rumor had it that one of the unmarried women and another woman shared a secluded river house an hour and a half from the university. The unmarried man was elegant and had three or four close friends in other departments who, like him, were officially "single," and who, like him, traveled to England or Europe at least once a year for a more relaxed and open life.

Of the six assistant professors hired that fall into the English department, I was one of the two women. This fact seemed miraculous to me, since so few women were placed at major research universities. When I asked the other new woman, also unmarried, to have lunch with me at the faculty dining club, she refused, saying: "Oh, I don't want to be seen at lunch with another single woman; I'm hoping to find a husband."

Efforts to make some kind of alliance with the tenured woman living on the river were equally daunting. Since neither of us was capable of speaking the "l" word, our social moves were opaque at best. Rather than reaching out to me, she seemed somehow threatened by my presence in ways I did not understand. Our offices were located in such a way that it was impossible for her to enter or leave without passing my door. One Friday afternoon when we were both still at work, she poked her head in my door to ask if I might read a poem given to her by a young male student in her modern poetry class and let her know on Monday what I thought of it. I spent too much of my weekend deciding how to respond and went to work prepared to discuss the merits and weaknesses in that rather tortured lyric which did, however, possess some effective imagery for the student's feelings about his girlfriend.

When I approached my colleague in her office, she barely looked up from what she was doing to listen to my comments. I tried to offer a mix of praise and suggestion for improvement, calculated to show her the seriousness with which I had taken her request and that I was trying to earn her warmth. When I finished, she leaned back slowly in her chair, poker-faced to the end, and said, "Oh, do you really think so? I found it sophomoric in the extreme."

I felt dismissed and demolished, consigned to some outer realm of cretonic readers. I would only much later comprehend that this woman feared I might encroach on the acceptance she had won for herself. Her need to establish permanent distance between us may well have been to keep herself inside the functional parameters she had established. The older patriarchs of the department admitted her to their sanctum in large part because she presented herself as "one of the boys" who could drink more than they could at extended lunch hours in downtown hotels, curse as vividly, and win regularly at their weekly smoke-filled poker marathons.

Genuine kindness and understanding came my way from the elegant unmarried man, though his carefully imposed silence about his own life and our shared terror of being "found out" by

2

colleagues left powerful omissions in our contact. Besides these immediate colleagues, I knew only one other unmarried woman in those early years. She was a full professor in another department in the College of Liberal Arts. We met after I was delegated by my chair to serve on a collegewide curriculum committee, and we liked each other from the start. However, she was so intense that she frightened me. One evening when the committee had met later than usual, she invited me to go for a drink. I refused before I knew what I was doing. Instinctively I withdrew from an invitation I was sure was for more than a whiskey sour; this woman, so senior to me professionally, was the subject of ominous rumors. After my rebuff, she never again extended herself, most likely for fear she had mistaken whatever silent cues I had sent out that we might both be lonely lesbians. A few years after I met her, she left the University of Minnesota to become an academic administrator at another midwestern university. A few years after that, she committed suicide.

Aside from these tortuous encounters, I was convinced for some years that there were no other lesbians or gay men at the University of Minnesota. Two decades later, Audre Lorde's *Cancer Journals* resonated deeply in me as she discussed women's hiding the fact of their radical mastectomies behind prosthetic breasts. Like them, none of us working at the university could find each other because, like them, we were in hiding, making heroic attempts to pass for heterosexual, usually being thought of as pathetically neuter.

Far from being neuter, I came to Minnesota with my lover, a woman who left her established life behind her to make a home with me and to pursue a graduate degree in counseling. Though very much in love, we each occupied a closet of considerable depth. Not even comfortable calling ourselves lesbian, we certainly had no intentions that anyone else do so. Consequently, we seldom saw one another on campus and then only in locations unassociated with either of our official domains. Our commitment to isolation prevented us from making efforts to find any other lesbians.

However, at some point during our second year in town, I became aware that my partner's academic advisor had had a somewhat older woman companion for many years, though they both maintained utmost secrecy. They never attended official university functions together or spoke of their shared household or personal lives. If my partner mentioned her summer vacation, her advisor might do likewise, both speaking as if they traveled alone.

I learned of this relationship primarily through observation. My partner's advisor owned a foreign sedan, unmistakable on a campus where most of us drove Fords or Chevrolets if we were buying American or Volkswagens or used Volvos if we preferred imports. In the late afternoon, I often parked near the advisor's building, waiting for my lover to emerge from another day of seminars, practicums, and office interviews with faculty. If she were later than 4:30, when the university closed the administrative offices where the advisor's companion worked as a high-level administrator, I saw the sleek car glide past me to pause briefly outside the adjacent building as a gray-haired, well-dressed woman hurriedly got in. Being both a good amateur sleuth and a lesbian desperate for assurance that we were not the only ones on campus, I concluded that these women were a couple.

The first time I asked my partner if she thought her advisor was "like us," she flatly denied any such possibility. But the more she described conversations she had with her advisor, the surer I became that I was right. I also became sure that the advisor sensed that her advisee was like her and that she was trying to make contact in the most convoluted codes imaginable. Perhaps because my lover was nearly the age of her advisor, perhaps because her advisor found my lover as appealing as I did, perhaps because she had also been watching as closely and had seen us together to confirm her hunches—whatever her reason, this deeply closeted woman eventually invited my partner to tea, adding that she should feel free to "bring a friend." After much debate about whether she should go alone or with me, we decided to make the trip together. Looking back, I see that decision as a tiny coming out on my part. At the time, it felt both dangerous and exciting.

The actual tea was inevitably awkward since no one acknowledged either their own or the other relationship. The two older faculty women hesitated to ask me questions about my work or department; I felt constrained from inquiring about their professional lives because they were so senior to me in academic terms and because they were in fields that were unfamiliar to me.

We chatted haltingly about sports and about visits to Lake Superior. The advisor talked with my lover about possible job opportunities for her as an older woman candidate while the advisor's partner and I remarked on the unusually colorful autumn outside their sliding patio doors. When we left, I was exhausted from participating in an afternoon full of simultaneous intensity and opacity.

During all the years between that strained afternoon and this advisor's retirement, we were thrown together periodically through committee work. Though she was always cordial, a tense reserve made it impossible for her to be of any assistance to me as a junior faculty member. In the absence of heterosexual senior women and in the unexamined presence of sexism, I had no mentors of either sex or any sexual orientation.

In this context I became mute as a teacher, a potential scholar, and a colleague. In my literature classes, I avoided texts and topics that might lead to any whisper of homosexuality. My writing was bland and ineffectual. Relationships with colleagues progressed nicely up to a point, but then stopped as if we had come up against a brick wall. My inability to mention my private life kept our conversations on a superficial, impersonal level. Those who liked me and suspected I was a lesbian were too polite to break the silence. Those who did not like me and suspected I was a lesbian watched closely, hoping to catch me in some glaring mistake. A third group, who ignored me altogether, seemed not to suspect that I had a sexual or emotional life at all, since I was neither married nor interested in dating men. Encased in silence, I nonetheless made my way in the academy, succeeding in the classroom and governance structure, while languishing as a scholar and person.

Design of the Project

Originally I had proposed to write a straightforward autobiography, tracing my 30-year trajectory as a case study for theorizing about the country at large. Very early on, however, I decided such an exclusively personal slant was too limited to reflect the immense variety within the world of gay and lesbian faculty. I decided to augment my own story with narratives taken from other faculty around the country whose long-term employment in their field gave them a perspective from which to judge change. I knew how to execute this project because previous training as a literary critic had taught me the structures and functions of narrative form.

The more questionnaires I read, the more I wanted to enlarge the portion of the book that did not relate directly to my own experience. I decided to use myself as frame rather than as center, to organize the book around aspects of academic life experienced by anyone working in such an environment. Because I was interested in studying change over time, I decided to focus on those with many years in their field. I sent the questionnaire to faculty who had worked at least fifteen years in a North American college or university. I focused on the impact of being gay or lesbian on three aspects of academic life that seemed to me to determine any faculty member's success and satisfaction. These themes are pedagogical choices, friendships and associations with colleagues, and research or intellectual development.

Whatever limitations there may be in Freud's theories, he was correct in asserting that happiness and fulfillment depend in large part upon our ability to find satisfaction in the realms of love and work. Institutions of higher learning in the United States usually emphasize the pursuit of knowledge as well as the development of all its citizens' full potential. The presence of lesbians and gay men on college and university campuses has long been undeniable and considerable, among students, staff, and faculty. Unmasking what it has been and is like to make our way in this context seemed to me especially important, because I knew from my own story the difficulty of integrating love and work. If others in similar situations could share their academic histories, surely we would have a compelling and revealing story.

I was encouraged in such hypothesizing by a letter I received early in the questionnaire collection phase. It came from a much younger colleague who had seen a call for volunteers on the Internet, been disappointed that her years in the academy fell far short of my 15-year minimum, yet was eager to encourage me to tell some of the complex truth about our experiences as scholars and teachers:

> I personally believe that academe is one of the most difficult places to be out because though we are often enveloped by a (supposedly) liberal environment, heterosexism has an insidious way of permeating that seemingly accepting exterior and striking at the core of people's deepest fears.

The ironies expressed in this brief condemnation are every-where apparent. Higher education, like its K–12 counterpart, all too often preserves and even endorses the prejudices of its sur-rounding culture. Simultaneously colleges and universities are seen as guardians of truth and sources of new knowledge. Formal studies of gay and lesbian history and issues, like those of racism and sexism, are either tolerated around the edges or disallowed al-together. This colleague at the beginning of her career helped con-vince me that I was on the right track.

Sometimes my own experience is mirrored almost exactly by that of colleagues, and sometimes we recount essentially different truths about academic life. I have tried to present divergent points of view wherever relevant. Additionally, Appendix C presents these points of agreement and divergence, in addition to reporting demographic data, a spectrum of responses registering how public faculty are about their gayness or lesbianism, and a discussion of the levels and kinds of institutional support available for faculty, staff, and students.

Requests for questionnaires were often accompanied by stories of a faculty member's own experiences with a homophobic cam-pus or colleague. People seemed eager to discuss the significance of working in higher education in the face of an indifference to their lives which rendered them invisible. They also wanted to re-count memories of individual and institutional hostility that had hurt them emotionally and professionally. My determination to complete the study strengthened with each stranger or friend who wrote that he or she could distribute 4, 8, 12, even 20 question-naires. I would be a conduit through which treasured and dreaded narratives could reach peers and administrators still hesitant about supporting legislation and programming intended to warm a cold and cruel climate. This book could show how destructive preju-dices can be, not only to the human beings involved but to the goals of their own institutions.

My hope is to reach department chairs or heads, collegiate deans, vice presidents and presidents, governing boards, legislative bodies, and alumni. I want to show the faculty who work with and for them but who feel ignored, discounted, and at risk because we do not conform to heterosexual patterns of behavior and thought. I want to reach heterosexual as well as lesbian and gay faculty who know that we avoid certain texts, data, and research because to engage with them directly could be too dangerous to our internal sense of safety and to our livelihood. I also hope to assist and encourage allies looking for additional ways to support their lesbian and gay colleagues and friends.

Theoretical Foundation

My theoretical position concerning memory and memoir is that remembering one's past, if that past involves oppressive elements, constitutes a radical political action. For those of us who have been told, overtly or subtly, that our existence is not quite valid, insisting on having and shaping memories into coherent form constitutes disobedience on a personal level and destabilization on a cultural level. Certainly lesbians and gay men wishing to pursue careers in academe have been among such groups. Some report that things are much better in the present for younger scholar-teachers. Although this may be true for those who are fortunate enough to be hired at institutions that at least tolerate research and teaching on gay and lesbian issues, I know that for many it is still necessary to downplay if not completely efface sexual identity in the pursuit of scarce tenure-track positions.

Just the other day, I had the unhappy job of advising a new Ph.D. in drama to wait until she had a job offer in hand before declaring her lesbian research and pedagogical interests. Like most of the humanities disciplines, drama has had significant reductions in new hires, a reality that has meant this young scholar did not have a full-time position two years after receiving her degree. A state university eager to bring her to campus is located in the rural Midwest, where her truest intellectual concerns are likely to be highly suspect because of their lesbian/gay cast.

It would have been irresponsible for me to assure this woman that things are categorically better today than they were when I was being interviewed in 1963. I certainly do not wish to dampen individual or collective celebrations of gains on some campuses and within many professional associations. But the stories offered here are a reminder of the reality of homophobia, which still demands serious attention.

This book explores three central facets of academic life—teaching, relating to colleagues, conducting research—in the expectation that readers will recognize themselves within its pages. I hope that all who continue to struggle with persistent and lingering degrees of invisibility within departments and institutions will be heartened by reading what follows and that we all will discover new ideas to use in overcoming the limiting conditions within which we attempt to carry out our work.

What We Know

No one should be surprised that only a few studies have been published that survey the workplace for gays and lesbians. Until fairly recently, with the advent of cultural studies curricula, most academics never thought to study themselves. We trained our research lenses on virtually every other subject, somehow taking our own histories and contexts for granted, assuming a dangerous status as investigators and never the objects of investigation. However, I want to discuss briefly the few published studies.

Perhaps the first such project was undertaken by Louie Crew in the mid-1970s (Crew, 1978). Published in 1978 as part of his book, *The Gay Academic,* his study surveyed the 893 English department chairs listed in the Modern Language Association mailing list for Associated Departments of English. In all, 24 percent (214) completed a questionnaire designed to measure hostility versus acceptance of gays by their chairs. The overall results revealed that 24 percent of all chairpersons were hostile, 32 percent were ambivalent, and only 44 percent were predominantly accepting of gays and lesbians in their departments. As Crew saw it, "these results justify a high degree of professional gay paranoia," since one out of every four chairs in English admitted to being anti-gay.

Additionally, Crew correlated the hostility–acceptance scale with types and locations of institutions, finding that the greatest hostility was to be found at private religious schools, southern schools, and schools with fewer than 1,000 students.

One aspect of Crew's findings is worth noting because of the similarity to what my own study turned up 20 years later. Crew lists the following as the most accepting subgroups of chairpersons:

those whose departments offer courses in gay literature; those reporting openly gay faculty in their midst; those in departments with more than 20 faculty members; those who are themselves gay or bisexual; those working at universities in the Northeast; those whose campuses have gay student organizations; those who are African American; and those whose campuses offer women's studies courses.

Studies of working conditions and attitudes toward lesbian and gay academics have been conducted recently in at least three social science disciplines—sociology, political science, and history. Professors Verta Taylor and Nicole Raeburn recently completed a study of lesbian, gay, and bisexual sociologists (Taylor and Raeburn, 1995). Relying on data collected in 1981 and again in 1992 from members of the lesbian and gay caucus of the American Sociological Association (ASA) and supplemented by interviews, Taylor and Raeburn wanted to assess the extent to which an increase in reported rates of discrimination and bias over the past 10 years were linked to variations in activist experience and political consciousness.

The broader sociological context of this study, social movement literature, suggests that participation in protest can have both short- and long-term effects on the personal lives and work histories of activists. Within this framework, identity politics are often seen as a retreat from political and institutional change. Taylor and Raeburn's results suggest layers of identity politics, however, only some of which may constitute such a retreat. Other aspects of these politics focus directly on broader change. The research findings distinguish between persons who disclose sexual orientation primarily for personal and individual motives and those who engage in "personalized political resistance," behaviors designed to promote public recognition of gays and lesbians in an effort to challenge institutional heterosexuality and/or to promote collective interests of lesbians and gays in sociology.

Sociologists who placed themselves in the first category reported experiencing virtually no prejudicial responses to announcing that they were lesbian or gay. Those faculty in the second category, however, attested to a wide range of biased or retaliatory moves from colleagues and the profession at large. These faculty also reported feeling energized and more powerful as a result of joining with others who shared their academic and professional goals and who effected tangible changes. Such changes are measured in terms of the number of panels held at annual ASA meetings where individuals offer testimony concerning positive and negative ways their professional careers have been influenced by being openly gay, lesbian, or bisexual; tables at such meetings featuring information about the caucus and how to join; and conference papers on lesbian, gay, or bisexual topics.

The final section of the Taylor and Raeburn study focuses on five consequences faced by gay, lesbian, and bisexual sociologists engaged in personalized political resistance: discrimination in hiring; bias in tenure and promotion; exclusion from social and professional networks; devaluation of scholarly work on gay and lesbian topics; and harassment and intimidation. Survey participants reported specific negative impacts in all five of these crucial areas of academic life, reflecting very little change between 1992 and a decade earlier. This lack of measurable improvement prompted Taylor and Raeburn to conclude the following:

> In an ideal world, the work of gay scholars and teachers would be seen as no more or less political than the work of any other academic. Because, however, the process of negotiating what it means to be a gay sociologists makes individuals a site of political activity, it not only alters the meaning of individuals' scholarship and teaching, but it increases their probability of experiencing discrimination and the likelihood that they will recognize it.

A survey of political science departments in the United States was commissioned in 1993 by the American Political Science Association's Committee on the Status of Lesbians and Gays and subsequently published in *PS: Political Science and Politics,* September 1995, Vol. XXVIII, No. 3, 561–574. Surveys were sent to chairs and association members. Of the 765 chairs of departments granting political science degrees who received questionnaires, 37 percent (280) responded. The membership survey elicited 459 responses, 25 percent of which came from professors identified as lesbian, gay, or bisexual. The authors of the report observed that their findings are significantly parallel to similar surveys conducted in sociology and in history.

A certain percentage of the profession "questioned one or more of [the] premises, and therefore challenged the legitimacy of the questionnaires themselves." These remarks from such political scientists in 1993 were representative: "This is a ridiculous questionnaire—a waste of postage!" "I resent having my dues money support this self-serving advocacy group!" "I seriously doubt the appropriateness of the APSA conducting a survey of this nature. It seems to be a basis for possible harassment . . . and has no relevance to the academic discipline."

Only 116 faculty defined themselves as gay, lesbian, or bisexual, while chairs reported knowing of only 49 full-time faculty members so identified. These figures assume significance when compared with the total number of political science faculty in the country—2,300. Because the survey was sent to all faculty in the field, the data adequately reflect a sharp difference between what lesbian, gay, and bisexual faculty say about the "extent to which sexual minority status does harm" and what most of their heterosexual colleagues believe. More than 40 percent of self-identified respondents claim to have "experienced or witnessed instances where the perception that a person was homosexual was prejudicial in hiring, teaching evaluations, and collegial relations." A dramatically lower percentage—only 10 to 25 percent—of heterosexuals report witnessing any such instances.

Open-ended responses like these suggest why more academic political scientists may not be out:

> I embrace the traditional point of view that homosexuality is deviant, abnormal behavior. I would not discriminate against a person because of sexual preference. However, I will not support or endorse what is clearly a contradiction to the natural order of things.
>
> I am frankly not interested in making their lives better, because I regard their behavior as repugnant. The more overt it is, the less inclined I am to have anything to do with them. Assuming they are discreet, I have fairly high tolerance of male homosexuals. . . . But I simply detest lesbians, whose sexual proclivities I regard as a betrayal of real female friendship. I can understand how men might find their male counterparts unacceptable. Would I discriminate against them? You bet—to exactly the degree their activities impinge on me.

What makes these comments so significant is their date of utterance. They are spoken by people teaching, forming collegial relationships, and voting on hiring, promotion, and tenure in the last decade of the twentieth century.

Again the data reflect a distinct difference in chairs' attitudes towards someone's being gay or lesbian or presenting papers or publishing research in the area as compared with their being public about sexual orientation. The report reveals mixed messages: despite clear and welcome progress in many areas of curricular and research work, "the status of sexual minorities, and of scholarly inquiry into gay and lesbian politics, remains marginal. That marginality is evident in the experiences and perceptions of a substantial number of lesbians, gay men, and bisexuals, but it is not always evident to heterosexuals in the profession. . . . Heterosexuals, and some gays and lesbians themselves, do not recognize the subtle ways in which academic culture in general, and the culture of political science in particular, discriminates. These issues assume particularly stark form in the case of lesbians and gays of color. . . . The small number of people of color who responded to this survey may reflect their particular experience of exclusion and enforced invisibility."

In addition to these two studies, the Committee on Women Historians published a report of a survey of lesbian and gay historians in *Perspectives* (Committee on Women Historians, 1993). Results of this study have not been made available and are not included here.

The Risks Involved in Change

Many scholars and artists currently speak about the devastating impact of not having language for who and what one is. Lesbian and gay faculty in the 1960s and later struggled with silence as we attempted both to protect ourselves and to find others like us. Yet we simultaneously joined many of the cultural change movements sweeping the country. We protested the Vietnam War on and off our campuses; we participated in sit-ins and demonstrations for the civil rights of other oppressed groups; we often worked vigorously to help form the ethnic and women's studies programs springing up across the academic landscape.

Though we were vocal and active on behalf of political causes, most of us remained quiet and passive in the face of discrimination

13

against us. I myself was unable to make simple social contact with women and men who shared my particular "outsider" status. For instance, I refused for years to go to the nicest gay bar in town, located quite near campus. Even though it advertised a "ladies' night," I was afraid that someone from school would see me. Irrationally, I envisioned a place full of heterosexual monitors poised to spot deviants who darkened the doors. I could not grasp that, more likely, people in the bar would be equally nervous about being seen there and were extremely unlikely informants. By staying away I denied myself any possibility of meeting potential friends, since at that time there were no safe alternative places for doing so.

Responses from other long-term faculty have showed that many experienced those early years as I did. As one participant who teaches philosophy at a liberal university put it so profoundly:

> When I began teaching (1966), no one even said those words ["lesbian" or "gay"] out loud. One heard rumors about certain faculty, but no one was open about being lesbian or gay. The card catalog listed only hostile materials, mostly by psychogists, nothing by self-identified lesbian or gay authors, and it didn't list much. There was no women's studies, no mention of the possibility of studying 'homosexuality' as anything but a perversion.

If my data and my own history are representative, this negative climate began to change on many campuses during the 1970s. Survey respondents who began their academic lives after 1975 report much less invisibility related to their being gay or lesbian than was the case for those of us working at most institutions of higher learning prior to that time. Several factors contributed to such changes. The formation of ethnic and women's studies programs played a vital role in changing faculty perception of what legitimately could be included as subject matter in our curricula and as topics of our research.

For middle-aged and older lesbians in this study, alignment with women's studies programs is most often cited as the chief external prompt for change. Suddenly information about our history and culture, as well as books by lesbian artists and activists, became available as texts we could teach in our classes. Students demanded information about this crucial phase of feminism's long and illustrious history. More and more lesbian faculty working in such programs gained the courage to come out to their heterosexual colleagues and to hope these relationships would be maintained after the disclosure. We were not always right in our assumptions, but even in cases where conflict erupted, there was great value for all who endured scathing and often excruciatingly long meetings. Even when losses and rejections occurred, the lesbians involved came away stronger and clearer about who we were and how we intended to teach and carry out research in the future.

For gay men on faculties across the country, the absence of any organized intellectual movement like feminism has meant a delay in the formation of specifically gay studies courses and programs until quite recently. As male scholars and teachers, gay men often stand to lose much more than lesbians by coming out academically. Many of them are leading researchers in their fields with decades of publication and reputation-building at stake. Even those not yet prominent in their fields sense that by being public about their sexuality, they will lose the possibility for preeminence. Many of the gay respondents said they do experience loss of credibility when they make their sexual orientation public. They speak of this loss in terms of student interaction and of career opportunities, specifically that they are passed over for high-level administrative positions:

> I believe my movement upward into an administrative position such as department head or associate dean is blocked permanently because I am gay. This is a conservative university, and while they tolerate and sometimes even support my openness, they would never go so far as to appoint me to such positions. They would get too much flak from alumni.

This state of affairs figures in the words of a professor emeritus at a large midwestern research university:

> In the mid-60s, I was interviewed for a prestigious professorship at my old undergraduate college in New England. I spent a weekend there, gave a public lecture, and was warmly entertained by the President and the faculty, some of whom had been my teachers. The interview went extremely well, and while I was being driven to the airport afterwards, the chair of the department told me that I would be receiving a very lucrative offer within 48 hours. But no offer came, and I was understandably puzzled. After two weeks the president of the college phoned to say that a

15

delicate problem had arisen which could only be discussed face-to-face in New York, and offered to pay my full expenses to this second interview. I knew immediately what the "problem" was. As an undergraduate I had had an affair with one of the young professors (fired after my graduation for questionable relationships with gay students), and we had remained close friends over the years. When my name was presented to the faculty for approval, one of the older professors (a closeted gay, but married, who had known of my relationship with the fired professor) objected to my appointment. He was obviously afraid I would expose him as a closeted gay.

When I met the President of the college in New York, he said that he was very embarrassed to question me about being gay, but felt he had an obligation to the trustees of the all-male college. If I would simply deny the charge, he was prepared to hire me on the spot at a very attractive salary. Without actually denying the charge, I angrily demanded to have the name of my anonymous denouncer in writing together with a written apology from this person, and was ready to walk out of the hotel room in high dudgeon. The President promised to have the accuser write me an apology immediately. He then wrote out a letter of appointment. I later got the apology, but declined the offer since I thought the climate had been so poisoned against me, that I would always feel uncomfortable there.

Because gay men on faculties have been able to gain the advantages that are unfairly afforded to men in general, they have been more reluctant to be public about their sexual identity than lesbians have been. It will continue to be difficult for some gay men to incorporate their sexual orientation into their intellectual and academic lives. Lesbians often see themselves as having less to lose professionally because unfairness based on gender persists at many colleges and universities.

In 1993, at a small liberal arts college in the East, an on-campus search for a new dean had been narrowed to two candidates. One was a white gay man, the other an African American lesbian; both were highly respected and supported by colleagues across the campus. The white gay man, described to me by a colleague at the college as "not 'in' and not exactly 'out'," was seen at campus and community events with his partner, a social presence that could be and was interpreted in a variety of ways. On the other hand, the black lesbian candidate had maintained a much higher profile as an out lesbian who expected her partner to be invited to official functions.

After being encouraged to stand for the post by faculty colleagues and administrators, these two candidates made vastly different decisions. The white gay man refused to run, saying that the college was not "ready" nor would it be "well-served" by having a gay man in such a visible position. Specifically, he felt his ability as a fund-raiser—an important element of his administrative duties— would be seriously hampered by the fact of his sexual orientation. The black lesbian stood for election and was widely supported. Now that she has the position, she is successfully raising funds and is performing her other duties with skill.

Some of the factors influencing such disparate decisions by people facing the same potential prejudices hinge on gender and race bias within the academic culture. The woman in this anecdote may have more at stake and less to lose by accepting this new challenge than did her white gay colleague. This story suggests how the academy simultaneously allows for new, more open stances by some of its citizens while remaining far too risky a place for others to step out of established expectations and patterns. Campuses reflect momentum for change countered by an undertow for the status quo.

How Change Occurs

In addition to the growth of ethnic and women's studies programs, faculty respondents affirm additional factors as having played a major role in the changes they see on their campuses. In 1973, the American Psychological Association (APA) removed homosexuality from its catalogue of diseases, reducing its classification from psychosis to neurosis. Especially prominent since 1980, student activists ask ever more insistently for inclusion of lesbian and gay material in relevant courses, for space and support services for gay/lesbian/bisexual student activities, and for coherent clusters of courses, if not full-fledged programs, focusing on gay and lesbian topics. Studies show that, during the 1980s and early 1990s, lesbians and gays have had the ambiguous distinction of being the only group not to lose previously hard-won civil rights. Some speculate that this fact has sadly depended on the inability even of a conservative Republican administration to ignore the threat of AIDS.

Survey participants also noted the importance of those few administrators who are beginning to advocate on behalf of lesbian and gay faculty, staff, and students. Scholars inside and outside the academy are quickly generating new knowledge through gay and lesbian research. The concomitant presentation of such research at conferences held by virtually every professional academic discipline fosters a growing context within which faculty members may feel freer to teach courses and conduct scholarship with a clear focus on lesbian and gay issues.

The burgeoning of queer theory in the 1990s has undoubtedly been helpful to some younger gay men and lesbians entering colleges and universities in the United States. Since much queer theory argues against identity politics as being too solipsistic and narrow to be helpful in understanding a post-modern world, it has become possible for a faculty member to conduct and publish research about gayness or lesbianism without necessarily being gay or lesbian. To the extent that this new field of inquiry provides a protective umbrella for some faculty who might otherwise refrain from integrating their sexual orientation into their work, it can only benefit students and faculty alike. To the extent that it runs counter to the ideas of an older generation or academic era, those who continue to advocate for greater visibility in asserting the existence of intimate and unavoidable connections between the personal and the intellectual, queer theory runs the risk of diluting gains made at great risk to individual faculty members.

Such a rift can be avoided if all concerned are willing to discuss similarities and differences and to value contributions made by members of each group. In the absence of such dialogue and mutual respect, however, queer theory stands to splinter the gay and lesbian academic community, once again allowing internecine disagreements to divide a vulnerable population. Such division would, I believe, play directly into the hands of faculty members who continue to wish that lesbian and gay colleagues would stay closeted, personally detached from their intellectual pursuits.

Ironically, the legal recognition of sexual orientation as a potential target for bias and its attendant verbal and physical harassment, together with the upsurge in hate speech on campuses are forcing some top-level administrators to come to grips with the virulence of homophobic attitudes, even in supposedly accepting environments. This change agent may be particularly galling to those who object to a more tolerant attitude toward gays and lesbians, but it is consistent with academic rhetoric that promises an open exchange of ideas as a centerpiece of academic discourse.

Probably the single factor rated most pivotal for change is the vocal and visible presence of out faculty on campus. Such individuals and small groups are credited with articulating, both by their being and their doing, the sheer existence of persons within a category that was often allowed to remain faceless in the past. Invisibility helps to preserve prejudice and injustice. If I actually know and work with another person who is part of a group previously defined as offensive, I have several options. I can reject someone who I admired, liked, and easily associated with moments before; I can view the person as an exception who does not fit stereotyped definitions of the group to which he or she belongs; I can extend my definition of acceptability to include a few representatives of the offending group; or I can begin a slow and usually unsettling process of redefining my own sense of acceptability in human behavior.

To demonstrate how central such a person or persons can be, I offer two accounts from respondents and a story of my own. In the first, a lesbian professor of education working in the Midwest describes an incident in which a closeted colleague died of AIDS, after which the faculty held a memorial service. This professor writes as follows:

> I thought maybe we'd change then, since our new president seemed so much more tolerant than his predecessor. But that's not enough—you need overt leadership—you need folks who will pick up the flag. I am going to try to pick up the flag—at least in some way. I may not have done that if: 1) I hadn't witnessed discrimination that was overt; 2) gay/lesbian students hadn't expressed need to be supported. So my interest is/was "others" oriented—I didn't seem to feel the need to do anything for myself.

The second account comes from a member of the science faculty at a southern university. After saying that he has never discussed his sexuality with any colleagues in his department, though most of them know he is gay and have socialized with him and his companion, he goes on to describe a campus event:

> I came out on the floor of the faculty senate when the president of our university took the words "sexual orientation" out of the anti-discrimination regulations, and then asked the senate for an endorsement. Two homophobic professors (one a classic closet case) took the floor in support of the president, saying that there was no need for this sort of language because gays and lesbians are not subject to discrimination on our campus. I came out right then and there in a 20-minute speech which outlined for the senate the real problems that exist for gay and lesbian faculty and students. I convinced the senate to vote against the president (first time in 10 years). In short, being gay and able to relate the experiences of gay people to others proved to be essential for changing the outcome of this situation.

On my own campus, a handful of faculty and staff began lobbying for greater visibility about seven years ago. I had been asked to write an essay exploring some ways campuses could assist their lesbian students for a book being published by the American Council on Education entitled *What Women Students Want*. Our president at that time was a man who enjoyed being in the academic vanguard. Capitalizing on this fact, I sent him an advance copy of my essay, accompanied by a note suggesting that Minnesota might be the first major research university to include sexual orientation in its nondiscrimination policy. Within weeks, he had established a task force charged with drafting a resolution that would include lesbian and gay faculty, staff, and students in the university's nondiscrimination statement. That group worked efficiently, consulting with the three or four out faculty members on campus about the relative merits of phrases like "sexual preference," "affectional preference," and "sexual orientation." We chose the latter, finding it the most precise and inclusive.

The president endorsed and took to the board of regents a phrase prohibiting discrimination on the basis of sexual orientation at all levels of the university, making Minnesota one of the first large public institutions of higher learning to have such protection. Since that regents meeting where, I was told, not a single word was uttered by way of inquiry, support, or objection before a unanimous

vote was recorded, tangible changes have been painfully and infuri-
atingly slow. It is as if the heterosexual establishment exhausted itself in this initial verbal gesture and has resisted harnessing additional energy or finding the will to move forward.

Passive resistance and neglect reflect the depth of self-delusion
at work on today's campuses. Administrators, seeing themselves as
benign liberals, do not define their current behavior as discriminatory to gay and lesbian faculty. Therefore, when they add "sexual
orientation" to anti-discrimination statements, they do not imagine
that such action will have any tangible impact on educational or
personnel policies. When faculty, staff, and students pressure
them for delivery of services and changed attitudes based on the
promised protection, such administrators are genuinely surprised
and often defensive.

Pressure at the University of Minnesota and on scores of other
campuses has remained constant, however, usually led by gay and
lesbian faculty and supported by invaluable heterosexual allies
and by ever-stronger coalitions defined by race or disability. Because this work is so important and administrative inertia so
deeply engrained, a relay team approach has proven most effective. As one or another of us has reached the limits of our energy,
someone else has stepped in to carry the baton, much like the person who spoke in her narrative above about picking up the flag. If
fewer of us had been vigorous in our dealings with the administration, it is possible that no changes would have occurred. This reality suggests that the more faculty who are able to be public advocates for gay and lesbian interests and rights, the more rapid
progress on a given campus will be.

A relatively small group of faculty and staff at the University of
Minnesota convinced our current president to set up a blue ribbon
committee reporting directly to him with recommendations for
warming the campus climate for lesbians and gays. He was finally
galvanized to act by evidence of hate speech in dorms, restrooms,
and even on university committees. He could no longer deny the
reality of such violence against a significant number of his staff
and student body.

At one point, the committee took voluntary testimony from
lesbian and gay faculty, staff, and students, closeted and out. The

resulting narratives were among the most convincing elements of the committee's presentations of its recommendations. Administrators who have hidden behind budget crunches, federal restrictions, and other external barriers suddenly saw the faces behind this issue. Professors and staff members they knew and worked with made them listen to the frustration and pain at being made invisible over and over again. Ironically, testimony also was given about the painful discrimination suffered by those faculty whose very visibility made them easy targets for discriminatory behavior and hate speech from some colleagues. Students told repeated stories of humiliating classroom jokes or innuendoes originating from their teachers as often as from classmates.

As a result, the University of Minnesota now has an office for gay/lesbian/bisexual/transgender concerns, headed by a full-time staff member with training in psychology and with experience as a community activist. Faculty members may register domestic partners who then are eligible for tuition and recreational sports membership benefits and who may utilize library facilities on the same basis as married spouses. In addition, a university employee in a domestic partnership may receive medical and bereavement leave and may be reimbursed a set amount to cover health insurance for his or her partner. As of this writing, there is still no direct coverage of domestic partners for health insurance, but the same group of lesbian and gay faculty continues to press the administration for this crucial benefit, arguing that until it is in place, the equal treatment of gay and lesbian employees is only rhetoric.

One objection put forth by insuring agencies is that the actual number of such faculty who claim benefits for a formally registered domestic partner is too small to make it economically feasible for them to extend coverage. On my campus, most of the faculty who have declared their partnerships are lesbian, raising the gender question. Not only may gay men feel more pressure to remain closeted than do most lesbians, but they also may be more likely to have partners in a work situation that grants them good health benefits in their own name. Like women in general, lesbians are more likely to hold part-time jobs that provide no health coverage. Finally, like most women in academe, lesbians are often paid less than their male counterparts and are therefore less able to help their partners purchase private health insurance.

A single voice or the voices of a very small group have been pivotal in gaining recognition and affecting change. The burden of this role is shown in the words of a gay faculty member:

> Being one of the only two openly gay or lesbian faculty members makes me the "official gay." I do not like being tagged as a gay faculty member; I would prefer to be known for my research and teaching abilities, which are formidable but being ignored in the glare of my sexuality. In addition, all the calls to lecture or participate on panels, etc., are time-consuming. Finally, my companion and I have to act as role models for the gay and lesbian students, and frankly, it is exhausting. I love these kids, but sometimes I just want to be left alone. There are many times that I wish I were back in the closet—not for lack of pride, but because of over-exposure.

Faculty like this one will continue serving as models for students on our campuses, but we must be allowed space to voice our occasional frustration at the demands that go along with being public. Such faculty also know that our own private and professional lives would be greatly enhanced if more of our colleagues felt sufficient support from administrators and co-workers to allow them to come out of their closets and stand among those already open about sexual orientation.

The Continued Need for Closets

While coming out to colleagues and students is deemed necessary by the majority of this study's respondent population, that population is skewed by self-selection. Although many faculty members volunteered to distribute questionnaires to their more closeted colleagues and friends in the profession, only 5 out of 304 questionnaires were returned totally anonymously. (Total anonymity in this case meant not only leaving the information portion of the questionnaire blank but also not putting a name on the mailing envelope.)

The overwhelming majority of respondents to the questionnaire were willing to give me their names and addresses for potential use in the follow-up phase of my research. Many subsequently wrote long and eloquent responses to my follow-up questions. These lesbians and gay men wanted to establish contact with me and help me in the writing of this book. However, they were much less eager to become identifiable from what they told me about their years within the profession. Their extreme generosity, linked with their fear of detection, prompted me to decide to maintain anonymity even as I quoted at length from their narratives. While some respondents probably hoped to be named in the study, protecting the majority has seemed more important as an organizing principle.

Additionally, the faculty who agreed to participate in this study were in many cases adamantly opposed to "outing" other lesbians or gay men. In fact, one of the liveliest conversations during my research involved how to get questionnaires to closeted faculty. In some cases, faculty were reluctant to distribute questionnaires for me—an option I suggested for obtaining much-desired responses from closeted colleagues. If a faculty member had not actually told a colleague about his or her sexual orientation, then it was assumed that that faculty member must prefer to remain closeted. Handing such an individual a questionnaire designed for lesbian and gay faculty seemed too intrusive to many faculty otherwise eager to assist in this project.

I puzzled over how to gather stories from colleagues who obviously do not feel comfortable enough at work to be more public about their lives. One goal in writing my own memoir and collecting narrative accounts from others was to measure changes in attitude and institutional policy concerning sexual orientation of faculty. So the very existence of colleagues with long and distinguished careers who find it convenient, wise, or necessary to keep their sexual identities separate from their academic lives may point to an absence of significant change in their campus environments. I am sure that many such individuals did not know about or participate in this project. I regret their absence even as I affirm their right to remain private.

Support and Hostility

In designing my original questionnaire, I asked faculty to tell me some of the primary sources of support for and hostility toward lesbian and gay members of their academic communities. The responses surprised me. I expected to read that individual colleagues and students, as well as members of the religious right, were vocal opponents of any supportive environment for lesbians and gays. I did not expect that respondents would cite as the primary source of hostility their colleagues on the faculty who remained closeted. This unexpected note forced me to think more closely about my own experience and to discuss the topic with lesbian and nonlesbian friends on campus. Old resentments surfaced. Some closeted faculty still resent associates whose coming out has occasioned a certain distancing and accompanying sense of loss on the part of the closeted person to preserve his or her position. Some out faculty still feel pain over withdrawn personal support and also anger over the lack of support for efforts to gain greater equity from administrators.

The worst part of this scenario in my own case is that these feelings make it very hard to build even informal networks among lesbian faculty. I believe my lesbian colleagues and I need a facilitated retreat at which everyone could say what she feels about colleagues who are situated differently on a continuum of outness. Even if such an exchange took place and was successful, all of us would still have to exist within the prevailing campus environment. Before more of my colleagues can teach and conduct research informed by their knowledge of and perspectives on gay history, culture, and politics, that surrounding climate must be warmed considerably. Making that happen will require leadership from the president and others in positions of academic power, together with a change of heart at the grassroots level.

As faculty on campuses across the country wait and work for this ideal world, we form what alliances seem possible in the world we have. Some survey respondents describe having groups of lesbian and gay faculty and staff that meet regularly both to socialize and to work on strategies for convincing administrators to recognize them more positively. In keying such responses to size and type of institution, I find that in most cases, the closest associations are located on campuses having relatively few gay and lesbian faculty and staff. Such groups realize all too well what a vulnerable minority they are, choosing to suppress whatever internal differences may exist in an effort to meet more urgent needs and goals of the group as a whole.

Contrarily, institutions that boast larger numbers of lesbian and gay personnel may think (erroneously, I believe) that they can afford to indulge in internecine conflicts. The usual debate in such settings turns around whether to have a campus organization that includes faculty and staff or a separate group exclusively for faculty. Some lesbian and gay faculty are reluctant to join with logical allies because we cannot get past a seeming refusal to see ourselves as employees of the institutions that pay our salaries and organize our working conditions to ever greater extents.

Smaller campuses, or campuses where being gay and lesbian is still a dangerous marker, succeed better at least in forming social alliances between their academic and support staffs. A professor at a large midwestern research university with an active feminist community, many of whom are lesbians, has written at length on this tangled topic:

> I would like to share an odd kind of hostility I feel as an "out" professor on campus. Although there are other "out" professors, there are many who are not as "out" or not "out" at all. Because the community among the "outs" is virtually non-existent and because the "ins" often seem to turn away from publicly supporting or giving energy to lesbian (and gay) issues, I often feel very lonely. I find this a hostile and painful aspect of campus climate. Sometimes, I really don't know how I survive, except perhaps for the rewards of teaching. I am hoping through Lesbian Area Studies to bring lesbian faculty and graduate students together, but so far no other faculty has appeared at our meetings. My interactions with lesbian grad students are always guarded and defined by professional parameters. My alliances with other lesbian faculty members are fragile and unreliable.
>
> Where are we, the lesbian faculty members? We had a lesbian supper group that dissolved (allegedly) because of class issues, because of lesbian faculty not wanting to socialize with lesbian staff. The lesbian faculty members have not seen each other as a formal/informal lesbian group for over a year. The lack of community or the ill-wishes towards such a community, I find frustrating, contributing to my sense of going to work on thin ice with nobody else out there with me. Now that I write about this, I realize how stressful this is for me.

This story makes clear that as long as groups historically shunned and opposed by a dominant culture shy away from internal conflicts, no lasting community can be forged. This reality slows the rate of significant systemic change by blunting the voices of those who must advocate for it.

How Being Gay or Lesbian Matters

After reading all the questionnaires and follow-up narratives, I came to a startling conclusion about how faculty members think about what it means to be "out of the closet." Although the language of the closet falls so easily off most of our tongues, my data strongly suggest that there is no settled idea about what such words and metaphors mean. Throughout this book, I will demonstrate through direct faculty accounts and through my own speculation just how varied and nuanced experience of the academic closet can be.

Regardless of whether lesbian and gay faculty are "in" or "out" of such a space, almost every one of my respondents sees the fact of being gay or lesbian as having a profound impact on how they conduct their business as teachers and scholars. One of the most interesting questions on the survey turned out to be: "Has being gay or lesbian had an impact on your teaching and/or research? If so, please describe in some detail." Although approximately 18.5 percent said their sexual orientation had no effect on their teaching or research, the vast majority felt it had played a significant role in their academic development and mental/intellectual health. Respondents noted these roles:

- designing new courses, or units in existing courses, that focus on lesbian or gay subject matter
- gradually incorporating gay or lesbian issues into conference presentations and eventually into formal research
- deciding to sponsor gay/lesbian/bisexual student organizations on campus, regardless of the possible criticism this might incur
- ordering books and other resources for use by faculty and students in campus libraries
- advising advanced undergraduate and graduate students who wish to study gay and lesbian topics for honors or senior papers, graduate papers, or doctoral dissertations

In addition to these perhaps predictable effects, faculty spoke eloquently of less direct impacts on their thinking and behavior: a heightened awareness of and sensitivity to other oppressed groups, knowledge of who has been historically suppressed, ignored, or trivialized by academic communities and the larger culture. These comments are representative:

- I teach family law. Being gay has had the indirect effect of making me more sensitive to difference, attentive to the "other."
- I do not teach specific courses in g/l studies nor have I done research in the area. But I do include the experience of gay and lesbian people in my general history courses. I would like to think I would do that even if I were not gay—as I include the experience of people of color and women even though I am a white man. I do believe that my sexual orientation has heightened my sensitivity to other oppressed groups.
- As a teacher and administrator I believe being gay helps me be more empathetic. In particular, I think that being openly gay *disrupts* a lot of the traditional gender tensions, power plays, etc. This is an area I really think might be worth examination even in structures other than academic institutions.
- I have always been more inclusive in a variety of perspectives in my teaching. I think this comes more easily because of my own experiences of exclusion in course material I studied.
- I believe I have always viewed the world from the outside because I am a Jew. Lesbianism continued this outside viewpoint which aided my critical attitudes, my detachment from accepted norms. As a result, I was one of the first in my department to teach Black literature and to accept a multicultural perspective, even though I was among the older teachers.
- I'm not sure being a lesbian has had the impact it should have on my teaching or research save for advising students. It did, however, have a major impact on my sensitivity to issues of discrimination, affecting my research and even more a temporary career choice to serve as Director of Equal Opportunity.

These accomplishments are important and may be significant over time, but it is also true that 18.5 percent of the respondents note little or no carryover into academic pursuits. I thought about this issue further because some of the language used by faculty registering no impact is emphatic (e.g., "Being gay has had absolutely NO impact on my teaching or research"; "Of course not, I've had great success"). When I showed these responses to friends in psychology, several remarked that some faculty may have interpreted my question defensively. It may be as if a woman were asked on a questionnaire about realizing career goals, "Has being a woman had any impact on your success?" For some, the "right" answer involves asserting their own ability to rise above their seeming disadvantage. In this case, some lesbian and gay faculty may be showing pride in their ability to put aside whatever discrimination may have been felt or to overcome self-doubt. Of course, simple denial may also lie behind these statements.

In addition, some gay and lesbian faculty who have been working in the academy for 15 years or longer view sexual orientation as having meaning only in terms of their sexual lives. Such individuals do not connect their personal lives with their work, whereas others see sexual identity as inextricable from intellectual perspectives on knowledge and research and thus integral to a fully realized academic career.

This book is a tracing of many journeys, the recounting of which casts light on lesbian and gay history. This tracing also reflects the history of higher education in the United States as it has impacted and continues to impact gay and lesbian faculty who work within it.

CHAPTER 2

"In or Out in the Classroom?"

If I as faculty member have a secret pertaining to my personal life, being in so public a venue as a classroom will be dangerous. On any given day, a student might ask a question that relates to the secret and threatens its exposure. My response will have to be in the nature of a cover-up or escape unless I am prepared to blow my carefully constructed cover.

During my years in the pedagogical closet, in the late 1960s and early 1970s, I routinely taught an advanced course in Shakespeare that was made up almost entirely of graduate students. Each time we discussed the sonnets, a bright male student asked if I saw something more than friendship going on between the poet and the young man to whom the first 127 poems are dedicated. My response was immediate and forceful: "Oh, no, but I can see what's happened here. You've misunderstood the poems in question because you are reading as a twentieth-century person. During the Renaissance, a revival of Platonic ideals was taking place; hence, platonic friendship was being practiced by many English noblemen. Within such a framework, the bond between two friends was actually superior to a sexual liaison because such relationships were susceptible to suspicion, jealousy, and anger, whereas friendships were more permanent and highly valued. The poet in the sonnets, then, is extolling the difference between the trust and harmony he can feel with his fair-haired young male friend and the consuming, destructive passion awakened by the dark-haired lady of the last twenty-seven sonnets."

My response was a flat denial of the text, because the poems to the young man describe jealousy over his youth, beauty, and the possibility that he is seeing other people. More importantly, I was misusing esoteric knowledge to protect my own identity. If I admitted the possibilities behind the student's question, I risked saying "we" when I spoke of same-sex relationships. The danger of outing myself prevented me from being of any intellectual or potentially personal assistance to the student who had most likely taken a risk in asking such a question. Similarly, I discouraged serious discussion of the relationships between Romeo and Mercutio, Hamlet and Horatio, Bassanio and Antonio, Rosalind and Celia, Othello and Iago or Cassio, and Hermione and Paulina. I broke into a sweat even when students expressed interest in the sixteenth-century stage practice of having young men play women's parts and the cross-dressing involved in this practice or the use of gender disguise in the comedies. Lecturing about such instances of sexual ambiguity and fluidity frightened me.

Thinking about these once so-frightening moments and the impact of being closeted on pedagogical effectiveness, I am reminded of a jack-in-the-box. Once presented with this toy, a child is prompted by curiosity to unlatch the brightly decorated box. A painted face springs up and the unsuspecting child often reacts with terror before feeling pleasure or enjoyment. Once out of the box, the jack is much harder to fold back into its hiding place. The springing out is sudden, whereas the replacement is slow and tricky. Often the jack pops back up rather than settling back into its container, and the toy is not enjoyable unless someone can put the coiled figure back in place.

My immediate impulse to lecture my student about arcane matters seemed at the time nothing more than a serious Renaissance scholar's intent to correct a reading of the text before us. What I see today is an attempt to fold the entire issue of homosexuality as well as my own secret life back into an academic container.

Ironically, by stuffing the issue back into what I prayed was safety, I practically ensured that students would continue to ask questions. My only real protection would have been to laugh back in the jack's face, to acknowledge the legitimate basis of this curiosity about same-sex relationships as they figured in Shakespeare's work. A second irony turns around my flying in the face of my own pedagogical philosophy. I held that by encouraging spontaneity in general, I could facilitate inquiry into the more complex and contested aspects of the Renaissance. I spoke about the pervasiveness of paradox and ambiguity during this period of English history and letters, and about the uneasiness with such ambiguity in our own culture. Yet on the subject of one of the most fundamental ambiguities of the period, sexual and gender identity, I did not allow discussion.

A gay professor of linguistics for 17 years, currently teaching on the West Coast, remarks as follows: "In the closet, I was always aware of 'neutralizing' any language marked for sexual orientation. I also felt that while straight colleagues could, in class, make reference to their personal lives to 'put a human touch' on what they were teaching and thereby develop greater rapport with their students, I could not." Similarly, a lesbian philosophy professor recalls teaching an introductory course before she was out. A student commented in a derogatory tone that if John Stuart Mill's liberty principle were "used to defend homosexuality, someone might suspect Mill of being homosexual." The professor countered by saying that such a suspicion could also lead its thinker to develop a better opinion of homosexuality, since Mill was clearly a respected thinker of his era. Once out, this same professor received several student complaints referring to her "exhibitionism" and saying they would never "advertise" their sexual orientation and wished she would have the "good taste" to keep hers to herself. She reflects on these circumstances as follows: "If I had been out, I doubt the first situation would have occurred at all; if I hadn't been, there would have been no occasion for the second."

There is no agreement among the respondents to my questionnaire about what constitutes outness, but they all speak about what it means in their own academic lives to teach and conduct research from inside or outside their own particular definitions of a closet. I myself define teaching as an out professor as being willing and even eager to integrate my lesbian perspective into my literary studies. Furthermore, I practice this willingness by introducing theoretical and interpretive remarks with a phrase like "as a lesbian-feminist scholar." For many respondents, such a stance is either not possible because of their subject matter or not preferred because of personal styles. I make no claims for my own definition.

Rather I offer it to clarify my own academic perspective and to open up the whole question of what the concept means to each person involved.

Teaching as a publicly declared lesbian scholar has allowed me tremendous opportunities to challenge lesbian or gay and also heterosexual students in my classes. I no longer worry about being surprised by student questions regarding possibly coded homoerotic energy in literary works. If anything, I now must be alert to the students who find it disquieting if not annoying for me to announce that Walt Whitman and Stephen Crane or Willa Cather and Emily Dickinson were among the American writers who felt and expressed love and passion for members of their own sex. In responding to them, I try to remember how terrified I was in the past so that I do not repress whatever it may be that motivates their discomfort.

However, I also am unwilling to stop telling students the truth. Since I teach literature written in England and the United States, and since many of the finest writers in and out of the canons of literary study were and are gay or lesbian, to bury this central biographical fact is to commit an injustice. To colleagues who argue that they never include biographical information of any kind, I can only point out that students, like the general population, assume heterosexuality unless invited or even forced to do otherwise. Silence about any biographical detail that has a bearing on plot, character development, tone, and language could prevent a full understanding of a text.

I have found that most students welcome the truth, even when it disturbs them. It seems only sensible to espouse a pedagogy built on the hypothesis that the more a student knows about the environment from which culture springs and within which knowledge and ideas are generated, the fuller that student's learning and understanding will be. Therefore, a fundamental principle of higher education is served if faculty of all persuasions tell students the truth about the men and women studied in courses, including their sexuality.

Many heterosexual faculty may well omit such information out of ignorance. We tend to teach what we ourselves have been taught. Others may withhold information out of anxiety over perhaps being thought to be gay or lesbian themselves. Those who are convinced that their sexual orientation is the only "normal" or "decent" one might lie about their subject matter when it comes into direct conflict with their moral beliefs or might fear that they will encourage their students to see erotic and sexual energy toward members of one's own sex as a viable option for human beings.

Gains and Risks

Lesbian and gay faculty who do choose to come out in their classrooms note both the gains and risks involved. A lesbian teaching at a midwestern graduate school describes her coming out as a process: "For years I stewed on whether I could be out in class—finally did it in one class, now do it regularly. I think it has a profound impact on my relationships with my students. I have become de facto counselor for many lesbian and gay students."

This faculty member also faced one of the more complex risks of being out, i.e., being unwilling to collude in any effort to continue burying gay or lesbian truths within their subject fields. She resigned from a lesbian graduate student's Ph.D. committee because that student was writing on secrets in Willa Cather's novels without dealing with the author's lesbianism as perhaps the most significant "secret" of all.

The lesbian professor mentions her relationship with the student's primary advisor, a heterosexual colleague with whom she had a mutually supportive history and who insisted that it was valid for the graduate student to ignore the author's sexual identity. The lesbian professor's response was emotional: "Young people are still dying regularly, literally dying, because they have nothing in their lives to let them know that being lesbian or gay is OK, that there are successful, healthy lesbian and gay people in the world."

This lesbian professor recalls another awkward conversation with the same colleague in which the appropriateness of her decision to come out in all her classes was questioned. Her colleague asked why she had to be a "lesbian" to her students rather than a "person." When the professor shared a letter she routinely sends to prospective students, her colleague grew more accepting. Reading a description of a person who loves the outdoors, comes from New Jersey, and is an avid gardener lessened the colleague's anxiety over the inclusion of lesbianism as a defining marker. The lesbian professor hoped through this exercise to convince her colleague of the possibility of being both a lesbian and a person.

Years of painful personal experience have taught me that a reductionistic view of sexual identity as total selfhood is entirely too prevalent among academics. These same academics would be appalled if I were to assume that their mentioning a spouse or children in class meant that they gave students only information tied to their sexual orientation.

Some respondents see other results from teaching from an out position. One lesbian faculty member added a postscript to her follow-up in which she reflected that being out had made her "more vulnerable than ever to becoming the object of student 'crushes,' which sometimes turn hostile when I am not as accessible as some students would like." She handles this by acknowledging to her feminist and lesbian classes that erotic attachments may be formed by her or them but that one need not speak or act on such feelings.

Some faculty report losing their previously held credibility as authorities in their field once they announce their sexual orientation. A lesbian with 30 years of experience as a professor of psychology, most of which have been at a large state university, reports that hostility toward her has come from "other faculty, mostly heterosexual and among them heterosexual feminists, who don't want to really hear about lesbian and gay issues even when they say they are interested. So once you are out they kind of discount what you say as if 'of course' you would say it." However, this same professor also remarks that "one of the nicest things is that I have been able to convince heterosexual students to incorporate lesbian and gay people into their research and that has been rewarding." This person attests to the perhaps predictable existence of more openness in students than in colleagues.

In some instances, respondents report a certain flattening of discussion of gay and lesbian issues as a result of their coming out:

> For a couple years when I was closeted I used an exercise in a sophomore level class that I really liked. When discussing Amy Lowell's love poems, identified in the text as being written to another woman, I asked the class in small groups to assume they were an editorial board of *The World's Greatest Love Poems.* Having already decided to use her poems, they now must decide if they

will include information that they were written to another woman. . . . This exercise had generated good discussion on a complex topic. However, one of the first times I used it after I had come out early in the semester, there was little good discussion. I suspected then, and still do, that their knowing I was a lesbian inhibited them.

In other cases, faculty feel marked conflicts between their attempts at objectivity and their own responses to students' negative comments, as one lesbian professor who has taught for 15 years in the midAtlantic region writes:

> The semester the classroom became an unsafe place for me, I decided to go back into the closet.

While teaching a first-year writing course on "Race, Class, and Sexuality," which included work by people of color, gays, and lesbians, writers from different social classes, and heterosexuals, the professor was surprised to learn that some students thought the course was "about" lesbianism. Of her 68 texts, only 4 were written by lesbians. However, the teacher realized that for at least male one student, her identification as a lesbian had become part of the course content. When asked by him if he might write on why lesbians should not be allowed to parent, she responded professionally: Of course he had a right to argue his beliefs.

The student's initial argument turned on these points: children of gay and lesbian parents would be subjected to homophobia; and lesbian and gay parenting, because subject to more planning and/or technological intervention, was a sign of selfishness rather than "natural" desire.

The class and the professor responded by pointing out that there is racism in the world but no one thinks of arguing that people of color stop having children. She continues as follows:

> We convinced him. He would have to come up with a better argument and evidence. He did. When he next presented, he had carefully researched Civil Rights law. He used the lack of civil rights to argue that legally gays and lesbians should not be allowed to parent since they were not protected. At the end of the semester, I asked myself what he had learned: to challenge his professor; to use effective argumentation as a means of voicing bigotry; he even earned an A− on the paper.

Later this professor asked herself what she had learned, and her answer is sobering: If she is to continue believing that by making students better thinkers, she helps make them better people, she cannot teach that course again. She used these words:

> Now I hide behind a text [that] is my closet. I peek out behind its pages to denounce the editors who remark that Kate O'Flaherty married Oscar Chopin while failing to mention anything about Langston Hughes' or E.M. Forster's sexual orientation. I inform my students "according to your editors, unless you are married, you have no sexuality." But I no longer teach many works I admire, enjoy, and have an investment in.

Faculty teaching in conservative areas or teaching the sciences, and some working in church-related or community colleges, often said they would lose too much of their students' respect to make it worthwhile to be out in classes. A lesbian who has worked at a community college in the Midwest for 26 years commented on the loss of credibility: "During the years I was more out in [first-year] English classes, one of my colleagues (lesbian) suggested I was trying to teach with both hands tied behind my back. She was likely correct; it's difficult to have credibility with many of our students." Whatever personal loss she may have experienced from a decision to be less out in the classroom, this faculty member has chosen to do so to teach more effectively. This dilemma was caused by a homophobic climate too deeply rooted for one teacher to combat.

Campus homophobia was often noted by faculty in this study. A gay faculty member who has been teaching for 16 years in a Catholic university reports: "Since the student body is so homophobic, I can never be a popular teacher. I can't hope for advancement based on my record with students. Only closeted gays can advance this way, so 90% stay closeted. It's a horrible set-up." This faculty member understands the pressures on his colleagues and describes a context over which neither he nor they has much control. His own decision to remain out even at the expense of his student evaluations must be taken seriously. He reflected that change is unlikely at his large private institution. "I'm really convinced of little improvement in 16 years teaching. A handful of people who are the official gay scholars can capitalize on being gay, which is OK, but it's of no help to anyone else." This context might be compared with

England during the reign of Queen Elizabeth I. Though a woman was on the throne, education and opportunities for the average woman did not change. It seems that, for many, benefits do not trickle down from those enjoying advantages.

In some instances, faculty report having encountered students who expect special treatment because of sharing a common sexual identity: "It was as if [her and my] being lesbian should have negated all other aspects of my review of her work." When I first was public in my classes, I found that I expected more from students who were lesbian or gay than I did from other students. I held them to more rigorous standards than I did the heterosexual students because I wanted them to progress in spite of their social circumstances. Once I realized this reverse prejudice, I understood why African American judges could have issued stiffer sentences to African American defendants than to whites committing similar offenses or why parents from minority groups might expect superhuman accomplishments from their children. I have attempted to be more even handed to the extent that I have conscious control over my responses to students.

In a few situations, faculty report being overtly threatened by students once they began to incorporate their sexual identity into their teaching. A gay professor told me of having the door to his office torched soon after he had agreed to an interview for the school paper about being gay. Then his new door was defaced with sexually explicit and violent graffiti. This man had initially assured me that he had suffered no ill will as a result of being out in his classes. Only as he was talking did he remember the door incident. A lesbian science professor reported receiving pornographic mail under her office door, which promised to rape her as the "solution" to her being lesbian. Recognizing the handwriting of the letter, she wrote to the student's parents to confront them with what their child had done. No more threats appeared.

For a few participants, coming out in classes became the wisest move to stop speculation that obstructed the conduct of lectures or discussions:

> Students had passed the word that I was a lesbian, but none said anything to me and it got to be the "big secret," a source of eyebrow raising among them. At the end of the course when a young woman failed the class, she was angry so she went to the dean and told him "she's a lesbian and she made a pass at me." I

learned that it is better for me to lead into that identity so it can't become a tool for student games or accusations.

As this narrative illustrates, lesbian and gay faculty often find ourselves in a pedagogical double-bind: our students can attack us if we are closeted but they suspect, and they can also attack us if we are open. In this regard, our students merely reflect the society in which they live and, in many cases, the academic world in which they learn.

For me, coming out in class took a very long time. Years after I had tenure and could no longer attribute remaining closeted to any fear of losing my job, I nonetheless held back from making this information public to students. More than one respondent notes that he or she lost a position offer or a promotion or advancement because of being openly gay or lesbian. Telling myself my heterosexual colleagues were not "ready" for my big announcement, I led a double life for several years. I was out in the local community but remained tightly closeted at the university. In the summer of 1975 I was teaching Introduction to Women's Studies. Knowing that I wanted to have a couple of class meetings focus on lesbianism, I found myself in a quandary. Finally I decided I would lecture one day about the history of lesbianism in the twentieth century; the second day I would invite a panel of women from the community to speak about being lesbians.

I got through the lecture, though my palms were sweating by the end and my heartbeat racing to the finish line. The people I had asked to participate in the panel had all agreed to come, accepting my inability to speak out myself and seeming to bear me no grudge for what could easily be construed as cowardice attached to privilege. Driving to campus on the fateful morning, I rehearsed my introductory speech: "Today we are fortunate to have a panel of local lesbians who are going to talk with us about their lives and about the levels of oppression lesbians suffer." The slight awkwardness caused by my having to repeat "lesbians" twice in the same sentence was more than compensated for by my relief at finding a way to avoid using the disassociative "they."

Class assembled, the panel members seated themselves around a table on the lecture podium, and the bell rang. Nothing else stood between me and the anxiety-ridden introduction. In the back of the room were two friends with whom I was currently working at a rural feminist center for women and young children. I had asked them to come because this panel was the first time a formal class at the university had included out lesbians.

I called the class to order, reminded them of our topic, and began my introduction. Soon I was appalled and excited to hear coming from my mouth, "They are going to talk with us about their lives as lesbians and the levels of oppression we suffer." My friends stood up for a moment at the back of the room, wide grins on their faces; the panel members exchanged surprised but pleased glances; I sat down. I have no idea what the generous women who spoke to those undergraduates actually said. All I could hear were my words, which may well have gone unnoticed by most students in the room, but which echoed loudly and triumphantly in my own head. I knew change had come for me for good.

My experience is apparently common to many who participated in this study. One woman, teaching at a small liberal arts college in the East admitted this: "Each year, every time I come out to students, I gulp. It's never really much easier. I have no doubt that my self-disclosure affects my classes. I imagine my classroom feels like a more personal space, a space where it is expected that certain kinds of analysis are encouraged. We talk—or at least I do—about sex a great deal. Some students find this unendurable and others like it for the wrong reasons, and some suddenly get very analytical, perceptive, complicated in their readings and understandings."

One of the most interesting responses I had to the question of coming out in class appeared in a questionnaire completed by a lesbian philosopher with relatively few years of teaching at a prestigious private school. Her city council passed an ordinance revoking rights of access to lesbians, gays, and bisexuals. In the months before the election, the professor wore a button urging defeat of the discrimination measure, discussed the issues involved in general terms, and spoke with students who asked about the upcoming vote. She reported being devastated the morning after the legislation passed, feeling sorry not to have spoken more directly, and she decided to come out to her classes. She wanted to explain that laws harming lesbian civil rights also could make it harder to teach radical feminist material.

Reflecting on the impact this incident had upon her, she concluded that she was mistaken in assuming that her being out on campus relieved her from the responsibility to take a public stand on specific issues. Also, she felt that it was riskier for her to speak out on civil rights issues affecting lesbians and gays than it was for her heterosexual allies.

About four years ago, I was teaching a large Introduction to Women's Studies course. I had delayed coming out until we were several weeks into the quarter and about to discuss the role of lesbians and lesbianism in the second wave of the women's movement in the United States. Though nervous as usual at such moments, I also felt prepared and confident. Several times I prefaced a factual or speculative remark with "As a lesbian . . . ." The next time the class met, I asked the 135 students to write brief evaluations of the last few weeks of class, including responses to this question—"How did you react to the teacher's personal announcement?" To my amazement, my big news had escaped the notice of almost a fourth of the class. The comments included these: "Sorry, I missed it"; "I can't remember what you said"; "I knew but it seemed to matter to you to tell us, so OK"; and "What announcement—will it be on a test?"

At such moments I wish I could distribute cards with "Your teacher is a lesbian—please try to remember this fact" printed on them in boldface type, or that I could suddenly turn deep purple and have done with "coming out." In the absence of such fantasy solutions, I can only continue to stumble through the process of making my sexual identity part of my pedagogy whenever I consider it to be the appropriate intellectual stance.

General Impact on Teaching

Lesbianism has acted as a strong motivator to become involved in women's studies programs. Several respondents describe ways in which their teaching within women's studies differs from that of heterosexual colleagues. While some respondents report feeling ignored or being taken less seriously than heterosexual feminists, most have felt supported by feminist colleagues more than by members of their own departments who do not share a feminist approach to knowledge and teaching: "I teach Intro to Women's Studies totally differently from straight colleagues, and students find my course more life-transforming as a result. Students, aware that I am a lesbian, ask questions they wouldn't otherwise." On a less positive note, some faculty reported reluctance to include in the titles of their courses the words lesbian or gay for fear no one would sign up.

These provocative responses were representative:

. . . my teaching is and has always been "gay," i.e. grounded in an (outsidered) position, passionate, and inherently critical of received forms of knowledge and wisdom. Some of this has to do with style, some with content. *(cultural studies, 24 years)*

As I came out on campus, I decided I should NOT any longer do a course on "The Philosophy of Sex and Love." I felt efforts to draw students out about their romantic and sexual thinking generally would be even more difficult, embarrassing for them, or manipulative. *(philosophy, 27 years)*

I am interested in ancient rhetoric. However, because I am gay, I have started teaching a course in homosexuality in the ancient world, which is currently the only course on this campus that deals primarily with homosexuality. I am involved with the administration in setting up what may one day become a curriculum in gay and lesbian studies. *(classics, 22 years)*

I try to make sure to include gay issues in courses where relevant. But I don't have any desire to define or market myself by my sexuality first. *That* belongs to my private life. *(English, 21 years)*

The pain of grappling with my sexual orientation and the total lack of any way to conceptualize related issues in economics led me to focus on teaching and to give up a tenured position at [a major university]. *(economics, 27 years)*

I avoided lesbian books and issues during my first eight years [in the 1970s]. I began to address such issues in my research and gradually brought those elements into my teaching. Now my research is entirely on lesbian literature and theory. *(English, 27 years)*

I am out in the classroom, so even if the course is not ostensibly concerned with gay, lesbian, bisexual, queer theory issues, my body as text brings lesbianism into the classroom in ways I had not even imagined. For example, if 5% of the class were devoted to such discussions/readings, the students would say 20% or more had been. *(field not provided, 15 years)*

It [being gay] probably added to any charisma [he might have had]. Also all my energies [were] channelled into teaching, as sexual expression was forbidden—a positive effect.

(history, emeritus 49 years)

I began to teach about lesbians as part of my feminist work, *before* I came out to myself, and I found I could more comfortably teach about lesbian themes when I was NOT myself lesbian. Once I was out, I felt "was this special pleading" and, how could I teach about "them" when I should be saying "we"? This led to my developing courses in lesbian studies.   *(women's studies, 23 years)*

The variety of these responses attests to the certainty that sexual identity matters to gay and lesbian faculty when assessing their pedagogical histories, successes, and dilemmas. For me, teaching as an open lesbian has freed me from intellectual tension in my classroom demeanor for the 12 years I taught closeted. It has made me more accessible to any student ready to explore the intriguing matrix of interconnections between one's sexual orientation and one's approach to knowledge and texts.

Advising and Mentoring

For many gay and lesbian faculty members, working in informal settings as an advisor or mentor has long been a less threatening setting than a formal classroom. Perhaps this is the case because such work often occurs in one's own office or laboratory, or, more in the past than now, in public places such as restaurants and even in one's own home. Respondents note how gay and lesbian students often seek them out for informal mentoring activities: "My being 'out' has made it easier for lesbian students to approach me for independent study projects and dissertation advising on matters of lesbian sexuality." Faculty members often agree to such requests even when they are already overbooked: "There are still not enough 'safe' places for students to gather and to find support for their chosen lifestyles. Gay and lesbian students are still considered quite renegade and others are reluctant to accept their feelings/wishes as the 'real thing.'"

In the past, when relatively few of us could afford to be public about our sexual orientation, the veneer of privacy may well have prompted us to connect with those students whom we believed to be lesbian or gay or exploring their sexual identities. Even today, it sometimes seems easier for faculty to be out in these less formal relationships with their students than it is in classes, one's department, or the broader academic community. Respondents express eagerness to assist students as advisors and mentors.

Such informal teaching connections can be invaluable, especially for graduate students considering writing dissertations on gay and lesbian subject matter. Lesbian and gay advisors not only encourage new research in their field but can assist their students in making invaluable connections with like-minded faculty at other colleges and universities. They can write strong letters of support when these students go out onto the job market or apply for fellowships and grants. If they themselves keep up with research and publishing in the fields of lesbian, gay, and queer studies, they can ensure that their proteges read important scholars and theorists who are currently shaping the intellectual landscape.

However, these caveats remain. I have found that if I am not public about my sexual orientation, it can be treacherous to work with students who are or who may be questioning their sexuality. To protect myself I erect conscious or unconscious barriers from which I try to carry out various advising and mentoring activities. Perhaps I deceive myself into thinking it is possible to discuss subject matter or career choices with students in this way.

One's office in fact constitutes another arena in which being closeted may have subtly negative effects on students. This became painfully clear to me about 15 years ago when a former student wrote me a long letter detailing her attempts to talk with me during office hours about literature and eventually about her plans for further schooling. Herself a published lesbian writer at the time she wrote the letter, she described herself waiting outside my open office door while I spoke with the student who preceded her. That student was a young man whom I remember quite clearly; he often visited my office as he grappled with his own wish to attend graduate school in English while his father, a successful doctor, pressed him to apply to medical schools.

The woman described the young man and me thoroughly engaged in conversation, laughing at times, intensely serious at others. She even described my body language—leaning forward in my chair, gesturing animatedly, looking directly at the student as he spoke. All these clues told her that I was offering unqualified support to the student. Then she enumerated with pain and anger the difference in my manner and behavior when she replaced the young man in the student chair. She said I sat as far back in my chair as possible after physically moving it further away from her own before the interview even began. She told me I was peremptory, withdrawn, and in a hurry. At one point I interrupted her to say, "I need to call a colleague, so what else is on your mind today?" As I read her letter, I recognized myself sufficiently to be unable to feel defensive. Even if her quoted statements were partially her remembrance of what I may actually have said, the point remains: my demeanor changed in the presence of a woman student about whom I remember having a distinct sense that she was a lesbian. My subconscious must have feared that if I exhibited the same degree of vitality and interest in her quandary as I just had over the male student's, she might leap to the truth about me.

The wild illogic of this psychological process astounds me today. I had no fear that the young man would connect my interest and pleasure in helping him with my sexual orientation, but the need to contain my secret impelled me to deny support to that young woman. Instead of providing guidance, I came across as cold and disinterested. The experience stayed with her for years, finally prompting her to write. She waited until I was thoroughly out in my scholarship as well as in my life, and the letter was not intended to shame me, though I felt considerable guilt after reading it. The woman framed that painful visit within the context of thanking me for coming out on campus so that I could be of much-needed assistance to present and future students.

On the subject of informal teaching situations, I want to reflect on some of the potential problems inherent in the increasing use of electronic mail systems (e-mail) in education. Because e-mail works electronically and is conveyed through computer monitors, it may seem an appropriately formal method for communication. However, this mode of communication can create a charged if not intimate atmosphere.

I first used e-mail in a class I recently taught on lesbian cultures. Having obtained e-mail addresses from all my students, I set up a list of the class. Not knowing at the time of any other available arrangements, I designed a system in which we communicated one-to-one, and no one in the class had access to anyone else's messages.

Because at least 50 percent of the students in the class were self-identified lesbians in a class taught by an openly lesbian professor, students wanted to discuss many aspects of their lives with me. Though I made it clear that I wanted e-mail messages confined to questions and responses to lectures or to the text under study, inevitably I got more. I was reminded of early days in feminist pedagogy when many of us used journals as a way to help students engage more immediately in the subject matter, only to find ourselves too often presented with extraneous material. Lesbians began to tell me about their private lives, often as a way of explaining why they were behind in the readings or why a particular text had been especially appreciated or painful. They expressed concern lest I think that they were not working as hard as some other lesbian in their small research group. Occasionally they just wanted to tell me about their latest political, cultural, or romantic adventure.

Fortunately I know how essential teacher-student boundaries are to providing uncluttered learning experiences. As the first personal messages appeared on my office computer screen, red flags went up and I delayed responding until I had thought my way through the cautionary reactions that set in. I pictured the solitary undergraduate who had sent the message from her dorm room, apartment, or study lab cubicle. Then I thought about myself, similarly encased and isolated from human contact by the computer screen. Finally I took into account the staggering size of my university (approximately 35,000 students) with its inevitable impersonality, remembering other instances in which students had revealed too much of their personal lives simply because I was a faculty member who showed interest in their welfare as future thinkers and doers.

I knew it would be inappropriate for me to respond to the personal elements of the e-mail messages. There are too many chances for misunderstanding when we express ourselves in writing to a physically absent recipient. I wrote about aspects of the messages that related to our work together on the announced topic, leaving other topics unaddressed or answered only in the most general terms. To one student who told me she was behind because her partner of six years had declared the relationship over, I said, "I hope your difficulties at home are soon resolved enough to allow you to catch up on the work for this course."

Faculty are always the ones in power in any relationship with a student. In exchanges between lesbian or gay students and lesbian or gay faculty, that imbalance can be eroded by the often joint need to speak openly with someone "like" us in a relatively hostile environment. Early in my own career, I turned to students for levels of support that I now understand were absolutely inappropriate. In follow-up interviews, I learned that some of my colleagues with 25 years or more in the academy did the same and regretted the potential harm it caused to the unsuspecting and often isolated students. We must see our responsibility for delicate and precious information about some of our students. We ourselves know, often from painful experience, how devastating it can be for an authority figure to violate professional or personal boundaries.

Recently, an established scholar with 17 years as an anthropologist realized her preference for relating to women, left a long-term marriage, and became a lesbian. Though her new status has not yet significantly impacted her research agenda, and though she has not yet discovered a comfortable way to come out in her classes (she is out to colleagues and individual students), one substantial change has occurred. She has become more careful around her women students as a group and especially around lesbian students: "As long as I was straight, it was delightful to have graduate student friends, but now, I keep a distance. With graduate students, I fear sharing personal information will open up space for inappropriate intimacies. With undergraduates, I don't want to get their homophobic responses or sexual harrassment charges."

In the present academic climate, faculty members know that some measure of distance is appropriate for both students and ourselves. This awareness should allow us to exercise restraint so as not to confuse the very students we are attempting to protect. It also puts some gay and lesbian faculty in positions of potential leadership among their colleagues who struggle with how to be both accessible to students and also remain distinct from them.

At the same time, instances of inappropriate conduct initiated by lesbian or heterosexual women or by gay faculty constitute only a small fraction of sexual harassment cases on campuses. Yet,

when reported, these are often prosecuted more publicly and vigorously than the overwhelming majority of such abuses initiated
by heterosexual male faculty against female students.

Teaching from Inside the Closet

As long as this country has no federal legislation protecting gays
and lesbians in areas such as housing, child bearing and rearing,
and employment, it will be necessary for many faculty to remain
private and fearful about their sexual identities. As long as campuses either refuse to add "sexual orientation" to their anti-discrimination policies and practices or go no further than such
rhetorical assurances, faculty will continue to pass in relation to
colleagues and to withhold potentially vital and affirming information from our students and others.

In the follow-up phase of this study, I heard often and clearly of
the negative effects faculty members felt from having to remain
closeted in their classrooms. They confirmed my own experience
that such teaching is muted at best and seriously distorted at
worst. While most attributed their remaining closeted in classes to
hostile campus environments, some criticized themselves for not
being out in class, feeling that they would not only serve as role
models for any lesbian or gay students in their courses but also
might open up classrooms to a variety of diversities.

One lesbian professor of English with 19 years of teaching in
the Midwest spoke of her self-censorship. While teaching the work
by May Sarton in a course on twentieth-century women writers,
she worried about how students would respond to learning that
Sarton was a lesbian. The professor was herself teaching from the
closet. She wanted to play a tape of Sarton reading her own work.
In the introduction the commentator identified Sarton as a lesbian,
and the professor could not decide whether to play that segment:

> I must have played it and rewound it a dozen times. What finally
> spurred me to include it was thinking about a lesbian student in
> the class who was out to me and I to her [in the community]. What
> would it mean to know that I would suppress information about
> an author being a lesbian? So I played it. The sky did not fall.

This professor's willingness to be public in the broader community while feeling it necessary to remain closeted on campus—a

situation noted often by faculty in the profession at least 25 years—belies the rhetoric that colleges and universities are committed to the active pursuit of knowledge and to creating a forum for the open exchange of ideas.

I too was able to be public in the community several years before I had the courage to come out in classes or to colleagues. This phenomenon, illogical on the surface, becomes quite sane in light of the usually severe insularity of academics from most other aspects of our surrounding towns and cities. It never seems to have occurred to the lesbian cited above (or to me), that a colleague might run into her out in the world. I think this is also possible because of the complete separation that existed between heterosexual circles and lesbian or gay ones until quite recently and that still persists in many locations. Separate spheres make it possible for some faculty to live double lives.

For me, this double life became schizophrenic. Like the lesbian who finally chose to let the "l" word be spoken about May Sarton, I increasingly felt guilty in classes where students knew me. Though none of them ever criticized me, they must have done a balancing act to determine how to be with me at a Margie Adam concert or a Mary Daly lecture as compared with a class on the modern feminist novel or Shakespeare. They also may have been distinctly confused about my seeming pride about being a dyke at a Meg Christian concert or an Adrienne Rich poetry reading juxtaposed with my implicit shame about that same identity as a professor on campus. They may even have failed to make what seemed the inevitable connection because of the force of heterosexism in the society at large. Living in such a culture means that most people assume everyone is heterosexual, no matter how unlikely that becomes based on observable data.

Two or three years after my timid coming out in a women's studies course, I took an unpaid leave because it seemed increasingly impossible for me to continue working at my university. The values I saw being funded were antithetical to my own empowerment theories of education. I wanted time to explore whether I could possibly earn a living outside an institution of higher education. While I was on that leave, the women's studies program was up for review as part of the process of acquiring permanent status.

One of the team of reviewers was Florence Howe, a pioneer in women's studies and feminist publications and someone I knew from professional meetings. We had dinner while she was in town, and I shared my intention to leave academe if I could find a way to support myself. After listening to my wish to remove myself from the cushy academic world, she gave me a stern lecture I have never forgotten: She said to return and teach as one of the (then) only tenured lesbian academics in the country; she said it was harder to maintain political and personal integrity (a virtue I had just espoused as desirable) working for a large university than it would be doing something alternative on the outside.

I took her advice and made an appointment with my chair, during which I said that I intended to submit work with a lesbian feminist slant, which I expected him to read and assess on its own merits. He surprised me by sharing the little-known fact that an Australian woman writer and educator on whom he had been doing research turns out to have had a woman as her life partner. He also promised to take my work seriously, a promise on which he made good in subsequent reviews of my performance. The older I get, the longer I watch the intricacies of homophobia and heterosexism on campuses across the country, the gladder I am that I did not leave the privileged position I had managed to hang onto through years of alcoholic drinking, depressed silence, and the inertia related to keeping my sexual identity secret and hidden. I also am increasingly able to acknowledge the responsible actions on the part of that chair to whom I first came out professionally.

None of us can legislate our colleagues' behavior, and none of us ever knows the precise context within which anyone decides about publicness or privateness. It took me nine years after tenure to feel good enough about myself to abandon the closet. I have never regretted that decision. I no longer teach under a cloud of false premises. My students no longer spend valuable class time conjecturing "Is she or isn't she?" but rather can direct their energies toward the course content or, if necessary, toward coping with the clear knowledge that they are learning from a lesbian. Additionally, my being out protects me from students inclined to "report" me. Most importantly, I am able to teach literature with the fullness of my critical faculties, slighting no connections that may exist between the sexual and the creative impulse as manifested by writers from whatever period and genre I happen to be exploring.

Teaching Out of the Closet

In the excitement and empowerment that flowed from my tiny announcement on a summer morning in the late 1970s, I did what converts usually do: I swung the pendulum to the farthest extreme from where it had been originally. On the first day of every class, after asking students to fill out index cards on which they told me such demographic facts as name, majors, and progress toward graduation, and such narrative data as why they were taking my course, what hobbies and talents they possessed, and the last movie or book they had seen or read, I told them about myself. Always included was the fact that my major interests were lesbian literature and culture.

I have no idea how most students responded, but several vivid incidents remain in my memory. In a class on Shakespeare in which I made my stock comments on the first day, I noticed that on the second day one student sat with two books open on her desk: Shakespeare's *As You Like It* and the *Holy Bible*. Initially I thought perhaps she had found some line in the play that echoed something she knew from the Bible, but this did not seem to be the case. When she continued to bring the Bible to class, often choosing to sit right beside my own desk in the circle, I began to ponder what was going on. On a late afternoon walk, a thought came to me: Perhaps the student brought her Bible to defend herself against me as the sinning soul she undoubtedly thought me. I flashed to scenes from novels and films in which people held crosses in front of their faces to ward off some attacking vampire.

Rather than becoming angry or defensive as a result of this epiphany, I felt genuinely amused and then sympathetic toward the student. How difficult her position must be. She needed my course and so had to stay in it. I went to the next class determined to make the effort less frightening for her. By then we were studying *Romeo and Juliet,* so I decided to give a short talk about the place of religion in Shakespeare's day and of Christianity in particular in the plot of that play. While some of what I said was critical of the character of the Friar, that criticism came not from his practicing his Christian faith but rather from his dangerous failure to do so.

My tactic seemed to succeed. The student in question returned the next class period still in possession of her Bible but relaxed enough to leave it closed and under the text of the play. By midterm, she had stopped bringing it altogether, had begun to contribute positively to discussions, and even visited me during office hours to ask whether Shakespeare was a Christian since she kept finding veiled references to Christian beliefs. Without fudging the truth (i.e., no hard evidence can be found to label him in this way), I managed to show her that some basic Christian tenets such as forgiveness and fidelity are central to any moral or ethical system. At the end of the term, I received a course evaluation from a female student who commented that she had learned about more than Shakespeare during the term and that the instructor had heard and respected her religious views. I felt certain this had come from the student who started out so frightened of who I was and what I had to say.

If I ask myself why this story has stuck in my mind for so long, I know the answer has to do with teaching out of the closet. It is absolutely my right to come out to students; it is equally my responsibility to consider their well-being and perhaps to take some unusual measures to ensure that my desire to create a safer context for myself and the gays or lesbians in my classes does not create a dangerous or frightening context for the heterosexual students. It doesn't matter that no heterosexual teachers of mine ever seemed to have given any thought to the likes of me when they taught. I want to act more inclusively than others whom I find ignorant at best, bigoted at worst.

Many students find it empowering to study in such an open setting. This is true not only for gay and lesbian students, who naturally appreciate my public openness about my own sexual orientation, but also for many heterosexual students. In about 1980 I offered a graduate seminar on the nineteenth-century American poet Emily Dickinson. Since a great many of her poems reflect homoerotic feelings for several close women friends, I encouraged students to read for coded lesbian content. While explaining the process of reading for various codes in earlier literatures, I mentioned my own schemes for recognizing lesbian references. These approaches depend upon an erotics and aesthetics based on physical and emotional likeness, constructs that have evolved at least in part from my personal experience of lesbianism.

My frankness in the seminar opened up space for the students to discuss their own sense of the relationship between sexual expression and linguistic or poetic practice. This became apparent from in-class discussions, from students' reading journals, and in their final evaluations of the course. I was wrong in assuming that such space was presumed by heterosexual students. Several of them wrote long, eloquent comments about how emancipating the seminar had been; they said they were able for the first time to incorporate body knowledge into an intellectual setting. I was moved by this and became even more committed to coming out in classes, seeing that the benefits spread to a much larger group than I had imagined.

In 1989 I taught a course on black women writers. One of our texts was Audre Lorde's *Zami,* an account of her childhood and young adulthood. Since Lorde remains one of the most outspoken African-American lesbians, much of her story concerns her early awareness of her attraction to women. Most students in my class were white undergraduates who had given relatively little serious thought to how or why they were heterosexual, though they were part of the campus feminist community and so had considered matters related to gender. In many cases, Lorde's book was their first unequivocal exposure to lesbian material in a college course.

Even though *Zami* is about nonsexual aspects of Lorde's coming of age, the lesbian scenes stuck in students' minds. Each session devoted to the book was punctuated with comments about matters such as "why" she became a lesbian.

Since the previously studied books had all been written by heterosexual black women, I had not made any reference to lesbianism. However, I did assume that everyone in class knew that I was a lesbian, and I was surprised when students began making overtly homophobic comments: "She probably became a lesbian because of her close relationship with her mother"; "I like the book except for the scenes about her being lesbian—they make me feel ishy"; "Why does she have to write so much about her sex life—the other books we've read have all sorts of other things going on in them"; "I can't relate to this book at all—not only is she black but since she's a lesbian nothing about her personal life makes any sense to me at all." During the second discussion period I felt compelled to come out directly in an effort not to squelch such remarks but to open up the discussion for me and any students who wanted to argue for a different emphasis.

Some heterosexual students felt immediately embarrassed, rushing to assure me that they were "just fine" with the subject, that some of their best friends were lesbian, that they had not meant anything negative or critical of Lorde even though they had voiced obviously negative and critical reactions to one of the central facts in Lorde's self-definition. One or two lesbian students came out, making clear to their classmates just how silenced and invisible they felt when judgmental remarks are made without any apparent concern for live lesbians who might be sitting next to the speakers.

Though the classroom atmosphere was decidedly tense for a time, the overall effect was productive. Not only was the remainder of our work on Audre Lorde truer to her text, but subsequent discussion of all books and issues was marked by a more rigorous analysis and a higher degree of self-reflection on most students' parts about their own sexual development and the ideas of the erotic in the works of such major figures as Toni Morrison and Alice Walker. On a broader scale, my intervention, together with the admission of invisibility on the part of lesbian students, encouraged many of the heterosexual women to acknowledge the limiting effects of unexamined heterosexism. They began to grasp how that system had kept them even from realizing there might be lesbians in the same room with them.

In their evaluations, students wrote movingly about the course's having prompted them to begin a serious consideration of their journeys into heterosexuality. Some spoke of being inspired by Audre Lorde's brave example to begin writing their own sexual autobiographies, a process that was obviously affording them new insights into their private choices and the way in which heterosexist hegemony continues to flourish. Lorde herself said that what she wanted most from all sisters, black or white, lesbian or heterosexual, was for us to live a conscious life; these comments seemed integral to the course.

Many students thanked me for interrupting the usual class discussion to come out, telling me that everything about the class had seemed to deepen from that point. Since then, I have continued to acknowledge my lesbianism at some point during the term, no matter what the subject matter. However, I realize that my being in literature gives me an advantage; coming out in science or math or engineering classes surely depends upon a determined stance about the need to be open with one's students about this particular aspect of one's life. In such fields, a professor must make a decision about when and how to incorporate the fact of being gay or lesbian into her or his pedagogical approach. While, as one respondent told me, "Molecules aren't sexed," the learning situation is. Furthermore, at some point in almost every discipline, we are obligated to offer examples to our students. A professor who values being out in class surely has an opportunity to make lesbian or gay reality a part of his or her discourse.

Surprisingly, being out in class is not at all common among gay and lesbian academics. Before conducting this study, I took my own experience as some kind of touchstone. When I came out, I did so in all academic arenas simultaneously, thinking one was either "in" or "out." My definition has proven not to be the rule. Gay and lesbian faculty speak of eager incorporation of their sexual identities into research and conference presentations, or of their willing sponsorship of student groups on campus, or of agreeing to be interviewed for community newspapers on issues of concern to lesbians and gay men, or of their openness about themselves (and, where relevant, their partners) at departmental and campus social occasions. However, these same faculty often say that they are not out in their classrooms. Some point out that it is not pertinent to what they teach; some indicate that they fear losing student respect; some see their "private lives" as none of their students' business; some have simply gotten used to teaching without being out and see no need to change. In an essay entitled "Personal Reflections on Coming Out, Prejudice, and Homophobia in the Academic Workplace," Ritch Savin-Williams summarizes a feeling that may lie behind all these explanations: "Little did I realize at the time the impact of the interview [about homosexuality, for a local alternative newspaper]: I lost control of who would know" (Diamant, 230).

A gay professor of English teaching on the East Coast recounted what may be a useful model for coming out to students in a class. Drawing a clear distinction between his role as a teacher and as a member of the faculty, he comes out to his colleagues. He plays an active part in campus lesbian, gay, and bisexual concerns. In the classroom, however, he feels the details of his life are irrelevant:

> Some students have said that I am very mysterious in the class-room, but I aim to make it a comfortable place for everyone in it—including myself. I don't care to deal with homophobia di-rected at me. (I've been teaching for over twenty years, and some of these ground rules were formulated when I began. I don't be-lieve I would face homophobic comments today. But I'm sure those feelings are still out there.) Of course, many students know I am gay because I am such a public figure.

Faculty cite additional reasons for remaining silent in the class-room about being gay or lesbian, as one professor of religious stud-ies at a southern university concludes:

> Because I teach about religion within a secular, public, pluralistic university, I have always been sensitive to my role as midwife to students of every type and persuasion. I am unwilling to simply represent one mode of being or inculcate a single orthodoxy of whatever form. Thus, by extension, I am generally unwilling to be openly gay within the classroom and to be seen as advocating particular gay positions exclusively.

Some faculty feel no need to come out to students, even if their campuses are accepting of diversity. A lesbian professor of com-parative literature makes no effort to hide her identity from indi-vidual students when asked direct questions. She includes lesbian and gay texts in her courses, but she has never come out in the classroom. She does not ascribe to the notion that being lesbian al-lows her to read differently from those who are not. Were she to teach lesbian or gay studies, she would see her identity as directly relevant and would consider it productive to come out.

However clear this individual is about not revealing her les-bianism in classroom settings, she nonetheless remembers two moments in her teaching career when she felt a need, "not acted upon in either case, to announce [her] sexuality to a class as a per-tinent part of discussion." The first was in the early 1980s, when she and several other women faculty were invited to a class taught by an African American colleague. The topic was feminism in Alice Walker's *The Color Purple*. "In the discussion, the instructor

57

deplored the lesbianism in the novel as denigrating to ideas about black life in America in a way that I found offensive and bigoted. I challenged prescribing content because of what we 'want' from texts." The professor did not make a personal statement because doing so would have distracted from the main point of the discussion. She was highly unsatisfied with the experience.

The second instance came in 1994 during the final class meeting of a course on forms of discrimination related to the history of infectious diseases. The lesbian professor reports "less dynamic discussion and less controversy than we had hoped, less lively debate than had occurred the last time we taught the course." The class was nearly half students of color, a far higher percentage than that on campus as a whole. Several of those students commented that discussions had "walked right up to issues of race but then skirted around them," an accusation the professor felt was justified. She asked whether beginning the semester with some discussion of overlapping identities would have improved the climate so that students might have taken more risks:

> This elicited a productive conversation in which students identified aspects of their identities that complicated their classroom lives. I did not come out, largely because the students were talking about themselves in important ways and I did not want to shift attention. However, as I think about my pedagogical strategies, next time I teach [this course], I will handle the issue differently.

Many lesbian and gay faculty who come out in classes do so in part to control who knows about our sexual identity. When I took the initiative in this matter, I disarmed several colleagues who might have hurt me. Once I was out to him, a close male friend told me a bizarre story. He was part of a weekly poker group at which talk flowed more freely as tongues were loosened by beer and bourbon. It seems that two or three of my most senior colleagues told of recording instances of my being seen with another woman—faculty, stranger, student, staff employee, or lover. They boasted at one of these marathons that if I ever had the nerve to sue them for not promoting me on sexist grounds, they would confront me with their record and threaten to disclose my private life. This tactic pleased them because it would transfer the problem from them to me. They saw it as their ace in the hole.

My friend assured me that I had taken away a potent weapon by announcing to my chairman and, through him, to the department, that I was a lesbian. No longer could my detractors feel capable of frightening me into silence about their refusal to recognize my accomplishments. Hearing this elaborate scheme confirmed my sense that naming myself took away others' ability to label me. To a lesser degree, coming out in my classes insures my safety from students who might wish to compromise my judgement of their work by accusing me of being lesbian in the face of my silence on this crucial subject.

For me, pedagogical strength seems to be attendant upon my coming out early in the term. In most undergraduate classes, I tell a favorite story on my "coming out day":

> Let's say I get to know, like, and respect someone through shared social or political activities or aims. At some point in our process, I learn that they occupy some category previously off my scale of acceptability. It's as if I had built a picture frame around what is "normal" or "good," which I assume includes the individual, who suddenly I find possesses characteristics that force me to exclude him or her from my picture. I can leave my friend or colleague outside the frame or I can revisit my lumberyard to purchase more wood to enlarge my frame.

This story usually works in getting students to think about the limitations inherent in prejudice against whole groups of people. On several occasions, the story has prompted notes from students who want to thank me for giving them a way to understand what happens when they find out something surprising about a friend or family member. One person wrote the following: "I just want to thank you, Toni, for your story about your picture frame. After class, I went right over to my lumberyard and bought more wood!"

At the graduate level, a declaration of my sexual identity assumes an entirely organic position in my pedagogy. Most seminars I offer focus on individual women writers, on implications of gender on genre, or on expressly lesbian-feminist theoretical concerns. Students know from titles and descriptions exactly what will be explored, and they anticipate my perspective. Whatever their own perspectives might be, they welcome a forum in which formal intellectual connections are made between the erotic and the creative, between sexuality and language, or between authorial bodies.

and literary strategies. Being out in such a context is essential for the success of the course.

In addition, my decision to be out is set in a context of a huge research university in a metropolitan area in one of the precious few states to legislate civil rights protection for lesbians and gay men. If I worked in a less liberal environment, my pedagogical stance might well be altered. Certainly if more of my students were members of fundamentalist Christian denominations with parents who monitored their academic studies, my choice to be open in classes would become rather quickly an unaffordable luxury.

As more becomes known about the rich diversity of approaches to teaching as gay or lesbian faculty, I need to remember that circumstances vary widely and each individual must make his or her own decisions. I remind myself constantly that none of us ever knows the innermost processes any lesbian or gay faculty member goes through in finding the best solution. For many gay and lesbian colleagues in this country, there is no genuine solution at all. People simply must do what they can to keep body and soul intact, and this is perhaps the saddest reality shared with me during this research. I want to carry that reality close to my heart and mind as I continue to argue for the highest degree of openness possible in a given context.

CHAPTER 3

"And What Did You Do Over the Weekend?"

A t a 1993 session for university staff intended to increase sensitivity to lesbian and gay issues in the workplace, I participated in a panel commissioned to speak about daily personal experiences with colleagues and staff. During the question period, the members of the panel were asked repeatedly in one way or another for helpful hints about how to let co-workers know that you believe them to be gay or lesbian if they have not spoken about their sexual orientation. I responded with the usual suggestions—put books, magazines, or posters by or about lesbians and gays in one's workspace; mention having watched a television program or newcast focusing on a relevant issue; make clear where possible that you have gay and lesbian friends or relatives; but my mind reeled back 30 years to my own early days in the English department.

Back then, I could not mention my life to the other lesbian on staff; she needed to remain separate, and she also could vote for or against my retention by the department. As an unaccompanied woman, I found it difficult to socialize within the department, at dinners or cocktail parties. Because my partner and I were totally closeted, I never took her to such functions. At the yearly departmental gathering in the fall, the wife of an older man in the department often tried to help me feel more a part of the scene by initiating conversations like this:

"Well, Toni, how are you finding Minneapolis [or your students/the winter/our art galleries/the symphony/your neighborhood]?"

"Oh, just fine, thank you," gulping my drink or sandwich in a frantic effort to buy some time while I thought about what I could say next to the person who was trying too hard to set me at ease. I usually muttered something about the latest movie or concert I had attended and smiled vacuously.

"Are you making friends, meeting people? Or are you missing someone special back in Madison?" The tone of the last question was hopeful, modulated to draw me into her confidence, and reminiscent of my mother's queries each holiday visit during college as she became increasingly concerned over my seeming failure to present some nice young man for her to meet.

Utter panic. My "someone special" was at home studying theories of personality development and deviant behavior. How to answer a question so innocuous on its surface? I didn't dare speak what was in my mind: "No, I'm not meeting people—it takes all my spare time to manage my secret life, thank you."

I fled such gatherings with headaches and stomach upsets; gradually I began to refuse invitations altogether, withdrawing into the seemingly protective shell of our apartment where my partner and I did not discuss what was happening to us. I also gradually relied on the bottle, finding my precarious position and growing loneliness more bearable if I were not quite sober most of my nonworking hours. The few times we had people over for dinner, matters were little improved over the cocktail party atmosphere. Since we presented ourselves as detached roommates, there was little opportunity for open conversation. These evenings were not enjoyable, and we were seldom invited to the homes of people whom we entertained.

The survey indicates that the isolation and pretense common in the 1960s continues even today. A lesbian who has taught at a large southern university for two decades reports that she did not ask to teach a course entitled Lesbian Culture until "*after* I had gotten tenure, and [I] waited to actually formally propose it until I had completed my [book] project. Then I had the full backing of my department and the college dean." Another lesbian who came out in 1976 writes as follows:

I've always felt alienated in academe, don't socialize with other academics, mostly don't know them. By now I probably could be out and be comfortable with my colleagues, but for so long it was not safe to show them who I was that by now my social world has completely diverged from them. This of course affects how seriously I am taken on campus as an academic and as "part of the team."

Other faculty report a "coolness" from colleagues, or an obvious "discomfort" with openly addressing "the topic" (gayness or lesbianism).

Heterosexual Assumptions

Most people tend to see what they are looking for. In the world of the academy, just as is the case in the broader culture, most people think in terms of a heterosexual orientation, giving little or no thought to the varieties of sexuality that may be present in their midst. For individuals with alternative sexual orientations, this myopic situation can be irritating, painful, ludicrous, or a combination of all three. As workplace issues continue to be monitored and theorized about, the exclusionary power of such heterosexual assumptions will become increasingly clear, not only to lesbian and gay members of the workforce but to our heterosexual allies and friends.

Studies of the consequences of such assumptions on various subsets within the academic profession are beginning to appear. In the 1994 study focused on sociologists and conducted by Verta Taylor and Nicole Raeburn (1), faculty respondents routinely reported being left out of both informal and formal social events on their campuses. Several connected this situation with difficulties they encountered in gaining tenure and promotion specifically and in advancing within campus professional networks more generally. One such sociologist connected being excluded from his campus social scene with his difficulty in obtaining tenure. It made a significant difference that neither he nor he and his partner as a couple were invited to most departmental gatherings, because this had an influence on how he was perceived by members of his review committee. Further, he believed that the fact that top administrators at his institution knew him only through his documented record, unenhanced by personal and informal contact, further disadvantaged his career progress.

On the more positive side, respondents to my study reported increased and increasing acceptance of themselves and their partners once they come out and begin to assume that they deserve the same considerations as their heterosexual colleagues:

One such perception comes from an administrator at a university in the southwest:

> My position functions at the level of a dean, so is fairly visible. While out, my sexuality is rarely at the forefront of my relationships so it's difficult to say how well it's known. The local paper did a feature article shortly after my appointment, and my partner was mentioned. A student paper featured our long-term relationship with photos—so we've been pretty public. It is rarely if ever mentioned. Social invitations from provost and president have been inclusive.

Even in this open context, this man still must wonder how well his sexuality is known. Second, is it altogether desirable to have one's most important relationship rarely mentioned by colleagues? One reason this silence persists is this: Most people working with lesbian and gay colleagues who have come out still do not really "see" such individuals in the same ways they do co-workers who have heterosexual partners. It may be necessary for gay and lesbian faculty members to keep coming out over and over to help colleagues register and incorporate this awareness into routine conversations. We may even need to tell others how lonely and invisible we feel when they do not ask us the same personal, family-oriented questions they ask one another.

Cultural myopia is glaringly present in the following narrative from a lesbian with 16 years of experience at a major midwestern research university:

> When I came to the [university] in 1984, I intended to be fully out in my department, and did nothing to hide my sexual orientation. I assumed I was doing this by just going about my life, hiding nothing (such as my partner, children whose lives I had been part of for years, and, eventually, grandchildren). Furthermore, because of her work, my partner was prominent in the g/l community, so I thought that if I did try to be closeted, it would drive me

nuts and be fruitless. I did not believe making announcements was necessary.

However, it seemed that for years, for the most part, only gay and lesbian students and faculty, and, of course, personal friends of whatever "stripe" knew I was a lesbian. While I wasn't always sure what others knew, there simply was no indication, one way or the other, from people like my department head. Over time, I became increasingly convinced that the head, as well as others on the faculty, didn't "get it." This was confirmed when my partner became ill with breast cancer. Because word of this got around, some faculty (including one person I had worked very closely with on some research for several years) finally understood and were very supportive. Prior to this time, I had taken my partner to departmental functions and we had social functions at our house, but apparently that wasn't enough for some people to realize what the relationship was.

Even after the breast cancer led to many people [understanding my circumstances], my head didn't know I was a lesbian until I sat in his office one day after being at the University about six years and simply told him. This was in the context of a discussion about concerns some senior faculty had about my "productivity." I had taken a quarter of unpaid leave because of my partner's illness and felt that I should explain what my perceptions of my "low productivity" were. Somewhat to my surprise (colleagues who knew I was going to have this conversation bet on whether or not he knew), when I told him I was a lesbian he was completely surprised, saying that he knew nothing about the cancer or subsequent difficulties we had been dealing with. He then said, defensively, that he didn't know about anyone's private life in the department. I pointed out that if a heterosexual's partner had cancer and they were having other serious problems, people were almost always aware of it. (Ironically, at that time, a heterosexual man in the department was on sabbatical in another country, yet we all knew he was having an affair and that he and his wife were getting a divorce. The department head did acknowledge that this was true and that we did tend to know about "big" things going on in our colleagues' lives.)

The point of this story is that I don't think I am now fundamentally any different in terms of being out, but others around me have become more conscious that gays and lesbians exist in the world and that they work with some. While I was not the first or only lesbian in the department, I don't think the situation was different for them. The difference was that I was consciously TRYING to be out and some of the others weren't. Now when a new gay or lesbian person joins the department, in addition to not having to hide the fact, the consciousness has been raised to the extent that people who didn't get it, even when it was right in front of them 5 to 10 years ago, get it now.

We can help co-workers in their efforts to make us feel more included and substantial within the workplace if we say, "Ask me about what my partner and I did over the weekend, for a major holiday, on our vacation. Once I tell you my partner's name, file it away just as you do the names of co-workers' spouses, so that you can refer to her specifically rather than having to resort continually to some distancing generic—'And how is your partner?' Think of me, my partner, and our cherished animals as a family that enjoys the same activities and feels the same kinds of stress that you and your family do, compounded by our not being legally recognized as a family at all. Speak out when you hear anti-lesbian or anti-gay jokes because you have friends, relatives, or co-workers who are gay or lesbian and you do not want to hear unfair and denigrating remarks about their group. If you're an affectionate person, extend your usual physical and verbal contacts to me when the occasion warrants."

The last item is important because so often I feel the person with me holding back from a hug or affectionate comment. Equally true is a degree of hesitation on my part about touching because I have internalized too many of the culture's poisonous assumptions that gays and lesbians are always on the prowl. This restraint makes for awkward and painful moments between me and some of my heterosexual co-workers, especially women who may fear being misinterpreted by a chance onlooker or even by me. What heterosexual colleagues need to remember is that most lesbian or gay faculty have our own networks for meeting people and for arranging and finding dates, lovers, and partners. We are not interested in them in this way. They might also see us the same way they see themselves; that is, often entirely too busy with class preparation, a scholarly paper, sick children at home, or a long list of errands to run before the day is over to be thinking of anyone in an amorous way.

In about 1990, I was a vocal gadfly urging our central administrators to deliver on their formal statement that the University no longer discriminates on the basis of sexual orientation. We had no health insurance or fringe benefits for our long-term life partners, whereas our heterosexual counterparts were blessed with instant and total coverage of a married partner. Accompanied by the associate vice-president for human resources, who is a staunch ally, I had an appointment with the academic vice-president. This individual would determine further measures intended to establish equity for lesbian and gay faculty, and I hoped to catch his attention by being personal rather than ideological.

After presenting information gathered by members of a blue-ribbon committee studying campus climate for gays and lesbians, I told him the following story. I have a good friend and colleague with whom I do odious household chores every other week, alternating between his house and mine. He and his wife are two of my oldest friends. Often he and I drive together on a freeway headed for Knox Lumber or a good hardware store. If we were to be killed in an accident, the University would send his wife, Martha, a letter of condolence, telling her of two options for collecting Martin's 30 years of retirement and pension funds. One option would be to receive a lump sum check; the other would be to be paid in monthly installments, beginning whenever she chose until she was 65. My partner, Susan, would get a letter informing her that as my beneficiary, she was receiving the enclosed check for the full amount earned in my 31 years at the University. Martha is smart and would delay payment until she was older, at which time she could pay fewer taxes because of reduced income. Susan would have no choice but to deposit and invest the check sent her. If Martin and I were killed tomorrow, given the total in my fund right now, Susan would have to write a check to the IRS for approximately $85,000 to cover her profit after losing her partner of 17 years. I asked if this seemed fair.

The academic vice-president was uncomfortable and agreed it was not fair, but he said the University's hands were tied by federal stipulations. Just as I was trying to feel kind toward him, he looked at me and said, "One of my concerns is that there might be so much turnover of faculty filling out forms to declare new domestic partners during an academic year."

My heterosexual ally and I exchanged a look of amazement before I responded, "Oh, most of us are too busy shoveling snow or grading papers to have the energy for all that high romance." My humor was lost on him, only causing his face to redden as he contemplated his own anxieties about this issue. My ally re-minded him that more than 50 percent of heterosexual marriages end in divorce, so maybe they ought to refrain from speculating about multiple partners for the few lesbian or gay faculty who would register for benefits. As we walked away from that discussion, we agreed that homophobia, like racism, requires the constant renewal of prejudice and fear through the creation of enforced differences between people like me and people like that administrator.

A few years ago, my partner and I were invited to a retirement dinner for an old friend of mine in history, a heterosexual man who had befriended women's studies in its formative days and advised one of the first openly lesbian doctoral dissertations on campus. He and his spouse had become friends of ours, so my partner and I were eager to attend the festivities. Arriving as close to the dinner hour as possible so I would not have to watch other people drink, we decided to purchase some mineral water to pass the time. As it happened, the person getting his drinks just ahead of us was the president of the university, someone I had known for years, who had always been quite civil, even after I came out academically. When he saw me, he turned his smile and his body in my direction and shook hands affably, not paying any attention to the person behind me in line.

"I'd like you to meet my partner, Susan" caught him totally by surprise, as if in his mind I might exist as an abstraction of something called "lesbian," but never as someone with a domestic and erotic life. There were a few seconds during which he was unable to hide his dismay tinged with distaste at having to acknowledge that, like him, I had a committed relationship that had a powerful dailiness about it. Recovering, he finally extended his hand to Susan. But the truth of his reaction will never fade from my memory, not because it particularly hurt either of us—in fact, we laughed about it at the time and later with friends—but because it so distinctly reinforced our shared conviction that many heterosexuals need desperately for lesbians and gay men to be different from them or else there will be no basis for continued discrimination, trivialization, and just plain neglect.

The persistence of a sense that lesbians and gays are different from heterosexuals continues to cause lesbian and gay faculty to be seen as a seemingly unavoidable embarrassment at best and a dangerous or unnatural force at worst. In the Taylor-Raeburn study, a significant percentage of subjects (27 percent in 1981, 47 percent in 1992) acknowledge difficulties in the workplace with heterosexual or closeted colleagues who exclude them and their work on grounds of negative differences. In my own follow-up narratives, I found repeated instances of similar "othering." One professor, retired after more than 30 years at a major midwestern research university, wrote as follows:

> In the early 70s I was a delegate from my local Episcopal parish to the convention assembled to elect our diocesan bishop. One of my departmental colleagues, a fellow parishioner, knew I would be voting for the new bishop, and tried to lobby me (he is a major homophobe): "Now, I hope you realize we need to keep homosexuals out of the church; be sure you vote for a candidate with orthodox [read anti-gay] credentials." I was not out, so the colleague didn't realize what my attitude toward homosexuality would be, though he suspected me of "liberalism." I was tempted to reply, "But I am homosexual myself." I didn't have the courage to come out or embarrass him publicly. But I DID say, "Well, on such an important question as homosexuality, I will have to vote my conscience." The candidate for whom I voted was elected and consecrated, and he has grown over the years to be a very tolerant—even loving—bishop toward gay Episcopalians in his diocese.

Many incidents from my thirty years at the University of Minnesota mirror this short-sightedness on the part of colleagues. In 1969, five years after my arrival in the department, one male colleague and his spouse were still inviting me to dinner parties made up of married couples, me, and an unattached man from some other department. Such obvious attempts to matchmake or at least balance the dinner table in an acceptable way amazed and amused me on the surface. Under that surface, I felt totally invisible to people who liked me and wanted to befriend me and yet were unable even to imagine a scenario in which they might invite an unattached woman as a potential "date" for me or ask me to bring a guest. Either my host thought "pairs" could only involve one man and one woman; or they were afraid to extend an open invitation for fear I would bring lesbianism into their midst. I remember hoping that the latter was true, since the former would suggest a paucity of imagination unappealing in people I might number among my friends.

Dangers of Working from Inside the Closet

Most gay and lesbian faculty who remain closeted at work do so to protect jobs and opportunities for advancement. I certainly did. However, I received tenure after only three years at the University of Minnesota, but continued to hide my sexual identity from colleagues for another nine years. Tenure came to me unexpectedly and for ironic reasons, at least partly because of the intervention of a disgruntled full professor who had recently been hired to chair an English department at a private college in New York State and was disappointed that there was no chance of his becoming chair at Minnesota. It was also true that I had won an outstanding teacher award; I had volunteered for such traditionally odious service as representing the department on the teacher education committee; I showed promise as a scholar of the Renaissance, having already presented papers at the Modern Language Association as well as at relevant regional conferences. I was awarded tenure, and a party followed at the soon-to-depart professor's house. I went alone, still terrified to acknowledge my relationship with my partner. The professor told me that when he asked himself what he could do to irritate for the longest period of time a department that was treating him shabbily, he thought of me and set about amassing data in support of my promotion.

When I reflect on what kept me in the closet for the next nine years, I come up with two major possibilities: my alcoholic drinking, a seemingly necessary accompaniment to my passing within the academy, kept me in a continual fog about how to conduct myself; my internalized homophobia fooled me into blaming the heterosexuals who surrounded me for my inability to be open and honest about myself. I told myself "they" were not ready for my story.

This self-censoring did not arise out of nowhere, nor do I blame myself for my fabrication. I came out in 1958 in Mississippi, where as recently as 1994 three white gay men had been brutally murdered and the authorities barely made an effort to discover why or by whom. At that time and place *no one* would have been ready to hear that I was a lesbian. In Vicksburg, where I had my first teaching position, I was criticized for driving a Volkswagen bug, for wearing slacks to shop on Saturdays, and for being seen entering the town's only movie house during a three-day run of *The L-Shaped Room*. My support of the "foreign" clearly branded me as suspect and dangerous by alumnae of the girls' school where I worked.

My original retreat into the closet was purely a survival measure. I did not understand it as an anti-survival stance until years later, when I made the inextricable connection between my closet and my bottle and decided on the same day to abandon both, no matter what the consequences might be.

Respondents to this study confirm that working in the closet may backfire in unexpected ways. A lesbian English professor with 20 years of experience writes as follows:

> In my first full-time job, I taught in an English department with 23 men and one other woman. I was out to the faculty and to students who chose to tell me about their sexual orientation. I did not feel comfortable with most colleagues, however, and was not out to them, nor did I socialize a great deal. Near the end of my two-year contract, they eliminated my specialty and told me that my contract would therefore not be renewed. They then turned around and hired someone—a straight woman—whose research interests were very close to my own, but who had less teaching experience.

> I was convinced then, and remain so, that I lost that job precisely because I *was* closeted. I didn't let colleagues know who I was; they guessed that I was a lesbian; they let me go. I'm not saying it was my fault that I was not re-hired, but that pragmatically, I'm better off coming out than not coming out. The experience taught me *not* to hide—that secrets probably make people more uncomfortable than uncomfortable things that they [actually] know; and if they are going to discriminate against me as a lesbian, I want them to have to do it openly.

> Coming out is, for me, the best way to *avoid* discrimination in higher education. I always come out as part of a statement on another subject, e.g. "Well, as a lesbian, I'm particularly aware of how Clinton's health plan will . . ."), to give my interlocutor an opportunity to pick up on, or to drop, the subject. I always say it

in a positive way, and I have never had anyone respond in a negative way. The "aura" I put around being a lesbian is "That's what
I am, so it must be the best thing since sliced bread."

A history professor with 29 years of experience teaching in the
Midwest writes as follows:

Back in 1970, when I was closeted, one of my colleagues warned
me about the friends with whom I was hanging out. He worried
that people might think I was an "H" (he was so paranoid he
could not even say the word homosexual). I dismissed his concern, but it really churned in my gut that I did not confront him
with being gay. Ten years later he had a severe mental collapse
when he "came out." The university had to fire him for his bizarre
behavior. Maybe if I had nipped all this in the bud in 1970, I could
have helped him. He was hiding behind marriage, kids, etc., and
never sent a clue until he crashed.

Finally, a lesbian with years at a religious-affiliated college in
the Midwest writes of the humiliating experiences she has had to
endure as she negotiates the treacherous landscape at her institution. In her first years, because she was one of the very few gay or
lesbian faculty, she chose to be out only to close colleagues. Living
in campus housing, she neither hid nor announced the fact that
she had a lover who visited from another town. When she was up
for renewal, she came out to a supportive senior colleague who
told her he had thought she was a lesbian because of her "body
type." He went on to assure her that the "god of love is beautiful regardless of how bruised and battered."

When this professor came out to the academic dean in her third
year on campus, it was in a context in which he was feeling concern
that their college would be seen as a "haven for homosexuals" because
it was considering an affirmative action policy to include gays and lesbians. Two years later, a new dean began suggesting that he could help
her find another job, even though she was enjoying such honors as
being asked by the senior class to deliver the baccalaureate address.
Their exchange went as follows:

The dean called me into his office, ostensibly to talk about
Women's Studies, and said, "I've been talking with the Board who
assured me "that if 'one' came up for tenure and if 'one' got it and

'one's' lifestyle then became public, 'one' would be terminated for moral terpitude. 'One' would be expected to resign." I said, "If one were to get tenure and one's lifestyle were to become public, one would have to decide what one would do at that time."

After 11 years of this delicate balancing act, the lesbian professor decided to stop limiting her behavior based on what she thought the college could bear. This was a freeing move, and now the college is headed by a president who has made gay rights a hiring-firing issue. The lesbian is herself an associate academic dean, working directly for the president who was surprised to learn that she had never said in a class, "As a lesbian, I." After he told her she could do so, an occasion eventually arose; but after taking so long in coming, it seemed anticlimactic.

During her 19 years at the college, she has watched a number of gay and lesbian colleagues come and go. She is, as she puts it, "the identified queer on campus, and being friends with me without a certified 'spouse and children heterosexual' card can have some stigma attached." Some of the Christian members of her community are intolerant, while others evangelize around the broken nature of humans. Colleagues on the right are openly hostile, and she is anxious about what will happen if the current president leaves. She concludes this way:

> You must be asking yourself "Why/how does she stay there." Because the teaching is very good—I like what students and teachers do together. I also live 30 miles from the college and have a life away from it. For the last 17 summers I've coordinated health care at a national women's event. I have always read a lot and books by other lesbians have helped me. I've benefited from the vision of folks like Daly and Raymond and Frye and Anzaldua and Smith and Penelope and Lorde and Rich. . . . I follow, teach, find fascinating, and am sometimes moved by the current "gender" and "sex" debates, and share worries about essentializing "woman." But what folks are calling "cultural feminism" with such disdain saved the lives of lots of rural, isolated dykes. I am one.

These narratives speak to the personal and professional costs of working day in and day out with people to whom one feels compelled to lie by omission.

Dangers of Working from an "Out" Position

Being ignorant or oblivious to material by and about lesbians and gay men turns out to be one of the more benign postures exhibited by academic colleagues. More often, overt or covert homophobia may be operating where colleagues refuse to accommodate lesbian and gay faculty members. Internalized homophobia showed itself once I came out at work. None of the lesbian faculty I met was publicly out on campus, so all our community building was done in private homes or at restaurants, where we discussed everything except our personal lives and where we never touched our lovers or made any other identifiable show of affection, erotic interest, or involvement.

When I came out on campus, this seemingly close-knit network began to experience discomfort and eventually to unravel. On one occasion in particular, I was ostracized by four lesbians with whom I had been having lively dinners several times a month for several years. I went directly from a volleyball game with some of my teammates to hear a talk by Kate Millett, a former undergraduate English major at the University of Minnesota. When Millet finished speaking and the lights went up in the auditorium, I saw four of my lesbian friends talking animatedly. As I approached the group, they all briskly turned and walked away from me.

The next day my best friend at the University, a heterosexual feminist, tried to help me sort out what had happened and how I was feeling. She suggested that the other lesbians might have been embarrassed by my sports attire, which set me apart from those in more conventional academic dress and made me look even more "butch" than usual. The part of her argument that struck home was that I definitely did not "pass" in that auditorium—either as a neutered and unmarried female or as a respectable faculty member. I was too out to allow my friends to associate with me in public, and so my decision to act in a manner conducive to my personal sanity and happiness endangered my relationship with former friends. In some instances, it even broke established ties.

While it has taken me years to develop a manner of being with colleagues that is satisfactory for me and manageable for most of them, some of the respondents to my questionnaire have been able to maintain one stance over long tenures at their institutions or within the profession. This response comes from a professor with 27 years experience teaching at a southeastern graduate/research university.

In 27 years, mine has been a posture of "keep them guessing." I was tenured within three years of arriving at the university; however, it was a very long time—21 years—before I was made full professor. A few have said I would have been promoted earlier but for my sexuality. There is evidence to support that position; however, there is also the fact that the university because a "research" university with "publish or perish" as its motto, and my academic style no longer fit. An equally strong case could be made that I was being punished not for my sexuality but for my laziness. This [may seem] a liberal place, but this is a facade carefully maintained by the administration. The student body is very homophobic, and I know that I would lose a great deal of respect were I to publicly come out. I think my gay students know this, for they have never once suggested that I do so, nor have they asked me why I am not publicly out. . . . No one ever told me, but I always got the impression that "if I kept my skirt clean, nothing would happen."

I met other gay faculty within a few months of arrival, and they gave me a sort of orientation though it was mostly a case of introducing me at parties and telling me about the bar scene. . . . Other than the "promotion thing," I have not felt put upon here. But this is evidence of something: it was only after I had been promoted to full professor that I did any writing about gay subjects. I wrote a journal article and subsequently a book about gay adolescents. I would not have written any of this prior to being promoted. Though there are plenty of official statements prohibiting discrimination, I had a decided fear about publishing anything having to do with homosexuality until I was safely in the fold.

In assessing me and my career, I believe it is a case of the celebrated "half-full, half-empty glass." If you look for victimization and repression, it is certainly here. Maybe I would have been a lot happier if I had come out years ago. We shall never know, and that is the point. I am bothered by the victimization crowd that posits that were just *one* element changed, life would be a bed of roses. This is simplistic reductionism; life may have been *changed,* but we have no assurance that life would necessarily be better. This campus is homophobic. I have not been free to stroll on campus, holding the hand of my male friend, nor have I been able to come out and at the same time preserve my considerable popularity among the student body. I have not been truly free to write until very recently. At the same time, I have not been hassled, bashed, stifled in my classroom, or threatened with dismissal. I have enjoyed a career which would be the envy of most. I have not felt any awful weight pressing down upon me. My young gay friends of a more radical stripe say that I have simply grown so used to it that I don't know it's there. How do you argue with that?

This professor, who accuses himself of "laziness" because he did not write more and sooner, is now engaged in a productive writing career focused on gay subject matter. By his own admission, his voice was freed only after he had achieved enough institutional security to risk speaking his own scholarly truths and theories. Yet he sets up an either-or explanation early in his narrative—either he is being punished for his sexuality or for his laziness. May he not have been being punished for a silence integrally related to his sexuality?

Embedded within this professor's articulation of 27 years at his university is a template for entirely too many lesbian and gay academics. When he invokes the half-full, half-empty argument, I feel entirely sympathetic. Family and friends often smile at my insistence on the half-full reading of some aspect of my or their lives. While I am not ready to abandon my way of interpreting reality, I do recognize that, like Boethius, I am consoling myself with philosophy, perhaps to continue functioning in the world as it is. I can still remain aware that the world as is remains a far cry from the world as it might be.

Hiring Practices

If a potential faculty member is open about his or her sexual orientation during the hiring process, he or she may not be taken seriously for the position. A lesbian professor of English working at a graduate university in the Midwest writes as follows:

A couple years ago I was on a search committee and very excited that an out lesbian scholar was among the applicants. She emerged as one of the two top candidates and was interviewed at our yearly conference. However, before it was decided who would be invited to campus, everyone on the committee was asked to read her newest book and comment on whether her approach was important and broad enough to be useful to graduate students. We were not asked to do anything similar for the other candidate. I told chairs of the recruitment committee and the department that it was homophobic to treat an out lesbian candidate differently than other candidates. But they were on their liberal "we need the best candidate" horse and wouldn't get it. I'm still bitter about this.

This kind of special scrutiny discourages faculty from researching gay and lesbian issues. When I read this account, I think of books on arcane aspects of standard topics; these books, which interest only relatively few specialists, are seldom questioned for their broadness or importance or, least of all, for their potential usefulness to students.

My department recently interviewed a creative writing candidate; she did not announce her lesbianism during her interview, but the subject figures in all her writings, as do parent-child relationships; common human motives like greed, jealousy, anger, and revenge; abuse of children by adults who should be trustworthy; and all manner of political engagements by the women and men who people her stories. At the meeting where we were to decide between her and our other top candidate, much coded speech focused on whether she could be of assistance to the young men in the creative writing program, given her somewhat harsh treatment of many of her male characters. In the interest of a positive vote, I bit my tongue and did not ask, "When did you worry about whether the three men we've hired in creative writing would be of assistance to the young women in the program, given their sometimes stereotypical treatment of the female characters in their fiction or poetry?" Nor did I dare name their behavior for what is was—blatant paranoid homophobia. The lesbian candidate got the job, but only after a distinguished professor stood up and named the elephant in the middle of our living room: "Aren't you really worried whether a lesbian can teach straights—and isn't that entirely beside the point before us?"

A senior professor in the field of recreation writes the following:

> Four years ago, I was invited to a university in New England to interview for deanship. After an exhausting but upbeat day with the faculty and some middle level administrators, all of whom made comments about my strengths, I met with the president. Toward the end, I asked if their would be any problem with me being an open and vocal gay member of the faculty. He blanched ashen, swallowed, and made an incoherent reference to that not being an issue at his school. I never heard from them again.

The situation is especially difficult for those seeking employment at colleges and universities whose partners are also lesbian or gay faculty members. While I have never had a lover or partner who taught at the University, several of the respondents in this study say pain and awkwardness characterize their personal relationships. The difficulty comes in making a move from one academic location to another. If one or both members of the couple are closeted, they must decide to declare their sexual orientation and their relationship with a colleague suddenly and under duress. Most gay or lesbian academic couples continue to work at different locations rather than risk coming out while attempting to find employment. While similar difficulties are encountered by heterosexual academic couples, especially as the job market as a whole continues to shrink, such faculty are at least able to complain openly and to get the benefit of sympathy from friends and co-workers.

At my own university, where partner hires are protected now that sexual orientation is part of our antidiscrimination statement, the situation seems to be more easily accommodated when both persons are at the beginning of their careers rather than more senior in rank. In the cases of new assistant professors, I often wonder if chairs and deans do not perhaps unconsciously assume that the relationships will have dissolved by tenure time. Presented with two established and tenured scholars who also share a life, however, the same administrators who have been supportive of getting the very best young people possible begin to focus on the budget, acting in bureautic slow-motion.

In my own department recently, we hired an advanced associate professor who requested the hiring of her long-time partner, a full professor in another field, as one of the conditions of her acceptance of our offer. Our chair, usually an aggressive voice on behalf of the department's personnel decisions, did nothing for several months. I forced the issue by scheduling a lunch with the new faculty member, her partner who was in town on leave from her own university, and me. Amidst much chat initiated by the chair, it became evident that he had not given any specific consideration to this matter crucial to the retention of a valued new colleague. This slow pace continued at every level of negotiations, causing both my colleague and her partner much irritation and pain. The process that should have begun as soon as the new faculty member accepted the English department's offer was brought to a positive conclusion three years later. This treatment blunted whatever celebratory mood might have been possible in better circumstances.

A social scientist at a major research university in the Midwest wrote at length about her vexing dilemma. Subjected to years of exclusion from the social life of her department, false accusations that she had an affair with a graduate student, and delays in promotion proceedings even though her publication record is substantial, she understandably wanted to work elsewhere. However, since her partner is a full professor in a field with more limited job possibilities than her own, she has

> judiciously pursued a small number of interviews for positions elsewhere. We feel lucky to be among the few lesbian couples we know of working on the same campus. In all three instances where I interviewed at major institutions (ironically with better or at least the same reputations as my school) I had to withdraw from the search because there was no possibility of their hiring [my partner]. I was simply unwilling to live apart from her.

This professor has to overlook any exclusionary and discriminatory practices out of gratitude for being able to live and work with her partner. She is clearly hindered by having to choose between advancement and her relationship. While it is certainly true that some heterosexual academic couples must cope with long-distance commutes or with delaying one or the other's move in order to remain in the same physical location, universities and colleges currently expect to be asked to work for spousal hires. No danger exists in asking for such special consideration, whereas for many lesbian or gay couples, doing so forces a public announcement about their sexual identity that may jeopardize any chance of either person's being hired.

Here is a story about a department's self-defeat in connection to a women's studies professor at a large state university on the East Coast:

> The most significant thing that happened in my department after I was tenured and out was when my then lover was nominated for a teaching position in the department, jointly with women's studies. Knowing our situation (and in recognition of her brilliance), women's studies enthusiastically and unanimously voted for her appointment. But my department fooled around, and it was clear to me that they did not support the appointment because they did not want two lesbian colleagues. All the people I had thought were so liberal turned out to be phobic. Of course they said no such thing; they argued about which literature area they should hire in. When they could not make up their mind, and it was clear that they were not going to come through, my lover took a job elsewhere, and the department LOST the line [i.e. the money for the position reverted to the college to be assigned elsewhere]. I personally think that is what they were wanting. Now, it must be said they were a feuding crazy bunch, but still, who would otherwise turn down a brilliant scholar one is being given as a gift?

A homophobic group will invent reasons for not hiring, tenuring, promoting, or valuing gay and lesbian colleagues. In my own case, I was denied promotion to full professor for six years after I had begun to publish widely and regularly. Until that time, the reason I had been given for such delay was that, while I was a superb teacher and citizen, I lacked sufficient publications. Once I had two edited books, several articles, and a third single-authored book in the works, the reason shifted and my publications were not "academic" enough. Finally, a chair to whom I am deeply grateful told me that I could turn into Northrop Frye overnight and it would not matter. He assured me that certain members of the department had made up their minds about me in my early years and nothing I could do would dissuade them.

Academic Leadership

Higher education resembles the U.S. military with its tacit policy of "don't ask, don't tell," especially if a person wants to advance within the administrative hierarchy. This theory is certainly borne out on my own campus. Lesbians and gay men occupy very responsible positions at all levels of governance, but virtually all of them keep their sexual orientation under wraps, perhaps telling friends but never making their "private" lives part of their professional lives. At administrative functions, they most often appear alone as if they had no family; they sanitize or refrain from discussing leisure activities. They cut themselves off from natural alliances with co-workers, many of whom guess that they are gay or lesbian but are in the awkward position of having to remain silent.

A few years ago, one of these highly placed and professionally closeted administrators developed cancer and underwent a successful operation. The woman then spent a long recuperation period at home, during which a co-worker called me to ask, "Toni, I think [she] has a life partner whom I would like to include in my message on the card I'm sending. But she's never told me, so do you think I should do that, or will it upset her or them too much to find out someone in the office knows their secret? I want to do the least intrusive thing, but it feels so cold not to say something to the person who is taking care of my friend and who's been through a lot of worry."

I told my scrupulous caller to follow her heart and no one could mind, but I kept hearing the confusion mixed with genuine care in her voice. Suddenly I remembered how stilted many of my friendships had been during the years I was closeted in the English department. Even my two best friends and I limited our intimacy. Since I never said anything about my home life, they were reluctant to share much of theirs. When I came out, I vowed to do something about this reticence. Realizing, like so many of the respondents to this study, that coming out once is seldom enough, I talked with my friends about the effects of my being closeted on our conversations. I admitted that I had focused on topics about the department in large part because they were "safe," and I said I wanted us to become more personal with one another. In cases where a deepening friendship with the other person was important to me, I asked her to read Adrienne Rich's now-classic essay, "Compulsory Heterosexuality and Lesbian Existence." My two closest friends agreed, and we eventually discussed it at length. I needed a sophisticated theoretical articulation to validate my experience and to justify bringing that experience into the scope of our conversation. My friends may well have read Rich out of their fondness for me.

My resolve to speak about my home life and to listen carefully when friends did likewise has truly paid off. Frozen friendships from the old days thawed and have become precious. Newer connections blossom or languish much sooner than when I hid my sexual orientation, since everyone can understand more quickly whether we wish to pursue a friendship. In fact, this clarity is the single most important reward I get for being open with co-workers.

In a few instances, this newfound clarity has brought a painful awareness about old university ties. Once again, some of the most difficult situations have arisen with partially or totally closeted lesbians. If such people have been closeted for many years, they have made certain accommodations. If any of us plays a role long enough, we tend to lose our ability to set it aside when circumstances no longer require us to pretend to some identity. In her feminist pamphlet *Three Guineas,* the English writer Virginia Woolf cautions women who are being admitted for the first time to colleges and universities to remain members of what she calls the "Outsiders' Society." She fears that women will be asked to give up their differences in order to gain admission to historically male preserves. Similarly, lesbians and gay men remain vulnerable to being expected to seem the same as everyone else, making it awkward and painful when any of their number declares his or her sexual orientation.

In the 20 years since I came out and began reconstructing my life at work, I have felt the effects of colleagues' attempts to steer conversations away from potentially revealing subjects and of their answering blandly when asked about life away from school. I begin to do what my heterosexual friends did when I behaved similarly—I withhold my own intimate information and eventually stop asking about the other person's. Our relationships drift for a while until it no longer seems urgent to make arrangements to get together, since no deeper friendship can develop.

Working from an "Out" Position

Lesbian and gay faculty members are often expected to accommodate homophobic anger that is often expressed orally. Colleagues may take "pot shots," banking either on the other person's being too polite to descend to their level of innuendo or too fearful to confront them directly. Part of why they can continue to behave in this debilitating fashion is the fact that in too many instances, the other person conforms to their expectations. They do not understand that the other person may just be stunned into silence by the speaker's cruelty.

In 1994, I served on a committee that was considering ways to make our campus less hostile for lesbians and gays. The committee was composed of four women and nine men, all white full professors elected from across the campus, all heterosexual except for me. The two people presenting a set of five recommendations intended to give greater equity to lesbian and gay faculty were a lesbian administrator and a heterosexual man who chaired the Faculty Social Concerns Committee. Directly across the table from me sat a longtime colleague from the History Department, a man with whom I had served on numerous college committees. Though we often disagreed about curricular and policy matters, we had always been quite civil to one another.

At one point, my history colleague began a speech which floored me entirely. Looking right at me, he said, "I and I'm sure a large majority of the faculty at this university continue to believe that the *only* situation within which to live and raise children is the heterosexual family, and I'll actively work against *any* efforts from any quarter of the university to change our public stance toward homosexuals on this campus." I maintained my composure, but his hostility affected me personally and I began to cry once out of the room.

I flashed to a freezing cold evening in January a few years back. While walking our bouncy English cocker spaniel, I slipped on a patch of invisible ice. My head hit the concrete and I was momentarily stunned beyond knowing where I was or how to get up. That was exactly how it felt sitting in the Regents' Room of the university to which I had devoted at that time thirty years of extraordinary service.

As I discussed this episode with my partner and close friends, I knew I had to either resign from the committee or to make a public statement at our next meeting. Several committee members called me to express their support for me, in light of the unfair comment that had been made. After a few days, I decided not to resign, since my point of view as a lesbian feminist would then be lost entirely and the homophobe would win much more than the battle of words over "homosexuality." So when next we met, I requested from the chair five minutes to make a personal statement.

The history professor was absent with an injury, but I spoke briefly anyway. I said that I appreciated the several committee members who had called me to make clear that they supported me, but I hoped in the future they would express their disagreement at the time and publicly. Then I simply asserted that the best way to live and to rear children was in loving homes. Though the man in history would have read my remarks in circulated minutes of the committee's proceedings, I never heard any more from him.

One survey respondent, a lesbian scientist with 25 years of teaching, recounted the following:

> The most significant exchange I have had with a colleague took place during open hearings hosted by a presidential committee on diversity and tolerance. The speaker ahead of me was a colleague whom I thought I knew fairly well after serving together on the Faculty Senate as well as on several committees. I was not prepared for what was to come out of this man's mouth since it was rhetoric that I had certainly read but not heard spoken by someone I respected. His message objected to the inclusion of gays and lesbians in the recommendations since they were immoral, recruiting young people, and responsible for much of the AIDS epidemic. My testimony, an account of the isolation, invisibility, and intolerance I had felt as a closeted gay faculty member, was difficult and emotional. I ended with a statement directed toward my colleague, telling him how personally hurtful his testimony had been. I will never forget his response, a response which made an enormous impact on the heterosexual members of the commission. It was, "but ____, I didn't mean you." I assured him that I was a proud member of the community about whom he was speaking. That exchange and the work of the commission with support from the administration has resulted in many positive changes in campus policy and culture.

A lesbian with 19 years in the academy, now teaching at a large and respected law school in the Midwest, writes as follows:

I seldom go into the faculty lunchroom. It has been taken over by (from my perspective) unfriendly types. Having not gone there for four or five months, I ventured in because I wanted to see if it could be made more friendly so that more people I cared about could visit comfortably. The day before, I had received a newspaper clipping about the appointment of a lesbian as a federal judge. It was claimed that she was the first openly gay person to be appointed to the federal judiciary. This clipping came to me unsigned and I was a bit angry about that. I suspected who had placed it in my mailbox—an older colleague who seems obsessed by my lesbianism. He came into the lunchroom, joined a group of four of us, and immediately asked what I thought about the news item. I made some noncommittal answer and others at the table wanted to know what we were talking about. I can't remember whether he or I explained the clipping. A conservative woman constitutional law professor said that she had it on good authority from an out law professor at another school that a Justice of the Supreme Court is gay, something this professor knew because he had seen copies of that Justice's receipts from video stores where he rented pornographic movies. My response was that I would have thought the professor would have been more careful about outing people. Her response was that he did not out the Justice because he just told a group of law professors, not in a public speech. I lamely said that I thought hers a problematic definition of outing. I continued to sit in this discussion which I realized in an other-body way was a "take a lesbian to lunch" encounter. At one point the question was raised by a male professor about when people at the table had first known they knew a gay person. I was numb and getting number as an older professor told a story of his college roommate's making a pass at him. Another older professor said he thought he must have known some at his all-male college. I again lamely said that I thought we needed to be cautious about evaluating events in the 20s and 30s with a 90s perspective. I said that I thought it might have been easier for men at an all-male college to come out than in many other situations. A contemporary colleague said "Well, that isn't true in the military and it's mostly male." I incredulously replied, "That's my point. There is a big difference between the consequences of coming out at a private college and in the military or on an assembly line." All I said seemed not to make a bit of difference; I only felt lesser for having engaged. I've told this story to friends— both straight and lesbian. The more I tell it, the more it hurts.

The most glaring aspect of this account is the near silence of the narrator, who is otherwise a productive and articulate legal scholar. References to pornography bills and to the college roommate's advances introduce two pervasive stereotypes of gay men— promiscuity and cruising. If the woman objects to such rumors on feminist grounds, she "sides" with the heterosexual detractors. If she silences herself, she comes away feeling impotent. In the end she is left with no effective avenues of response.

Conditions in the Workplace

When I consider the latest generation of lesbian and gay faculty, who are teaching courses in gay/lesbian/bisexual studies; publishing dissertations, articles and books on queer theory; or organizing panels on these topics at professional meetings, I feel a rush of excitement. I also feel a little like the late eighteenth-century English poet Thomas Gray, who wrote a poem about looking down at some young students at his old prep school, Eton. From his vantage point, their flamboyant play was shadowed by knowledge gained from bitter experience. These wonderfully open and assertive individuals sometimes look at old-timers like me with a mixture of indulgent sufferance and sentimental trivializing, sure that the world has changed permanently. Yet progress could be rescinded by the same liberal bodies that have allowed it to occur.

We must look at the realities of American culture squarely and then persist in celebrating sexual orientation as a fact of our intellectual, pedagogical, and professional lives as much as it is of our home lives. The older generation of lesbians and gays within the academy will need to give way to more youthful enthusiasms even when we want to urge alert caution. The younger generation will need to recognize that the persistence and bravery of their more senior predecessors contribute to their freedom to work as people more open about sexual identity and its relationship to teaching and research. Most of all, we will need to listen to one another.

For example, here are words from a veteran academic:

It's a battle. Those of us who have been in the trenches longest have the most scars, but it is good for those who have come after to face a less hostile environment.

A young lesbian was eager to describe her circumstances at the prestigious eastern private university where she teaches:

It is absolutely clear to me that my life (as an out lesbian theorist) is possible in ways never before realizable, and also that dykes in academia of my generation have a sense of entitlement because of this.

Finally, consider these cheering words from a head of a journalism department in the Midwest:

Being gay or lesbian in this university makes no more difference than color of hair or eyes. My dean and the president inquire about the health of my disabled partner (of thirty-nine years). A lesbian and I were appointed to the fringe benefits committee to try to negotiate spousal benefits for unmarried couples. In the directory of faculty experts that is distributed to the media and various organizations, I am listed as an "expert" on gay and lesbian rights, among other of my specialties. In such an open environment, it is difficult to pinpoint any single exchange where my being gay mattered.

The world advocated and described here was unimaginable in the mid-60s, when I began my long career.

Even with such changes taking place in many locations, most campuses still refuse to acknowledge lesbian and gay faculty as part of their "diversity" population. When my college's curriculum committee met a few years back to design a cultural diversity requirement, followed by a listing of courses that would fulfill such a requirement, an out lesbian happened to be serving on the committee. We talked about the best strategy to use in trying to get the committee to include gay and lesbian history and culture courses. We devised an argument for such inclusion: In a deeply homophobic society like the one in the United States, lesbian and gay groups constitute a genuine minority, discriminated against in many of the same ways as racial and ethnic minorities and hence eligible for some of the same gestures of recourse. We also developed the ultimately academic argument that so much of the material studied in many departments within the College of Liberal

Arts had been produced by gay and lesbian artists, writers, and thinkers that continuing to cloak their contributions by hiding their sexual identities from students would run counter to the definition of a liberal education.

My friend made these and other arguments cogently and with conviction, but the committee refused to include gayness and lesbianism as an element of cultural diversity. Many lesbian and gay faculty feel themselves to be valuable resources for diversifying their department's curricular and research agendas, but most report resistance from their colleagues. One respondent, a social scientist, expressed the following:

> I believe that part of the reasons that I had to engage in a long struggle for tenure (that I eventually won) was because of very subtle, covert hostility in the form of lack of appreciation for what I brought to the department in terms of diversity. This has become clearer to me now that I have been "at the table" for others' annual reviews and tenure decisions. I have observed that those who tend to be very progressive have on occasion been more verbal, in a negative sort of way, about homosexuality than about other issues of diversity. Homosexuality seems to be the issue that is perceived to be 'safe' in terms of thinking that it is being addressed 'too much' in the classroom, compared to other issues of diversity.

Gains in the Workplace

Tangible gains have been made in terms of relationships in the workplace. In my own case, I no longer need to skulk in corners to eat lunch with my partner or speak in generalities about what I do on weekends, holidays, and vacations. My chairs routinely extend invitations to my partner Susan by name, and she is listed in the departmental directory under the column labeled "spouse." In fact, her placement there is a story about the vestigial remains of my own internalized homophobia. Long after I had declared my sexual identity and proposed and received approval to teach courses in lesbian literature, I still allowed myself to be listed in that directory as if I had no one who loved me specially or with whom I made a household. Shortly after my fiftieth birthday, I asked Susan if she had any objection to my sending in her name to be included under "spouses." She did not, so I wrote a note to the secretary in charge of collecting data. Between that time and the appearance of the directory, my dominant feeling was fear. What was I afraid of? Feeling younger and more vulnerable than I really was, I fantasized about being called into the chair's office to be reprimanded for introducing sexuality into an innocuous list of addresses and telephone numbers. It took conscious effort to remember that every heterosexual faculty member who listed his or her spouse was introducing sexuality. I still remember the day the list appeared in our boxes, the thrill I experienced to see my lover in the same category as my friends' husbands, and the pride with which I showed the directory to Susan that evening at dinner. While I have grave reservations about marriage as it has been framed and practiced historically, I want public recognition that my intimate connection carries similar weight and moment as more conventional unions.

For a welcome cadre of my colleagues, I constitute a valuable resource, someone to whom they can turn for books by and about lesbian or gay life and literary theory. Responding to such queries gives me a feeling of being useful, though no one can any longer boast about having read even the majority of current work in this area. But having to tell colleagues that I do not know the answer to a question about contemporary English gay poets or African lesbian novelists fills me with pleasure. At the very least, such questions point me in new directions.

One of the follow-up narratives brought up a moving aspect of being viewed as a resource. The speaker, a lesbian teaching English at a university in the midwest, reports the following:

> I have had several significant conversations with colleagues who have lesbian children, who have come to me ostensibly to talk about something else but have ended up "coming out" as a parent of a lesbian or telling me something that is troubling them about their lesbian daughter. They're seeking some kind of reassurance, "inside information" from me that it's OK. One colleague and his wife talked to me, and at one point asked me to have coffee with their daughter when she was home from college. (They claimed that it was "OK" with them, but they didn't understand that she seemed to live almost entirely in a lesbian world, since they themselves had all kinds of friends, "even" gays and lesbians.) In a recent conversation, the husband told me that his daughter and

her partner were thinking of having a child. Clearly this upset him. We talked about how a lesbian could become pregnant, and he asked if I had friends who had done this. I had, so I could tell him about their experiences. This guy is a not-show-your-emotions-stiff-upper-lipper from Maine. He hasn't said anything to me about appreciating being able to talk, although I know he does. Every once in a while he'll give me an update in an offhand kind of way, like "Oh, you'll be interested to know that my daughter and her partner decided they can't afford a child right now." I feel this has enabled a closeness that we wouldn't have otherwise. And, since he's vice-chair and makes teaching assignments, I suspect that may have subliminally influenced my teaching schedule for the last several years, when I have taught women's lit almost exclusively, a gay and lesbian lit class, and a lesbian lit class of my own devising.

Stories like these not only warm my heart; they confirm my own experience that when I am comfortable about my life as a lesbian within the academy, many faculty who know and like me are more comfortable with me and with the subject of lesbianism and gayness. Since I work in an area where from a third to a half of the writers taught and researched share my sexual orientation, there is a great need for a ripple effect caused by increased faculty comfort levels.

Sometimes I am unable to determine whether exclusionary practices and persistent hostilities toward me accrue to my being a lesbian or to my being a feminist working in the predominantly white-collar hold-out of sexist ideology that is higher education. On at least one occasion, I detected an attempt to divide my two close heterosexual women friends and me along lines of sexual orientation. We had all received letters informing us of our raises. In each of our cases, the chair had failed to award us our deserved merit points. As we had in the past, we drafted a single letter demanding a review and reassignment of points according to the record we submitted. A few days later, I had a note from the chair to come in to see him about my salary. Wary, I kept the appointment and found myself in his office with the door closed. What he wanted to tell me was that he had considered my request for additional merit points and realized that he had indeed miscalculated. He offered to change the documents to reflect the additional points I had proposed.

When I asked what decision he had reached in the cases of my two friends, he was visibly surprised. "Oh, I'm not going to change theirs—their arguments don't hold water, they're just sour grapes. But yours . . . ," he paused to clap me around the shoulders with a force I felt would be more appropriate in a locker room than a chair's office, "yours stands up to objective measures, is something I can get behind and defend."

I looked at him pleasantly but firmly and replied, "Well, then, I won't be able to accept your alterations in my case; all of us were unfairly treated, so if you can't see the merit of their arguments, I don't want any changes for myself." His incomprehension was unmaskable. I was putting friendship before monetary gain, loyalty above competition. I was not falling in with his clear attempts to separate me from the two heterosexual women with whom he often flirted at meetings.

In retrospect, I believe my words prevented him from categorizing me, the lesbian, as someone more like him with a rational claim to his attention while my friends remained "women" complaining and wanting special treatment.

In a follow-up interview with a lesbian faculty member at a prestigious private college in the East, I was startled but validated to read the following analysis of how things are on her campus:

> I think it's actually easier for some of the older men at this school [historically all-male] to have gay than straight women on the faculty. After all, we don't infect the campus with feminine sexuality. Of course, if that is true, it's a very dark vision of gayness, isn't it?

Some colleagues obviously continue to cast lesbians as not quite female. The fact that this occasionally may work to our advantage in no way lessens the fundamental insult imbedded in the definition.

In regards to recent responses to openly gay and lesbian colleagues, some narratives suggest that gender issues may have an impact on how one's faculty colleagues react. Perhaps the single most revealing instance of this turns around a fortuitous coincidence: a lesbian and a gay man from the same highly ranked college in the East spoke to the issue. The lesbian is the person cited above who believes that lesbians have caused fewer ripples than have heterosexual faculty women at this historically all-male college. Her theory makes fascinating reading when juxtaposed with the narrative returned by a gay faculty member with 22 years in the classics department of the same school. He writes the following:

> The experience of faculty lesbians and gays in the last decade has been eerily benign. The institution traditionally had the intense homosociality and tormented homophobia of a single-sex institution. Once women arrived, traumatically (for the women), in 1978, those mean old tendencies found focus and vigor in misogyny, leaving gays more or less untouched (indeed, in some ways as the inheritors of the all-male traditions), and leaving lesbians to be undervalued and overnoticed not as queers but as women. (Some very butch colleagues have fitted in comparatively easily.) Curiously, one of the problems for faculty is that being out for us is so much easier than for some students, who feel all the guiltier for their hesitation and fears. The constituency of my classes may have shifted since I came out, some of the legions of male jokes in lecture courses may have migrated elsewhere, with the result that the quality of the course has increased. The major resistance I got last year from teaching Women's and Gender Studies was not from the women students, who seemed completely uninterested in my gender, but from the male minority (1/6th), who felt marginalized and undervalued. My main insight may be that in a community that can make remarkable strides in overcoming homophobia, a major result may be to reveal how intractable sexism is.

This professor espouses the same ideology about some of his lesbian colleagues as does his lesbian colleague, i.e. many heterosexual males still stereotype lesbians as "mannish." The gay faculty member, however, finds that in certain circumstances this fact can work in favor of an individual lesbian who may or may not see herself in the same light. In this gay professor's reading of his campus, many heterosexual males are less disturbed by the presence of lesbians than by women who have been culturally stereoptyped as "feminine."

The damaging aspect of this phenomenon, as I myself have experienced, is that such a view leaves lesbians with no identifiable sex in the minds of many male colleagues. This status may provide short-term protection from deeply intrenched misogynist attitudes, but it certainly offers no genuine support for being who one is. Falling off the map is never merely an adventure; I suspect it always feels like a wipe out, like being put "outdoors" must feel to the African Americans who write with powerful dread of such total exclusion from family and community. For the gay man quoted above, the academic climate may indeed be benign. But no campus populated by large numbers of faculty who respond stereotypically can boast a truly warm climate for its lesbian or gay faculty. The *world* of work remains for many of us a tricky *place* indeed.

CHAPTER 4

"Any Room for Me Here?"

Virginia Woolf writes in *A Room of One's Own* that it is impossible for women to do their best writing when their only audience is Professor X. For Woolf, this impersonal male recipient represents everything that is repressive and static in the established worlds of scholarship and thought, a recipient who will inevitably squelch her most daring or original ideas and words in favor of something bland—if there must be a "something" at all.

For the twelve years I worked at the University of Minnesota closeted, my research and writing languished. Though I arrived on campus with a dissertation manuscript on a virtually unmined field of literary inquiry (rhetorical strategies found in the 160 extant sermons by the infamous seventeenth-century poet-turned-preacher, John Donne), none of my senior colleagues was willing to help me get it published. As all promising graduate students were told to do in those days, I asked a senior scholar in my department if he would read my manuscript and advise me about needed revisions and prospective publishers. He agreed with a smile and took my year's labor into his book-lined office.

When two months had elapsed without any word, I timidly asked him one morning in the coffee room, "Oh, Dr. ____, have you had a chance to glance at my work on Donne's sermons? I'm not in a rush, of course, but was just wondering. . . ." In the moment during which he could not entirely cover his confusion, I knew that not only had he not read my work, but he had not even registered my request sufficiently to feel bad about not doing so. Once he had regained his equilibrium, he made a series of half-sentences in

95

which he described his busy schedule and his own writing deadlines, ending with an invitation to come by his office in two weeks to discuss my next steps.

Appearing on his doorstep once again caused him momentary confusion, but in his effort to recover, he offered me a chair and a cup of coffee. (I was an inveterate tea-drinker but accepted in the hopes that social accommodation might enhance my chances of getting some sound advice about my future.) At first he could not even find my manuscript, but after disrupting several stacks of papers on his desk, he finally unearthed it from a pile which appeared not to have been touched for some time.

I tried to hide my disappointment, and the scholar tried to hide his neglect. My intended mentor managed one comment about my rather esoteric research into Donne's prose style: "Well, Toni, you've done a fine job here, and with just a little polishing, it will be ready to mail off to a publisher. Thank you for letting me read it." I thanked him profusely for doing nothing for me or my advancement.

Before I could get out of that office, however, I was invited for cocktails in a tone full of self-confidence, by a man suddenly possessed of *savoir faire*. I knew in an instant what was in my senior colleague's mind. My distaste was complete, not only because his was an inappropriate "move" upon a very junior faculty member in no real position to refuse, but also because it signaled his total insensitivity to me as the lesbian I was.

My colleague's invitation sprang from his heterosexist assumption that since I was female I was fair game for his flirtatious impulses. Over the years, several heterosexual women in the department were similarly invited by this man for dinner or cocktails. They accepted, fully aware of his game, but able to play along because they often responded with pleasure to male flirtation. From the depths of my lesbian self came my involuntary response to his overture: "Oh, no, I won't be able to do that with you. I wanted intellectual help, not social contact." I fled his office and never showed the Donne manuscript to anyone else or pursued its revision further.

Why I was not able to recover from and put behind me this multiply insulting incident is all tied up with my inability to share the fact of my lesbianism with my colleagues. The academic context in the mid-1960s certainly was less accepting than it is today, and I had no immediate models for being public about sexual orientation. But, in my field, pioneering scholars like Louie Crew and Virginia Noll were already beginning to publish articles and present conference papers which were richly informed by their gay and lesbian critical perspective. In my case, however, the most important operative fact was that I had internalized the world's negative views of me at some deep level of semi-consciousness. That unacknowledged and unexamined internalization kept me essentially silent not only about lesbian or gay literary matters but as an intellectual.

Not being able to claim and celebrate my innermost life had a serious impact on my ability to claim and celebrate my ideas. Again Virginia Woolf is instructive: in *Three Guineas* (1939) she states unequivocally that anyone dependent upon their "father" for financial support or approval will hesitate to express ideas that conflict with his; more particularly, she remarks that women living in a world that attaches tremendous "atmosphere" to the appellation "Miss" will stunt themselves in a pathetic effort to recede from critical view. My method of stunting myself was to rely increasingly on alcohol to dull the pain I felt over how my senior colleagues were treating me as well as the fear and shame I felt over a sexual orientation the culture had taught me to loathe as immoral and offensive to decent people.

In the short term, I accepted and mimicked my potential mentor's trivialization of me and my work, abandoning Donne as a subject of research. For the next few years I wrote a second book-length manuscript focusing on Shakespeare's late romances, *Pericles, Cymbeline, The Winter's Tale,* and *The Tempest.* During a final phase of my work, I applied for and received a summer grant that allowed me to hire a graduate assistant to check bibliographical references in the library. This student, a gay man himself and someone who eventually became a friend out of school, was excited about my approach to the plays. In a moment of naivete, he had shared my hypothesis with his dissertation advisor, a man who had always competed with me as a classroom teacher. Out of what I assume was some complex matrix of jealousies—personal and professional in nature—he wrote an acquaintance who worked at the press that had accepted my book for publication, telling him that much of the McNaron manuscript had been ghostwritten by a graduate student.

Once again, I folded my research tent and crept away to my apartment where I spent many days drinking far too much bourbon. I believe that no one can handle internal homophobia and external rejection without developing some kind of mechanism for easing the inevitable pain and self-doubt. My mechanism was alcohol. I spent my first decade in the academy on a steadily downward slope first acknowledged in undergraduate school when I could no longer bear to admit that I was failing utterly at the serious business of dating boys or moving toward marriage and family life.

In 1974, I sobered up, began coming out to a few friends at work, and began keeping a journal. At first the journal was something to do with all the open time I suddenly had. Drinking and hangovers had consumed many waking hours for years and left me a little foggy about how to spend free time. Gradually, the focus of my journals shifted from interminable monologues about how to survive another day without a drink to ideas about what I was teaching, seeing on film and television, or discussing with colleagues and friends. I filled 26 thick journals in the space of two years—a lot of writing for someone who had stopped saying anything about anything on paper a long time before.

Soon after this epiphanic moment, I began to write about literature from a feminist perspective, followed shortly by my first piece of lesbian-feminist criticism. It was a speech about lesbian poetry delivered to members of the local women's community. In it, I dealt with Adrienne Rich, Olga Broumas, and Audre Lorde and speculated tentatively about ways in which their poetry might differ from work produced by heterosexual poets. Though it has taken years to develop those initial speculations into a full-fledged theory of an alternative aesthetic based on likeness rather than opposition (the dominant aesthetic), that work began on Valentine's Day, 1977, in a church meeting hall before an audience of about a hundred lesbians eager to learn more about their culture.

Increased Productivity

My experience is mirrored by many of the survey responses I received. One gay professor with 24 years at a major research university in the Midwest wrote: "My research and scholarship languished until lesbian/gay studies came of age in the academy and I realized I had something to say that was connected to my lived experience and to my teaching." A lesbian librarian with 24 years' experience at a large state university said this:

> I feel more *alive* than I've ever been because I am being *me.* I have compiled a 100+ page bibliography of lesbian/gay material in the library system for the campus community, am writing an article on [a new museum], am the chair of [two gay/lesbian caucus committees of her professional association], taught a [women's studies] course (spring of 1994)—"Out of the Closet and Into View, Art History from the Gay/Lesbian Perspective."

From the moment I began interpreting literature from a lesbian perspective, my scholarly career took off. Finally, I had a clear voice and an audience with a face. Before going too public with my work, however, I determined that I had to talk with my chair to insure his taking such scholarship seriously in terms of merit and promotion to full professor. The man in that position had worked his way through college on a boxing scholarship, still played rugby weekly, and prided himself on being a no-nonsense fellow.

After several practice runs, initially in front of my mirror and eventually in a role play where my partner assumed the persona of my chair, I made the appointment. I had a speech committed to memory and even had the presence of mind to ask the chair to hear me out before responding. (As a somewhat impatient man, he had a habit of interrupting colleagues who seemed to be thinking their way through some idea at too slow a pace for his taste.) "I plan to return from my year's leave without pay as a lesbian-feminist scholar. I'll be writing articles and eventually books as well as making conference presentations from that approach. I expect you to read and take such work as seriously as you do all the other kinds of literary research conducted by your faculty. Can you do that?"

The response has supportive. Since his goal was to help his faculty be productive, my chair said he was delighted to hear of my rejuvenated writing career. He then spoke of an Australian woman on whom he had done extensive research. She had lived for many years with another Australian woman, and he offered to show me his book about her. This attempt to establish his credentials as someone who indeed could judge lesbian-feminist criticism seemed touching. I thanked him and told him I would take him at his word. The next spring when I presented two articles having a lesbian focus, my chair did indeed read them and award me appropriate merit points.

Since then, all of my research and writing has assumed a lesbian-feminist point of view as backdrop if not actual subject matter. After 12 years of virtual silence, I became a consistent and substantial scholar. I am convinced that without having come out professionally, my career would have continued to be founded on superb teaching and generous service, even as my salary and status in the department would have continued to slide backward. As it is, I am among the five best-paid professors in the English Department, a fact which depends almost exclusively upon scholarly productivity.

Many other gay and lesbian faculty speak of an increased excitement about and execution of scholarship once they have chosen to conduct such work from a perspective informed by their sexual orientation. An English professor in California writes, "My career as a scholar has been about 75% in lesbian studies (and growing)—my reputation is entirely due to my lesbian work." A professor of French for 20 years at a small midwestern university describes his scholarly trajectory:

> Up until 5 or so years ago, my work on [a lesbian writer] was primarily based on a feminist approach. Now I'm interested in analysis of the lesbian content and forms of her work. Recent publications have treated these questions. And I'm no longer interested in women's issues, but rather, lesbian issues.

A gay faculty member with 37 years at a prestigious private university in the East writes: "Being out has allowed me to develop sensitive analyses of HIV issues . . . . I could not DO what I do without being gay and out." A professor of social work on the West Coast concludes as follows:

> In the last 6 years, I have worked in AIDS-first care services and now in prevention. I bring a great deal of passion to this work—in large part because AIDS first appeared in this country as a "gay disease." In the midst of this tragedy, there is work and there are relationships about which I care deeply. I feel that I

have been successful in blending my lesbian identity and my research interests.

Finally, a groundbreaking scholar in gay literary criticism reflects from retirement:

Teaching and publishing research in gay and lesbian studies was a challenge and a path to fulfillment during my last twenty years as an English professor. In 1970 I organized an interdisciplinary course in "Homophile Studies" which ran into political difficulties. A state legislator introduced a bill to make discussion of homosexuality illegal at state colleges. The bill failed but the course was abandoned after one semester. However, I was able to give the gay/lesbian component of a "Human Sexuality" course for many years and introduced a course in "Sex Roles in Literature" which I taught until I retired. This work was enormously rewarding. It brought me into contact with gay and lesbian faculty at a very closeted campus and led to my becoming the advisor to the campus gay students for 14 years. It also suggested a fruitful way of combining literary, historical, and legal research to reveal how a major poet (Byron) expressed his homoerotic side in a very hostile milieu. Though I came out nationally and in my writing, I never came out in any dramatic way on my home campus. I simply let my academic interests speak for themselves. Not that I don't think coming out is a good and positive idea. But college teachers should realize that they can operate effectively within traditional academic bounds even if they are temperamentally shy about making public personal statements.

These testimonials, from faculty in a wide variety of disciplines, affirm the possibility not only of doing gay and lesbian research but of being recognized and rewarded for this work. However, among the 304 returned questionnaires and 99 follow-up studies, such glowing accounts are not in the majority. For far too many, it still seems to be a distinct risk if not professional suicide to bring sexual identity issues to bear on formal academic research.

Using narrative data from this population of lesbian and gay faculty, I can only conclude that in the area of research, progress is spotty and complicated. Thirty years of pioneering and substantial publication in the field of lesbian and gay history and culture has not eradicated the deeply held prejudices against such scholarship and its authors.

Is it "Safe"?

For some faculty, the safety factor has been replaced by a survival factor. For such academics, it is no longer possible to conceive of doing research and scholarship that is not reflective of and informed by knowledge and experience arising from their being lesbian or gay. Three testimonials to this total commitment to fusing the personal and the intellectual or professional will suggest the passion with which many faculty integrate the various aspects of their lives:

> My research is so thoroughly imbued with the consequences of my orientation, I wouldn't know where to begin. Suffice it to say, that as of coming out in 1970, I have based my research on the insights that being a woman and a lesbian have given me. I have brought my gender and sexual orientation fully to my writing and it has paid off handsomely [an English professor with 24 years of teaching at a variety of institutions in the East and the Midwest].
>
> I do not believe I would be a functioning scholar if I did not have a compelling personal and political reason to write. Virtually all the scholarship I do is related to issues of sexuality. In addition, I have worked for the last 4 or 5 years as advisor of the g/l/b/t group on campus. I am more open discussing issues of gender and sexuality in class. I do not raise my own sexuality in class, however, although I assume most students know it. I am one of the most visible gay or lesbian faculty members on campus. Others have expressed great anxiety about being "out," but I have experienced little opposition directly [a professor of English for 21 years in the East].
>
> In a move [recent] toward a more committed, more political, and more accessible kind of writing, a move I am far from alone in making, I have shifted my focus from narrow studies of 18th century literature. First, I began to do feminist work, both theoretical and critical. Then, in an essay published [recently], I wrote about cultural markers of homophobia. That essay led to a co-edited collection on gender ambiguity, and became part of a book. . . . I have written on being a lesbian mother of racially different (from me) children, and am working on an essay on parenting and racism [a professor of English for 17 years in eastern colleges].

The fact that all three of these affirmations come from professors in the humanities highlights a troublesome reality: It continues to be relatively easier for faculty in disciplines such as English and American literature, the foreign languages, comparative literature, and cultural studies to infuse sexual orientation into scholarship than for our counterparts in many of the social sciences and virtually all of the physical sciences.

Within the social sciences, history, philosophy, and sociology seem the most compatible for gay and lesbian scholarship, perhaps because they can easily include work on subset populations composed of lesbians and gay men. Faculty in other fields who attempt to carry out research involving issues of sexual identity report having considerable difficulty with acceptance and funding for such work. For most respondents in this study in the physical sciences, the question of impact of sexual orientation on research seems moot. Such faculty who are out more generally on their campuses report devoting time and energy to a wide range of student and faculty programs and issues, but they cannot in most cases imagine how they would make overt connections between their scientific research and their personal and political lives.

All of these explanations aside, the most often-reported reason for refraining from conducting gay or lesbian research is much more basic: fear. Much debate currently swirls around the question of whether that lingering reluctance is grounded in reality. A respondent with 27 years as a professor at a midwestern state university commented as follows:

> Initially I avoided doing any research that involved lesbian issues—partially because I'd be doing database searches and using interlibrary loan and that meant the staff who worked for me might know I was a lesbian. As I've become more comfortable with myself, I really don't care what people think. . . . I think my own fear of what people might do or say is more inhibiting than reality. Perhaps this results from internalized homophobia; I don't know—I do suspect that if we all took more risks, we'd be amazed how much support we have.

While my own experience mirrors that in this narrative, I know I had the privilege of a tenured position as a safety net. No matter how badly individual faculty might treat me, I was not in danger of losing my job if I came out. Had I done so as an untenured professor in the mid-1960s, I might well have found myself fired for other causes. And, some of my respondents caution against the conclusion that North American campuses or all professional journals and publishers are uniformly receptive to work incorporating sexual orientation into their hypothesis and findings. Let me offer a few of the less positive comments from survey respondents.

A gay professor of family studies graphically reports: "I conduct unfunded and unfundable research. It has kept me in the university however—otherwise I'd be bored and would have quit by now." A philosopher writes the following:

> My being lesbian has contributed to my research in the area of lesbian culture and lesbian ethics. I have just this year published two books in the area. . . . I haven't been able to get ANY outside grants for research support.

A professor of sociology sadly remarks:

> "It [being gay/lesbian] has *completely* informed my research; as a result, however, while it has positioned me in leadership at the national level professionally, it has prevented my finding full-time work. I've been job-hunting without success since January 1982!"

A widely published science professor who was the fourth woman to be tenured at an historically all-male private school reports with some resentment:

> I publish under two names—one for my regular science work and one for writing on gay/lesbian subjects. I do that because I'd lose my grant funding for my scientific research if my sexual identity was known.

Finally, a professor of communication for 15 years writes the following:

> Being a lesbian has taken away job opportunities for me—has led to my not receiving tenure at one institution and has curtailed my research in that I have been hesitant to publish anything feminist—let alone lesbian.

Clearly, there are many faculty across this country do not dare produce scholarship informed by their sexual orientation, and others insist upon doing so at great cost to their professional advancement.

Though most faculty who report negative responses to their research efforts refer to academic or professional colleagues, a few focus on more personal relationships. These comments came from an English professor with 19 years of experience:

> The only negative impact has to do with my family. Because they are not accepting, I no longer show them my academic work, or talk about it (unlike the James Joyce articles and books, still displayed on the coffee table). I assume that they won't come across the journals and books in which my lesbian writing appears. But eventually, I will have to write in places/of things that will be harmful to them. That's a hard thing for me to face and I haven't dealt with it yet.

Unfortunately, many in academia are ignorant of the writers and theories important to lesbian criticism. Furthermore, many of them feel no need for correction, though people like me have had to learn to read and interpret heterosexual literature to be members of our profession. Continued ignorance eventually feels like dismissal or trivialization of my cultural context by people who pride themselves on their sensitivity as well as their intellectual acumen.

As with many of the faculty respondents in this study, my career as a publishing scholar did not truly take form until I was able to be out at work. Shortly after I stopped drinking and began to tell close friends what they already knew at some level, I became aware of the discrepancy between my life at the university and my life in the larger community. By 1975, I had been able to volunteer as a worker at the fledgling women's bookstore housed at that time in a dingy storefront next door to an even dingier pool hall. Doing this allowed me to make use of my knowledge of literature and to meet radical heterosexual feminists and lesbian activists. My weekly shifts engaged me in lively discussions with the lesbians who managed the store over which books to buy with our meager resources. Both of them were social scientists by training and inclination, women with an intellectual stake in historical and measurable data. My position was one I had developed over years of teaching Shakespeare and Milton: Social and personal change often begin as a result of exposure to so-called fictional representations of human motivation and aspiration; great literature has the capacity to enter our consciousness before defenses can be erected or rational faculties marshalled to protect us from feeling the content of what we are reading.

Shortly after I began working at the bookstore, I joined the editorial staff of a local lesbian publication, *So's Your Old Lady,* a journal of poetry, prose, and essays that enjoyed a life span of about eight or nine years. Once again, I felt useful as a literary critic, no longer attempting to write ineffectual and impersonal essays to faceless readers of academic journals. In our lively staff meetings, I applied what I knew about good poetry and prose to the varied manuscripts we reviewed. I also learned about the composition and production of a little magazine, and I practiced using my growing feminist consciousness about juggling the urgent need to publish silenced and usually inexperienced voices with the equally important need to maintain standards of structure and language. Finally, those years taught me to work cooperatively; I learned something invaluable—how to mesh ego into community without losing self.

This community involvement strengthened my sense of having information and perspectives that were worth sharing with specific audiences of my choosing. It was in this context that I agreed to deliver my Valentine's Day speech to an openly lesbian and radical feminist group. But I remained closeted to academic colleagues about my most original insights into literature until the early 1980s, when I began to include lesbian novels in my courses and to present papers at scholarly conferences that assumed a lesbian-feminist point of view. Like a colleague quoted earlier in this study, I found the academy the last safe place to come out, notwithstanding the thick liberal veneer of the place.

The Paradoxes

Most colleges and universities in the United States issue high-minded statements in catalogues and other public relations documents about being locations where the free flow of ideas is unhampered by any of the usual social or financial constraints found in such crude arenas as politics or business. Yet a significant subgroup of the 304 lesbian and gay professors participating in this study remain closeted in their primary research and their professional organizations. This group is large, even if I exclude people whose research does not easily lend itself to gay or lesbian perspectives, e.g. plant physiology, molecular biology, physics. But even those faculty teach graduate students who are lesbian or gay, attend professional meetings where others in their field are lesbian or gay, and deliver lectures that include examples involving human situations.

In follow-up comments, faculty repeatedly told me that my questions about ways in which being gay or lesbian had impacted their research and intellectual or professional development were the most difficult for them to handle. Much greater ambivalence marked their responses in this area than in either the pedagogical or colleagual areas. Bitterness and disappointment surfaced often because respondents had never or had only relatively recently found ways of incorporating their sexual identities into their research, scholarship, or creative production. A gay professor of religious studies for 20 years said this:

> These are the hardest questions that you have asked. I think that the experience of social and intellectual marginality attendant upon growing up gay but trying to live straight in a straight world has everything to do with my intellectual awakening, and with the shape and direction my mind has taken. . . . It was not a particularly pleasant experience to live through but I wouldn't trade it now for the world. And I don't just mean the end result, I mean the experience. But I have a strong Calvinist/American streak that prizes adversity as the school for the soul.

This man cherishes his perspective from the margin and attributes his greatest pain at work to the "cold, distant posture" of closeted gay colleagues who do not want to be "known by association." His daily price for maintaining an openness toward his subject matter and professional pursuits is severe but worth it for the clarity and comfort that results from being out in his intellectual work.

A major paradox exists around publishing research findings that explore instances of homoerotic content or that predate the twentieth century. On the one hand, many scholars are excited to reconfigure such historic periods and uncover the sexual variety and anxiety under more conventional approaches. On the other hand, scholars whose own careers depend upon more conventional readings of history and culture naturally feel threatened by such research.

The following case in point comes from a literary scholar of the Renaissance whose first book was an edition of one writers' homoerotic poetry. This writer was a sixteenth-century English poet who wrote a sonnet sequence exculsively to a male lover. Until fairly recently, he has not been included in literary studies of the sonnet form, even though second-rate heterosexual sonneteers and their compositions have been taken with more seriousness than their talents warranted. The professor recounts as follows:

> The publishers wanted a long introduction after they tentatively accepted the manuscript, so I rewrote the introduction and included some strong paragraphs against homophobic critics of [the writer]. One reviewer apparently was aggravated by those paragraphs because she singled them out in her hostile review. I do not regret writing what I did and think that section of the introduction is the bravest writing I have done in academia. At a conference I tried to give a homoerotic interpretation of a 16th century poem and was surprised to hear a nasty comment from the small audience. Many had heard an earlier paper I had given on the subject so I was not an unknown quantity. I was shocked that someone would be so vocal in a *public forum where one should expect views to be aired however unusual* [emphasis mine].

Happily, such negative responses were not able to squelch the intellectual curiosity of this gay scholar of sixteenth- and seventeenth-century English poetry. He has gone on to publish on the presence of homoerotic elements in the work of other poets previously known only for seduction and love poetry having an undeniably heterosexual bent. In explaining his persistence in reexamining such early modern literature in light of newly articulated theories of the pervasiveness of homoeroticism in the period, this scholar comments as follows:

> The most significant moment in my academic life where the impact of being gay figured was the first MLA [Modern Language Association] convention that I dared attend the gay/lesbian sessions. I remember sitting in a large gathering to hear papers and feeling that there was something special in the place. Then I went to the small business meeting where I sat next to Eve Sedgwick [well-known author in gay/lesbian studies] and was able to hear people discuss future caucus sessions. At the same convention I found myself at a lunch counter next to Paula Bennett [lesbian critic of Emily Dickinson and other 19th century American women poets]. It was a wonderful way to become part of the gay academic movement.

Clearly, for this faculty member, negative criticism and reviews cannot compete with the sheer excitement and energy of gay and lesbian scholarship in his field.

My own experience is quite similar. Until I began writing from a lesbian-feminist perspective, my writing tended to accent pedagogical matters simply because I enjoyed success in the classroom as opposed to the two devastating experiences of attempting to begin a career in Renaissance criticism. But under my silence and occasional obscure academic prose lurked a passionate reader of English and American literature. That reader kept her knowledge and findings very much to herself until she was able to come out at work. For me, as for many in the humanities and social sciences, being a lesbian extends far beyond sexual practice; it influences and shapes virtually every perception we have.

It is refreshing to hear of instances where the production of new gay or lesbian knowledge is well-received. A professor of English teaching for the past 6 years at a research university in California articulates the impact of his gayness of his research by saying:

> My research is generated neither by my identifications as a gay man nor by my identifications as a theoretical historicist, but rather the ways in which these two terms map out both competing and complementary claims has carved out a space of inquiry and existence for me.

This professor admits to having felt some initial restrictions on his study stemming from what he perceived as "compulsions" to acknowledge his own subjectivity on the one hand and to refrain from speaking for anyone other than himself on the other. He was troubled by silences this brand of identity politics inscribed, feeling that his act of supposed responsibility forced him "to make people of color and women exist only as absences." He now posits "an 'us' that, depending on what I am writing about, may or may not include women, and may or may not include non-Anglos."

The best part of this academic's story is the reception of his work on writers (from the English Renaissance again) whose sexual relations with other men clearly influenced their work and easily might influence later interpretations of that work. His book on this subject was the basis for his being granted tenure five years early. His own reflections on all this are instructive:

I think that one reason for this acceptance is that, aside from being a gay book, it is also a "good" book—the homework is in place, the research is thorough. It is sometimes whispered behind my back that the main reason I got tenure is *because* I am gay—which is ironic since the personnel committee at the university originally blocked my tenure on the grounds that teaching homosexuality amounted to proselytizing and that this indicated a lack of "maturity."

In one of the first questionnaires to be returned, I found the following reflection that literally stopped me in my tracks: "Being lesbian has an impact on *everything* I do. *Every* 'beat' of *every* day is straight. Therefore it takes an effort to work into the day an alternative view." Being lesbian has an impact on everything I do, too. Every beat of every day for me is inflected or skewed by that sexual identity. I watch the news in a different way than I would if I were not lesbian; I find scenes in movies or TV programs compelling that are inconsequential to most of my heterosexual friends, and I hear chance comments at work with different ears than they do. "Lesbian" is an intellectual lens through which I sift all the data that enter my consciousness daily. So all the years I was closeted, the gigantic effort was not to introduce an alternative view but rather to continue to stifle that view in my need to pass in the corridors and classrooms of my building, in committee meetings and at lunches, and within the scholarly circles of my profession. Only after I came out could an equally gargantuan effort be directed toward introducing my alternative view into what the survey participant called the "straight days" of our lives.

For instance, doing this research has brought me quite unexpected and sometimes distinctly paradoxical gifts. In the process of weaving material from colleagues into this book, I often needed to correspond with a particular gay or lesbian faculty member. These correspondences usually involved clarifying some point made in a follow-up or checking with the author before I used long sections verbatim to be sure I was not revealing more than their narrator might wish. Under usual circumstances, attending to such "fussy" details strains my patience. In this instance, however, I actually welcomed an excuse for further contact. Occasionally, the respondent and I began a more personal exchange based on shared intellectual or personal interests.

One of the most salutary involved my exchanges with a colleague whose work, like mine, is in the English Renaissance. I knew that I was referring to his research in such a way as to identify him to certain readers. In the course of assuring me that he wanted me to discuss his work, he recounted his memory of first meeting me. We were both at a regional conference in our field. Someone was presenting a paper on Shakespeare's sonnets, the bulk of which are now widely understood to have been written to a young man with whom the poet was intimately involved. In fact, of the 154 sonnets in Shakesepeare's sequence, 127 are to the young man, while only 27 are addressed to a "dark lady" who saps the poet's self-respect as well as his sexual energy. My respondent still recalls, over 20 years later, that the presenter on the sonnets at our session had consistently erased all homoerotic or homosexual elements from these poems. He also remembers that I responded by asking the presenter about the physical existence of 127 poems to a young man. The respondent, then completing his dissertation, remembers feeling both excited and frightened at my unconventional interruption. Finally, he recalls wanting to talk with me afterwards but refraining from doing so out of fear and shyness.

I had not thought of that incident for many years, but as I read his recollection on my e-mail screen, emotions came flooding back. I was excited and frightened too, since it was my first public acknowledgement that I read these famous and often quoted poems differently because I am a lesbian. My unplanned outburst opened another door in my own scholarly closet, freeing me to begin teaching what I actually saw in Shakespeare rather than what I was supposed to see.

Part of my recovery program from 19 years of alcoholic drinking tells me not to dwell on the collosal waste involved in those years. However, every now and then, when I am thrown back into my earlier life by something "chance" like this e-mail exchange, I have to face all the articles that have not been written because of my response to the academy's need for me not to intrude my special perspective on literature into my classrooms or my publishing record. The message I hear at such moments is always the same, and always crystal clear: "If you *must* be out, please have the courtesy NOT to be out professionally; the institution can tolerate personal disclosure in the name of liberality and employee well-being. But don't expect us to condone that disclosure when it is coupled with the currency of the place—ideas, theories of knowledge, and modes of interpretation." I believe this message, heard by so many who have participated in this study, is one of the most crippling deterrents to integrating our personal identities into our intellectual pursuits.

Closing and Opening the Professional Doors

Most faculty who suppressed impulses and interests that would cause their research or scholarship to reflect their sexual identity did so in graduate school and beyond. A typical comment comes from an English professor with 41 years in the profession: "When I was young, I was afraid to research what really interested me if it touched on lesbian/gay issues." (This particular instance of self-censorship has a happy ending. This same professor concludes her comments on her intellectual development by saying, "But the development of Gay and Lesbian Studies has done wonders for my self-esteem and intellectual confidence! Especially to have my book included in the New York Public Library's Stonewall/Gay Games list of recommended works in Gay and Lesbian Studies—what a joy!") For most of the respondents in this study with twenty years or more in the profession (60 percent of the total pool), research and intellectual development has undergone a profound change over time. At some point in our careers, something happened to allow or compel us to open the doors we had either unconsciously or consciously closed, to begin speaking and publishing our theories and ideas about the intersection of sexual identity with various other aspects of our research agendas.

As a gay professor of history who eventually moved his tenure into a program in recreational administration put it:

When I was still in the history department, and eventually open, my colleagues asked me to make a classroom presentation on the history of gays in the U.S. This consumed my attention for almost an entire semester, bringing me "up to speed" in a way I never imagined. This was about 1979 or 1980. I never felt so intellectually emancipated or enriched. All of my other research interests seemed so mundane compared to the importance of lesbian and gay history.

A lesbian professor of humanities and women's studies, who has taught for 20 years at a community college in New York State reports the following:

> When I first published [a book on parenting, 1987], I was at first hesitant to share this with my colleagues, but I made a definite attempt to push myself past those fears. When I was in the research and writing stages, I was aware of how rarely I gave my materials to the Word Processing Center for typing or duplication. I was resentful of this hesitancy because colleagues used these services freely. I knew that the staff of the Center would do the work I asked them to do because it was part of their job and because I was a faculty member who could ask them to do this, but I realize now that I was afraid of what some of them might say of this material and of me. Nevertheless, when the book was published, I sent copies to my division chair and to the academic dean. I brought it to a division meeting and passed it around. I wanted people to have to hold a book in their hands with the word "lesbian" in the title. In spite of the fact that this was scary, I wanted them to see that I was proud of the work. Nobody though, in my division, said anything to me about the book or gave any indication that they might be interested in reading it.

The moral of this story seems clear: Self-censorship can hold us back but self-declaration can move us to safer, happier ground. And, with self-declaration, we can see more clearly that the problem of reception of lesbian and gay research often lies with the receivers, not the producers.

Further evidence of the about-face phenomenon in relation to one's research comes from a professor of religious studies whose years of formal teaching just barely qualify him for this study. His career has been interrupted by a decision to switch his focus; now middle-aged, he still holds only a part-time position at his university. His story speaks to the professional lives of too many gay and lesbian intellectuals in this country who seldom if ever are appropriately employed. Reflecting on the positive and negative impact of being gay on his research and professional life, he offers the following narrative:

> My being a gay man has entirely shaped my life as a scholar and as a theologian, beginning in graduate school when I shifted my focus from studying women writers to gay male writers and did the [university's] first gay-identified dissertation [in English]. After an initial period of depression about job prospects, and, once my first friend died of AIDS, my energies kicked in big time and everything I've written for publication since graduate school is openly gay and liberatory in nature—as was my interest in meeting with and then co-founding the Gay Men's Issues in Religion Group at the American Academy of Religion (AAR). (A lesbian group had formed 2 years earlier; all the men attended but weren't doing anything for themselves and I couldn't put up with that! The lesbian-feminist group helped us get started.)
>
> All the negatives are in the professional development side of this question. I've had none! The one shot I finally had was, on a dare, submitting a very empty cv for a part-time job here; I was hired and came out within a year or two to my chair, but part-timers almost never get to cross the line to full time, plus I teach writing, not my field of research. At the same time, I love the classroom and student interaction, and if I have to work as somebody's drone a few hours a day in order to be in the classroom, I'll do it, even if that means, as it does this year, teaching Business English!
>
> I think my being out in religious studies has prevented my finding a full-time position. My cv is more loaded than many of our full professors (12 books, 24+ articles), but since gay scholarship is still too often considered "not real," and since so many of those institutions with departments of religion are church-related, there's a lot of homophobia in hiring; I've got roughly 300 letters of rejection, all vaguely worded of course. Most of us who are out in the AAR are in the same situation. Only one out person has a tenure-track position; all the rest of us are working as adjuncts if we're working at all. But as our written work accumulates, being marginalized from classrooms and departments doesn't keep us silent!

When asked how he felt about hiding his publication record in order to apply for a part-time job, the respondent said this:

> It made me feel like I looked awfully green. . . . It made me feel VERY dishonest, since I was and am out in every other area of my life. What amazed me even further was that it worked; I got the

interview and the position virtually in the blink of an eye. I certainly felt like I had taken a spiritually cleansing bath when I was finally able a couple of years later to "come clean" and come out to the then new director of lower division studies and subsequently to the then new (and female) chairperson. . . . Since then it has been nice to have my publications included in departmental newsletters and to have copies in the graduate student lounge.

Contrarily, some faculty see the connections between personal and professional maturity in much more ambiguous terms. A gay man with 16 years of teaching at a graduate university in the South is quick to tell me he does not believe in the concept of gay identity. Furthermore, he denies the existence of groups of non-sexual characteristics which are shared by all gay people. However, he does acknowledge the following:

> Being gay is too large a part of my life for it not to have affected my career indirectly and I will recount the most important positive and negative effects, which are, as often, interrelated. I met my lover in 1976 when I attended an eastern private university. In 1978 I moved to a southern university. For the next 14 years we had a long-distance relationship.

This professor was physically in residence at his southern institution only when classes were in session. For 14 years, he spent summers, vacations, and term breaks with his partner. Because he was often in the East, he kept up not only with his former teachers but with the next two generations of graduate students in his field. Admitting that he is not a gregarious individual and that he "hate[s] organized groups," he admits that he refused to attend conferences where he could begin to build his career.

In the early 1980s, things changed for him, as he notes:

> My dissertation advisor and two colleagues started an annual conference in our specialty, purposely keeping it small, by invitation only. Since I was in the area, I could hardly avoid giving a paper. The upshot is I have participated every year.

Eventually, this professor attended a major international conference in his discipline and is clear that "relationships established and nurtured through this [personal] activity have enriched my scholarly life and enhanced my professional standing." In 1992, his lover died, forcing him to face the fact that he has few close personal ties at his university. But he does not regret any of his choices, since they have brought him both personal satisfaction and professional success.

The lingering pressure on faculty not to conduct research involving issues of gay and lesbian identity is reflected in the two narratives that follow. The first is written by a professor of political science and public affairs with 15 years of teaching at a large southern university:

> I was discouraged in graduate school from pursuing research on the then emerging topic of g/l politics. After much work in more established fields, I finally began to research g/l/b politics but have had much trouble getting materials published. Manuscripts sent to journals tend to receive positive reviews of the research, methodology, etc., but it seems each evaluation will contain one letter criticizing the *topic* and neglecting to review the paper. In the most competitive journals in my field (those with 90% rejection rates), all it takes to receive a rejection is one reason not to publish in the mind of the editor.

The second account comes from a lesbian professor with 25 years in the academy, the last 15 of which have been in women's studies at a midwestern state university. When asked why she feared including "lesbian" in the titles of her publications and conference papers, she spoke of the low tolerance for such work at her school.

> Even two or three obviously lesbian items on a 10-page vitae are perceived as being many; whereas to list six or eight such items would constitute a focus that is inappropriate and embarrassing for both the English department and the Women's Studies Program. There is a conspiracy of polite silence in the Midwest around personal differences from the normal, usual, or ordinary person—who is presumed to be white, straight, Christian (by heritage if not practice), and male. Gender is finally being perceived as something one cannot help or alter—but the assumption is that anyone would choose to be male if a choice were given. To be Jewish or Buddhist, lesbian or bisexual, Black or biracial is looked upon as being in rather bad taste, a matter of inexplicable choice; it is often implied that one ought to have the decency to downplay such tendencies, not explore them in public.

Believing that having too much lesbian studies material in her dossier would "brand [her] as some kind of pervert whose intellectual beliefs and personal conduct are suspect at worst and ludicrous at best," she feared she would not receive tenure. Now that she has tenure, she fears she will be denied promotion, taking as part of her reason the fact that a former colleague is currently suing the university. He believes that he was denied tenure because of homophobia at his institution, and his fear is infectious. She reflects on her feelings about continuing to efface her lesbian scholarship on her vita:

> How do I feel about performing evasive maneuvers from time to time? Relieved that it is possible to walk this thin line, furious that it is necessary to do so, and guilty that I am betraying myself and other gay people in this cowardly fashion. I feel caught in a double bind: I must do this in order to protect myself and my family, yet in doing it, I humiliate us as well.

Attempting to lead a vigorous scholarly life under the multiple clouds found in these scenarios is arduous if not impossible. No member of a college or university faculty should have to juggle such painful variables or perceive their options as so inherently flawed as these professors must. No mental relaxation or sheer play of mind is possible under such circumstances. The scholarly world loses what may well be these professors' best research efforts to necessary considerations about self-protection in the midst of ignorance and prejudice.

The Path to Scholarly Integration

Many faculty tell stories of starting out in their fields by confining research and publication to topics well within the parameters of their established professions. My own case mirrors this determination to "color within the lines." In graduate school, I simply learned what I was taught; for the first 6 or 7 years of my career, I struggled to write professionally acceptable articles and book-length manuscripts. These prescriptions never even approximated the inclusion of information about writers' homosexual lives or works. Nor did they include the kinds of lesbian-feminist interpretative and analytic constructs I now routinely apply to literary works.

Similarly, the following story of a gay law professor is representative of many respondents to my questionnaire:

> I actually started this [doing lesbian and gay legal research] before entering law teaching by writing for a weekly gay newspaper long since defunct (although I did it under a pseudonym, since I was not "out" at my law firm and rather doubted they would appreciate having one of their young attorneys writing a column for a gay paper). In terms of academic work, I got into writing about gay issues through the side door. My field is labor and employment law. As an untenured professor, of course I was concerned to write things that would get me tenure, so my initial publications were on traditional labor relations law subjects. At the same time (1982–88), I answered the call when Lambda Legal Defense requested that I write a chapter on employment discrimination for their first "AIDS Legal Guide," published in 1984. Since then, I've written on both AIDS and lesbian/gay legal issues in a variety of fora, including traditional law reviews, a monthly column that ran for a while in *The New York Native,* continuing publication in a law newsletter.
>
> I got tenure in 1988 and since then have done little writing on traditional labor law topics. The degree of national recognition I've gotten for the AIDS work is well-received at my school, and they have been fully supportive of the work I've been doing. A few years ago I published a book on sexuality and the law and the school co-hosted (with my publisher) a publication party. But then we're an unusual law school, with 7 openly lesbian or gay full-time faculty members, several of whom are tenured.

An even more subtle scenario is found in the following narrative, sent me by a gay professor of English with 35 years at a major midwestern research university. Well-known for his research, this man recently published a scholarly edition of a early modern work long thought to be written by a gay author. Reflecting about the impact of his own gayness on his research, he said this:

> The series in which I published my edition had originally asked another (heterosexual) scholar. When he abandoned the project because of the press of other commitments, the editorial committee approached me to take it on. I don't believe my sexuality had anything at all to do with my being chosen for the job, although of

course I can't be certain of this. But when I did get into the task it became obvious that previous editors had virtually ignored the sexual issues of the play and that it was necessary for *historical and intrepretive* reasons to address these. In the meantime, of course, a good deal had happened in the emergent field of gay-lesbian studies, so it became my task to relate certain aspects of the play to this body of work. The stage history involved a gradual transition from productions which almost totally censored the homosexual content to those that blatantly emphasized it and that involved actors who are openly gay. I'm afraid it's too early to say what sort of reception the book will receive. And the distribution of the book will probably be limited because of the high price of works published in England. I could hardly write the kind of analysis of the sexual politics of the play that I provided in my rather detailed introduction without revealing my own sexual orientation—at least by implication. So, in an indirect way, this book constituted a kind of coming-out of its author. But all this is a by-product of the scholarship. I didn't undertake it for that reason. . . . Even though I've no desire to conceal my sexuality, I'm also not eager to advertise it. After all I'm a scholar first and I wish my professional reputation to rest on that. My sexuality is incidental, nor do I consider it by any means the *principal* ingredient in my professional identity.

This senior professor in his field and at his university appreciates ambiguity and elision more than he favors more obvious positioning within his area of scholarly expertise. Simultaneously, however, he has no illusions as to the complex matrix within which that scholarship takes place. Most importantly, perhaps, he is brave enough or truly scholarly enough to report all the truth about the works he studies. And, finally, he is self-reflective enough to grasp just how inextricable his own sexuality is in relation to his professional theory and writing. I was moved by this colleague's elaborately choreographed presentation of himself within his work and find his conclusions about "impact" entirely credible.

Barriers to Integration

Though most faculty speak of gradual progressions from conducting more traditional research and scholarship to focusing on gay and lesbian issues, a few acknowledged that their sense of being misfits in high school or earlier had implications on what they would study and write about in college as well as afterwards. One of the most moving of such narratives comes from a lesbian with 27 years in the field of education, primarily at a medium-sized midwestern university:

> I was cognizant at the time I was in high school and early on in college that there was really a lot of danger of non-acceptance in certain career paths. I had been active in my church and wanted to study for the ministry. As I pursued the first steps toward that, it became very clear that they weren't fond of the idea of a woman in the ministry (1959–62). The men kept suggesting that I become a deaconess or a religious educator. Neither of those appealed to me and I knew I was in for a struggle if I became a serious student of theology. So I got serious and really began working in that direction. During my first year of college, I got involved in a very sexual same-sex relationship and it became clear to me that not only was I going to have the struggle of a woman in unwanted territory, but I was going to have to navigate the waters of being discovered as a lesbian. When my enthusiasm for religious matters waned, I took up the idea of teaching, but again I feared that I would have to spend my whole professional life hiding my sexual identity and my attractedness to women.

Once this woman completed an undergraduate degree in philosophy and history of religions, she entered graduate school in philosophy. At the end of her first semester, a young ABD [all but degree] white male instructor from an ivy-league school failed all the women in the philosophy program. Stranded mid-year, she enrolled in the College of Education's program in Philosophy of Education and Educational Policy Studies. Her survival in that program, however, hinged on her not choosing to enter a secondary or elementary school classroom:

> I knew all too well that would be the worst place to try to be me. Fears of homosexuals and the construct of prejudice that made every gay or lesbian person suspect for acts of pedophilia was more than I could imagine surviving. I knew [by then] that kids loved to share their emotional lives with me and that I would be all too likely to get accused of spending too much time with them. Getting a doctorate and teaching in a university was the only option within the educational profession that would even be

half way tolerable. To this day, I am amazed at the number of lesbian and gay family members who hide out in their closets in fear for their jobs.

Because of her interest in educational policy, this professor has been asked to and often thought about running for a school board position. She has not pursued or realized this ambition:

I am faced with the fact that my identity would be as a lesbian and not as a "good" educator. My credibility is always challenged by two factors: I am not a parent; I am a minority who really cannot possibly understand or advise on policy that would nurture good heterosexual youngsters into their life choices and educational needs. These are not phantom views. Such accusations are implicit in the entire oppressive framework of governance and the constructs of "job credibility."

As an exception, a workaholic, and a professional and public lesbian, I could probably survive now both as a public school educator and as a school board member, but what hell it would be to put up with that smoke and confusion every time I engaged in a risk-taking behavior or took a minority position on an issue.

My initial and deepest response to reading this story is to lament the waste of this woman's considerable talents as either a minister or a public schoolteacher. While she has influenced many young people preparing to be teachers, her persistent sense that her own struggle could not be outweighed by her contributions in either of these two crucial positions within society saddens and angers me. No society can afford to lose dedicated people called to serve. Yet this lesbian and many like her have taken themselves out of the running for certain professional careers. The difficulties that stem from other people's unexamined assumptions and prejudices are simply too daunting.

That one of those "dangerous" careers is teaching young people to think critically and to love knowledge should be a cause for shame on the part of school administrators at every level. Yet this professor reports being told in 1963 by a college professor that she could not be a philosopher because she was a woman who had five days a month (during menses) when she would be illogical. Her internal retort was "Ye gads, what if he knew that I was a lesbian!" As a final insult, she recalls the following:

In the stress of studying for my doctorate, I was especially un-
nerved by the sexual passes and harassment from the division
head. I always was aware of how some of the other students were
sleeping with profs (male) and getting their paths salved to receive the degree. I felt I had to hide my lesbianism to make sure I
wouldn't be even more of a target for sexual harassment. That
was very very difficult and I was angry and scared almost the
whole way through my doctoral program.

When gay and lesbian faculty find the courage to integrate our personal and professional lives, we often find ourselves in the midst of
cruel ironies. Experiencing powerful awakenings about what we
know about our subject matter areas, we may simultaneously find
ourselves no longer accepted or respected by some of the very
same colleagues who formerly sought us out as experts in some
branch of our particular fields. This sorry phenomenon is comparable to what often happens to lesbians or gay men who are parents: A person who until the day of coming out has been seen as a
fine mother or father suddenly is "unfit" to rear their children because someone with very narrow definitions of family learns of
their sexual identities.

A chilling case in point comes from a faculty member whose
professional reputation as an artist was well-established before he
began doing work with a gay focus:

I began to show my art in professional venues in graduate school
in 1963. My paintings were stylistically abstract, about color and
pattern. I received a high degree of critical and commercial success due to the fact that my work fit comfortably within the accepted artistic norms of that period. As most of us did, I hid my
sexuality behind an acceptable mask in order to rise rapidly
within the art world and academia. This carried me along until
1977. Although I came out to my family as a gay man around
1966, I was closeted as artist and educator until 1968 when I
moved from a southern university to Baltimore to teach visual
arts at a women's college with my former student and partner. Although we didn't talk openly to colleagues or students about
being gay, we entertained these colleagues and students at our
house. My artwork remained abstract—it was also critically and
economically successful—until 1977 when I began to paint the
male nude. I demonstrated figure painting using a nude male
model in front of 20 women students!

From 1977 until the present, I have painted no other subject. In 1978 I had my first public exhibition of gay male imagery, initially in Baltimore and then NYC. At that point I came out publicly as a gay male and gay artist. My first two shows were totally unsuccessful both critically and economically. I didn't sell a single painting for the next 12 years and I have never received a criticly successful review of my gay art. Offers of shows and acceptance into juried exhibitions ceased. That state of affairs remains about the same today. Spiritually, emotionally, intellectually, and artistically, I consider my art to be the best it has ever been—a view not shared by my professional colleagues in either the art world or academia. I became an honest artist in 1977 and have remained so to the present day. My career as an artist has suffered. But it doesn't make any difference because I know what I'm doing is right.

While it may well be true that virtue is its own reward, the facts of this case beg the question of academic freedom. Lending weight to the hesitation to come out professionally is the following account from a faculty librarian with 24 years of service at a graduate research university. Shortly after she came out at work, this professor began to experience resistance and hostility from the chair of one department with which she had worked for years. In a powerful follow-up narrative, she recounts this:

I had NO TROUBLE with that department until after I came out. The faculty say that problems with me are a result of my too frequent absences for a period (a couple of years ago). . . . When I tried to explain to the chair that my absences happened when my partner was hospitalized . . . and again when two of our children were hospitalized, I was told never to speak of these things again. NOW REALLY! How supportive was that? When one of them has illness or death in the family, they are VERY supportive. And they were human with me when my father died recently. That was a safe topic.

In one instance, I received a long negative letter about my performance from the department chair only a week after I supervised an artistic and educational exhibition of lesbian/gay materials. Although she did not say so directly, I'm sure she does not consider that in my job description. The impact of my sexual identity on my professional work has caused some people to erect a wall between themselves and me—of course, they think I am the one who has constructed the wall. Basically they are suspicious of anything I do, relate to me as a person even less than they did prior to my coming out, and in fact seem to continually TRY to find small reasons to have me removed.

This example of harassment and ostracism, also suggests the ineffectiveness of academic freedom pronouncements when a professor decides to fuse the personal and the professional in ways that challenge unexamined precepts about the parameters of scholarship and professionalism.

A gay professor of music with 31 years in the profession, 28 at a research university in California, writes as follows:

I'm sending you a letter from the Royal Opera House, Covent Garden, disinviting me from writing a program note for the production of Benjamin Britten's *Peter Grimes* that they brought to the Los Angeles Olympics (1984). This occurred because at the end of a phone conversation with the editor, I had said, "Oh, by the way, I guess that by now it's all right for me to mention the word gay in my article—and I referred to a previous occasion when the editor of the house's magazine had (in 1978) withdrawn an article of mine on *Billy Budd* (Britten's opera) that he had asked for because I wouldn't remove the reference to Britten's homosexuality.

A commonplace in human psychology asserts that fear of rejection can have pronounced effects on the ideas or behaviors an individual develops or manifests. Even when such rejections stem from the private sector, as in the case of the opera review, there is a stifling effect on scholars trying to express the most complex truths about their research subjects. To have censorship originate from the academic world itself casts an even more profound pall over scholarly and creative research.

I myself recently have been subjected to such behavior at my own university. Writing this book has been trickier than I thought would be the case. On any given day, I might receive an e-mail alert about some new infringement of equal access to campus facilities, or the latest brutal attack on gays or lesbians in my own or some other community, or a fresh indignity to which a colleague somewhere in the country had been exposed. These events have only heightened my sense of urgency about completing this book.

Given the larger political and social context in the United States, the stories contained here became ever more vital and useful to gays and lesbians trying to get or deliver an education.

Recently I was approached by the associate editor of our alumni magazine to write an essay on some aspect of my lengthy career at the University of Minnesota. Not wanting to distract myself from this project, I volunteered to write about my 30 years as a lesbian faculty member, accenting my own and the institution's positive changes. In my telephone acceptance, I told her my proposed focus, asking her to let me know if that topic fit into her idea for the issue.

The response, recorded on my voice mail, was perplexing: The associate editor had assumed I would write about my lesbianism since that seemed to be a recent focus of my work; her first response had been excitement because she knew that many readers of the alumni magazine would enjoy such an essay. Then, midstream in the recorded message, she hesitated, saying perhaps she should check the topic out with the general editor and get back to me.

I must have heard that hesitation as a courtesy gesture to her superior because I was completely unprepared for her eventual call that I took in person. It seems her editor refused even to discuss the matter, saying something like "we're just not going to fight this one." The associate editor was clearly upset to have to refuse me when she had been, in her own words, "hoping to get you to write for the magazine since I came to work for it six years ago." Trying to smooth things over, she said, "This probably doesn't surprise you." I responded involuntarily, "Oh yes, it does; I thought my university would behave better."

I wrote the president, asking him to discuss this matter with the editor. I copied the equal opportunity officer, the director of the gay/lesbian/bisexual/transgender office on campus, my college dean, and my department chair. But I also felt kicked in the teeth by the same publication that two issues before had highlighted me with a full-page article and photograph as one of the first inductees into the University's Teachers "Hall of Fame."

Shortly after delivering my letter to the president, I received a courier-delivered response from the executive director of the alumni association "explaining" the decision to turn back my article:

she felt the magazine had to be "conservative" because the alumni association was eager to enroll 50,000 new members. I puzzled over this statement, concluding that to this person, the cliched ten percent of the population we occupy must either be unknown or unbelieved. Printing my essay might just conceivably prompt some of the maverick lesbian and gay graduates of the University of Minnesota to join their alumni association. This letter ended by assuring me that my story was "powerful" but that the alumni magazine was simply not the venue for it.

Having the temerity to state discriminatory decisions on paper cools the atmosphere considerably. Once again, I have to wonder if most institutions of higher education (and their alumni associations) believe that including "sexual orientation" in their anti-discrimination statements will entail no tangible alternations in daily policy or behavior. Surely the executive director would not have written a comparable letter to an African American faculty member whose work had been vigorously solicited by a member of her staff. Or would she?

Refusing to let this blatant instance of discrimination stand, I subsequently met with the editorial staff and the head of the state's volunteer board. Taking with me the Director of our Gay/Lesbian/Bisexual/Transgender Office, I intended to be clear and curt in the face of all the rhetoric coming my way. However, I learned that the voluneer board had voted unanimously to accept my projected article since it represented precisely the direction they wanted for the alumni association and its magazine. The woman who had so offended my sensibilities and sense of justice had to back down from her position and ask me please to write the piece I had intended to write at the outset. One simple theme for this story is that the membership of the alumni association is more open to and knowledgeable about the world they live in than their executive director seems to be.

The essay appeared in the magazine, prompting several alumni now in leadership positions at their own schools to write thanking me for having the courage and taking the time to put my views on paper. I copied these to the homophobic editor in hopes that she can gradually come to understand that the world around her is changing.

Now and Later

Even when faculty feel supported by their colleagues in relation to their research, their reflections and memories are sometimes peppered with ambiguity, contradiction, and even a hint of ancient resentment at the unequal standards to which they have been held. This follow-up narrative, from a retired professor of English who spent 45 years in academic life, illustrates my point:

> Generally I've had no static whatsoever from colleagues, and have been appreciated by them—judging by my frequent promotions. While I've been reticent about letting students know [that he is gay], that's not been true with the faculty; it's never seemed to matter. I realized, though, that being gay I had to write and publish as much or more than any of them did, garner good reviews from around the country, etc. I have been multi-talented—publishing much original poetry, criticism, and scholarship, and have had the reputation for publishing more than anybody in the department. On these grounds (the most important to academics) I am beyond reproach. I believe professional pressures are placed on those in a persecuted minority to be exceptional, i.e., better and more prolific than colleagues.

Overachievement has long been a coping strategy for some members of oppressed groups within our society. While the strategy sometimes works, as alluded to by the narrator above, it also exhausts the inner and outer resources of the people who practice it. Surely a saner policy would be for institutions of higher education to be even-handed in their reward systems, evaluating lesbian and gay faculty along the same criteria and holding us to the same standards of professional and personal conduct as all other employees.

Until such even-handedness prevails, gays and lesbians will continue to do the institution's work for them by informal conversations with younger colleagues. A case in point originates from a lesbian law professor working in New York State. Her questionnaire was not counted in my official data computations because she had only 10 years in academia. However, her comments are noteworthy, precisely because they stem from a more recent past than do the majority of narratives quoted here. Recalling how her colleagues responded to her work in lesbian theory, she says:

I was heavily advised against it—especially before tenure. I was told by many, including lesbians, that the way to do the work I wanted to do was to first do "safe" scholarship, get tenure, and then do what I wanted. I was heavily advised that even if I was going to engage in foolish pre-tenure risk, I should do it in an exclusively academic manner, meaning that I should not do community based scholarship. My goal to do a book that would be accessible (both in language and price) was considered naive and "selfish." (The latter criticism is one that I have never understood.) Thus, I have been very interested in the ways in which we "police" each other with regard to our scholarship. This experience, which turned out to be positive although I realize it could have been different, has made me very reluctant to "police" other lesbians. My work is generally received well, although better by students than by colleagues. I am invited to speak at many universities, although I always get the feeling that the faculty is "interested" to have me for a few hours or even days, but would not consider me a viable full-time colleague because of the nature of my work. I thus feel very fortunate to work at a "progressive" institution.

This lesbian legal scholar has absolute clarity about the subtle and internalized process of censorship operating within the ranks of any population subject to institutionalized discrimination. All too often, the price of admission to such arenas of power and privilege entails exactly the kinds of "safety" this professor documents. Not to pay it is to risk losing entry into a profession for which one is admirably suited and to which one could contribute significantly. To pay it is often to be deflected from one's more original work. Situations like this one obviate liberal notions of "choice," since neither option is healthy or self-affirming.

I want to end this chapter on a positive note because so many faculty who returned questionnaires have been able to integrate their sexual identities with their professional and scholarly careers, often after long years of suppression and self-censorship. One respondent reported this:

Since I have come out to myself and at work, I have become very involved in the faculty-staff l/g group. In that capacity I wrote and was awarded a grant of $7,000 by the state humanities council for a year-long series of events to commemorate Stonewall 25. I have been the chairperson of l/g groups of various sorts within library associations. . . . Opportunities runneth over and I feel very creative now. Opportunities are literally falling in my lap.

Another colleague with 22 years of teaching and writing at a graduate research university in the Northwest concludes as follows:

I have always advised students to choose topics that matter to them, to be emotionally and intellectually engaged; I'm only now getting around to following this rule.

A third faculty member with 22 years in a school of social work said this:

Because I am gay, I have been able to secure funding to complete three studies of gays and lesbians: one on the behaviors of gays and lesbians who have married and had children; another on the help-seeking behavior of gays and lesbians who have experienced social problems; a third on the effects of hate legislation on gays and lesbians. I don't think I would have done this if I were in the closet.

In each instance, the faculty member deems being public about their sexuality to have directly affected the research they do and their success.

A gay professor of communication for 25 years concludes his follow-up comments:

In my career development, being gay has been a positive advantage. It propelled me into high level university circles, because when the president was looking for a professor to head his Select Committee for Lesbian and Gay Concerns, I was one of the few who were out. Chairing that committee brought me into frequent contact with the president, vice presidents, provosts and deans, something that would have been very unlikely otherwise.

This professor has found being out on campus to be a door opener rather than a door closer as witnessed by several others quoted earlier in this chapter.

In addition to providing many faculty with a renewed sense of enthusiasm and focus, lesbian and gay research raises new questions in the minds of the researchers. For me, one important and fruitful new question is: How are intimacy and intensity between the women characters in a given work lit by the author? Are such moments placed at the center of the narrative or, more likely, are they shadowed or parenthetical? Reading the novels of Jane Austen, for example, from a lesbian perspective can be quite different; reading through a heterosexual lens reveals a predictable series of marriage plots culminating in more or less conventional unions however wittily framed. A lesbian slant on the same novels yields stories in which sisters predominate over heterosexual couples, and marriages may not be settled upon until the sister bond has been honored.

To take a more complicated case, Shakespeare's comedy, *As You Like It,* is usually seen as a predictable tale of heterosexual young lovers, foiled by a dominating father, but united in the end. I see this work as containing a significant shadow plot between the ingenue, Rosalind, and her best friend, Celia, with whom she runs away into the Forest of Arden. These two young maidens could have chosen any number of disguises in order to make their escape from Celia's father who has become jealous of Rosalind's beauty which he imagines is upstaging his own daughter's ability to attract a suitor. But they pretend to be a peasant couple, and take up housekeeping in the woods. Because I read as a lesbian, I place more emphasis on a set of lines they exchange fairly late in the play than most heterosexual critics or directors. Celia tires of Rosalind's using her friendship as a secure emotional base from which to explore more tempestuous feelings for her male lover. In a fit of pique, Celia accuses her friend of prolonging her male disguise far longer than necessary for safety reasons. This scene is sometimes omitted from stage productions, I assume because the director can find no dramatic charge within it. I and many other lesbian and gay students of Shakespeare, on the other hand, find this scene extremely dramatic, especially if the stage practice of having young men play women's parts is taken seriously into account.

A paradigmatic shift in scholarly questioning of one's subject matter can be exciting to gay or lesbian researchers. It may be perceived as distinctly threatening, however, by homophobic colleagues or colleagues who simply do not want the traditional set of questions disturbed by researchers from the margins. I want to cite two comments to suggest the energy inherent in such alterations. When asked how being a lesbian impacted her work as an historian, a professor for 18 years at a major midwestern research university wrote:

Since all my work focuses on women, and especially on the women's movement, the relevant thing for me is that I am aware of and sensitive to questions about the nature of women's relationships that I think might have not necessarily occurred to me if I were not a lesbian. I always think of Blanche Weisen Cook's comment that she once tossed aside love letters in her search for important information; I find myself wanting to toss aside everything else! Then there's sensitivity to the dynamics: again, Blanche Cook puts it nicely in the Eleanor Roosevelt biography: "coded words and costumes, pinky rings and pearls, lavender and violets." In my current work on the international women's movement. . . I get a sense from their letters of their emotional ties and commitments. I just don't know if these things would be so important to straight women historians—or so obvious. (This isn't about essentialism! It's about culture.)

In an extended follow-up comment, a lesbian professor working for the past 11 years at a private university on the West Coast, speaks for many of her colleagues in this study, especially those with fewer than 20 years in the academy:

It's given me an "oblique" (often ironic) angle of vision on the world which I treasure and which is remarkably useful *whatever* I am thinking about, whether it's 18th-century English novels or 20th-century popular music culture. One is always slightly outside the mainstream: that enforces creative flexibility and imagination. One tends to be suspicious of authority, conventional thinking and the whole world of *idees recues,* and that can only be beneficial for an intellectual. Nothing can be a given.

Beyond that, of course, have been the pragmatic benefits: over the past 10 years, as the history of sexuality and gender studies has been mainstreamed in American academic life (at least at major research universities), one suddenly finds oneself at the forefront of what it seems like everybody is interested in. My work has often had a lot to do with sexuality questions, and I think that's in part why it has been well-received. People are fascinated by homosexuality. I can't really think of any negative impact my lesbianism has had on my research or professional development. Rather, I say, thank God for it.

The writer of these emancipated words places into a parenthesis what seems to me the crux of the matter—"at least at major research universities." Comments immediately preceding that parenthesis ignore the mixed findings that I have had to accept as the complex truth of being a gay or lesbian academic in 1995. The directive seems clear: As some of us benefit from the present fascination with our work, we need to renew our vigilance about such matters as nomenclature. The two are intimately related, of course, since a rush for funding of research may come to entail subtle pressures to soften that research or distance it from the material lives of actual lesbians and gay men. As mentioned in an earlier chapter, the acceptance of queer theory by departments and institutions that have historically turned a cold shoulder to openly lesbian or gay studies makes us think. We should ask why queer theory wins official support. We must not produce scholarship that is inaccessible to the people who need it the most. We must ensure that we are not talking to ourselves or to a tiny circle of colleagues who understand our terminology and hypotheses.

At least in academic publishing circles, there is an undeniable interest in homosexuality as both a social and an aesthetic marker within contemporary society. This means there is a geometric increase in the number of books and articles appearing in catalogues and at some bookstores. The following comment from a professor of social work who has taught for two decades at a state university in the Northwest simply could not have been made 22 years ago when he began his academic career:

> *Because I am gay,* I have been able to secure funding to complete three studies of gays and lesbians in this area. . . . *Because I am out,* I was able to focus on this kind of research and solicit local funding [emphasis mine]. I don't think I would have done this if I were in the closet.

The following example shows the research agenda conceived and realized by a professor of communications with 27 years of teaching in the mid-Atlantic region and reflects the growing ease with which some of us are able to follow our scholarly dreams. Beginning in 1971, this man considered the content and the effect of mass media on the values of audience members. Focusing on television, this professor analyzed content of dramatic presentations over a period of years. Then in the late 1970s, the focus shifted:

I began to pay attention to the growing (though still minuscule) visibility of lesbian/gay characters on TV; but the numbers were not sufficient for them to be represented in a random sample of programming. However, I began to look for ways to determine the possible role of TV's generally conservative tendency in shaping attitudes toward lesbigays, and used questions that were included in the annual General Social Survey of the National Opinion Research Center. The first study I did on these data was published in 1984.

Since then, this gay academic has simply broadened and deepened his analysis of such media programming, writing widely about correlations between programming and audience opinions of gays and lesbians, presenting his work at conferences, and encouraging graduate students to conduct research and write dissertations in the field. In fact, one of those students recently published his dissertation, which analyzed the effect of the closet on those attempting to succeed in the corporate world.

At the same time, lesbians and gays living outside metropolitan areas and working at one of the many smaller, less progressive institutions but hungry to read such scholarship still must ask friends in major cities to send them these works or order them directly from publishers. These people do not enjoy the relative liberty of proposing a course whose content is explicitly lesbian or gay. And in far too many cases, they perceive themselves as unable to be open about their sexual identification to any but their closest friends on the faculty.

As I consider this cultural phenomenon, I feel cautious about proclaiming the onset of anything remotely resembling a post-homophobic era in higher education in the United States. My own campus is a good example in relation to women in leadership positions. As recently as 1993, senior women served in two deanships, two vice-presidencies, and one vice-provost position. All four have been hired elsewhere, and we suddenly find ourselves once again being led by a group of white men. Academics of color have known for a long time that whatever modest gains occurred in hiring and graduate school admissions during the late 60s and early 70s have eroded because colleges and universities are reluctant to pursue affirmative action policies for fear of being labeled politically correct. Similarly, the happy situation in which some gay and lesbian scholars currently find themselves is not guaranteed to continue. Our research support is subject to the winds of local and national politics, religious and moral prejudice against our "lifestyle," and, most crucially, academic funding trends.

Throughout the writing of this book, I have been reminded of certain of John Milton's political sonnets, written to prominent or heroic figures in government, the military, or the church—the three most powerful institutions in England in the seventeenth century. Milton began each sonnet with an octave of praise for the celebrated figure's accomplishments and leadership in his field. The last six lines, however, turned into a cautionary tale; Milton adjured these same men to remain alert so as not to allow matters to backslide, reminding them that "victory" is not a static condition.

That is how I feel as the scribe of the stories entrusted to me by those who took the time and pains to tell me particulars of their lives as scholars. At this moment in United States history, publishers solicit manuscripts with a gay or lesbian focus. This phenomenon is to be enjoyed by those of us who want to write such books and articles as well as by all who are curious or compelled to read them. But as long as so many tenured, long-time faculty write narratives of pain and ambiguity, I cannot feel confident the struggle is over. Backlash is alive and well. We cannot relax our vigilance regarding stresses placed on anyone whose research agenda includes a perspective informed by sexual identity.

CHAPTER 5

"Are We in Your Mind?"

Elsewhere in this study, I have quoted various faculty who understand how dangerous it has been and still can be to try to teach gay or lesbian subject matter in courses, to contemplate conducting and publishing research about or from the perspective of lesbian or gay reality and theory, or to come out to any but one's most trusted colleagues. What I want to do now is reflect on ways in which the larger institutions reinforce such restrictive parameters on all within their control. I begin with the view from institutional officers whose job it is to oversee an even-handed administration of protection and equity to all members of college and university communities.

View from Inside

In an attempt to measure how institutions see themselves in relation to their gay and lesbian citizens, I sent questionnaires to equal opportunity officers at seventy-one colleges and universities, randomly chosen from a national directory of such persons (see Appendix A.) Twenty-four surveys (34%) were returned, consistent with the return rate from faculty (35%). The geographical distribution as well as the rate of return of those questionnaires is, however, much more skewed than is the case with the faculty surveys. I sent 22 surveys to equal employment opportunity (EEO) officers in the Midwest and got 13 back; New England received 9 and returned 2; of the 8 sent to schools in both the South and the Southwest, only 3 came back from the South; 5 were distributed in the

Great Plains states, 3 of which were returned; 4 went to the mid-Atlantic locales and 1 was returned; 2 were distributed in the West, with no returns; and 1 was sent to and returned from a school in the Northwest.

My concentration on midwestern institutions was based on the fact that most large, state-supported research universities are located in that part of the country. The Midwest also reflects a wide political and demographic spectrum ranging from progressive populists to Bible-belt fundamentalists, from large urban areas to tiny, rural communities. My sample included 11 colleges and 40 universities, 20 private and 31 public schools. Questionnaires were completed by EEO officers from 3 colleges and 21 universities, from 8 private and 16 public institutions.

Quantitative data concerning various levels of support for lesbians and gays show that 91.66% of reporting campuses have anti-discrimination statements in place; 95.83% recognize student organizations; 79.16% provide counseling services for gay and lesbian students; 87.5% provide space for student meetings and activities; 83.33% report that faculty are public about their gay or lesbian identity; 62.5% have faculty and staff support groups; 54.16% offer courses on lesbian and gay subjects; 33.33% extend fringe benefits to gays and lesbians—citizens—29.16% to faculty, 29.16% to staff, and 12.5% to students; and 8.33% have at least a fledgling gay and lesbian studies program.

Similar data responding to a question about occurrences of hate speech or action on campus revealed that demeaning name-calling was most prevalent (70.83% of schools report such incidents), whereas physical assaults or threats on gay or lesbian students, faculty, and staff were least prevalent though still alarmingly high (41.66% for students, 25% for faculty, and 16.66% for staff). In between these extremes, surveys revealed a high incidence of graffiti in restrooms and of the defacement or theft of notices of gay or lesbian activities (62.50% of campuses reporting in each case).

The bulk of information provided in the questionnaires was qualitative, reflecting my wish to find out something about self-perception within the same institutions where faculty are struggling to win increased visibility and acceptance. The two prevailing themes in the narrative portions of the questionnaires are self-congratulations and caution about the fragility of reported gains.

One significant finding is that almost no faculty have filed formal complaints of discrimination based on sexual orientation. This fact corresponds with the majority of faculty respondents, who report not feeling safe enough to declare their sexual identity to central administrators. In those few cases where someone has voiced a grievance, the subject matter has revolved around the faculty's wanting benefits extended to them and their partners, a faculty member's being outed by a colleague or chair, a professor's commenting to a student that he could not agree with a colleague's work because she was a lesbian, and a complaint that the selection process for a prestigious campus award is guilty of homophobic bias.

In response to a question asking for the position of the institution's top level administrators vis-a-vis lesbian and gay faculty, student, and staff issues, most EEO officers assured me that such individuals were positive. Evidence for this was almost entirely limited to the existence of a statement in the official anti-discrimination policy including gays and lesbians. A typical comment is this: "The Affirmative Action and Equal Employment statements include sexual orientation. This should demonstrate that the University seeks to create a climate of tolerance." As reported here earlier, however, most faculty do not find such paper protection sufficient; it must be accompanied by programmatic outreach before most faculty will believe there is anything behind the liberal rhetoric.

Occasionally, an EEO officer recognized the gap between language and effect:

> The institution has formally included sexual orientation as a part of the non-discrimination policy, and it is included in most statements about diversity which come out of the central administration. However, efforts to address homophobia and heterosexism programmatically have met with little encouragement and little funding support.

Occasionally, as well, a respondent acknowledged the painfully slow road to recognition:

> Seven of eight Regents, the President, the Provost, and various VPs supported the inclusion of "sexual orientation" in the University's non-discrimination by-law. The inclusion was mandated by a vote of the Regents (7 for, 1 against) in 1993 after a *twenty-one*

year campaign to effect such inclusion. Two newly elected Regents precipitated the change." [emphasis mine].

This situation pertained, shockingly, at a major research university long known for its progressive policies on a host of academic issues.

When asked to report whatever changes might have occurred in the past 10 years relative to lesbian and gay members of their institutions, respondents commented predictably. Changes reported include inclusion of protective language in anti-discrimination documents; formation of committees or task forces to gather information for central administrators about campus climate for gays and lesbians; vocal agitation by students for recognition and relevant programming; the presence of a growing group of faculty and staff who are public about their sexual identities and who then expect colleagues and administrators to value them accordingly.

Point of origin is the key variable connected with the growth on campuses across the country of committees and task forces to study conditions for lesbians and gays. If an institution's president or provost creates such a body with the expectation that it will report its findings to him or her, there is a high degree of probability that things will begin to change. If the group arises from the ranks in an attempt to convince a president or provost, results are far less certain, though perhaps no less necessary to obtain. The latter situation can have the immediate benefit of empowering those immediately affected by a campus's laissez-faire or hostile attitude; but without open support from the administration from the outset, such groups often will experience internal frustration and external inertia before anything is actually accomplished.

My own campus is a good case in point. A group of gay and lesbian faculty, staff, and students decided to conduct a campus climate survey in order to convince our central administration that the university was unfriendly to lesbians and gays in its midst. The group found it virtually impossible to get any funding support for the massive survey that was proposed, meetings tended to rehearse wrongs without being able to effect remedies, and energies flagged even as tempers flared. Only after the president was forced to acknowledge incidences of hate speech in undergraduate dormitories did he sit down with some of the leaders of this grassroots group, charge them under his auspices, and ask for a report in short order. Given this visible and financial support, the committee completed its work in record time, presenting five major recommendations to improve life on campus. These recommendations then moved through the governance system and won the endorsement of the University Senate, which in turn recommended implementation to the Regents.

Even with this tacit presidential blessing, the recommendations are still being implemented, meeting major funding hurdles as well as the less tangible obstructions that come from any attempt to alter social attitudes within a large group of people. Without this blessing, however, virtually nothing can be accomplished. Those EEO officers who were not congratulating themselves and their superiors for having put two words into a document agree with my analysis, accenting that verbal and financial backing at the top is mandatory for lasting or deep improvements.

At the end of the questionnaires, EEO officers were provided space in which to make any additional comments they might wish:

- It's not what it needs to be, but it is certainly better!
- There is frustration of GLB faculty and staff at lack of progress, particularly on benefits.
- Although discrimination still exists, many of our gay, lesbian and bisexual employees and students say that they find this community is more hospitable than most. They are especially appreciative of our help finding employment for their partners.
- Many college-age students are severely homophobic. We must do more to challenge them and protect the gay and lesbian students who are hurt.
- Generally, we need more awareness, education, and sensitivity to GLB issues and more education for employees, especially staff. The Affirmative Action Office has a sexual orientation workshop/conference planned to take place in the immediate future. It will be held for students groups, staff, administrators, employees' unions, and local city reps.
- A gay/lesbian lifestyle is not tolerated on a broad basis in the state. The strong religious right influences continue to condemn gay/lesbian behavior.
- The most difficult and problematic issue, benefits for same-sex partners, is still under study.

- This is a fragile enterprise. Even maintaining these gains will require vigilance as well as constituencies and alliances with other nonmajority groups.

If time and resources had permitted, I would have surveyed many more institutions. I also would have sent additional prods to those EEO officers who did not return questionnaires within the requested time frame. However, I suspect that the results of a larger polling effort would not differ significantly from what appears here. Like the institutions they serve, EEO officers want to believe they have addressed inequity if they have formulated inclusive statements about equity. And, like the institutions they serve, they seem much less eager to embark upon the kinds of proactive ventures that faculty say are necessary to insure the protection promised and, more importantly, to create the surroundings in which teaching and research about gay and lesbian history and culture could be not only tolerated but also nourished and valued.

The Professoriate Speaks Back

Of the 304 returned questionnaires for this study, 220 report the inclusion of sexual orientation in campus antidiscrimination policies. In a study conducted at the University of Florida in 1994, lesbian, gay, and bisexual students, faculty and staff were surveyed about their perceptions of the quality of life on campus. Representative evaluative statements included these: "As a l/g/b person, I fear the oppressive behavior of faculty on the UF campus"; "I have experienced an atmosphere of harassment regarding l/g/b persons on the UF campus"; "As a l/g/b person at UF, I feel pressure to keep my sexual orientation a secret"; "I try to tell even people with whom I am casually acquainted that I am l/g/b"; "As a l/g/b person at UF, I experience equal access to on-campus activities" (Quality of Life Survey: Campus Climate for Lesbian, Gay, Bisexual People on Campus," 1993–1994). The results, reported in a series of pie charts, were visually impressive. Every segment of the pie representing faculty revealed the chilling fact that lesbian and gay faculty see their lives in a more oppressed and endangered light than do their student or staff counterparts.

At the University of Delaware, a study of campus climate for lesbian, gay, and bisexual faculty, staff, and students was completed and reported in April 1994. Many will remember this university for its 1973–1974 firing of an openly gay theatre instructor for "advocating" homosexuality. The 1994 study is predicated on the following hypothesis: "Work is the major place where people gain a sense of purpose." The administrator reporting findings from the study further asserts the following:

> Research on gay and lesbian experience in the workplace has been hampered by two assumptions: first, that sexuality is a matter of the private realm and, second, that studying gay and lesbian experience is only a matter of studying sex. These two false assumptions have led scholars to ignore studying sexuality in the workplace, thinking instead that it is irrelevant to public institutions, like education and work. In fact, sexuality is very salient in the workplace, as we now know from research on sexual harassment and are beginning to learn from studies of gay and lesbian experiences at work (Anderson, 1994).

In this study, undertaken from the very best of motives, 1,019 questionnaires were sent to a random sample of the entire campus community. Out of an encouragingly high percentage of returns (45%), only 7% came from faculty self-defined as lesbian, gay or questioning sexual identity. Even using the conservative "ten percent" figure, there clearly are many more faculty at such a large university who are lesbian, gay, or bisexual. Their school includes them in its anti-discrimination statement. Why did they refuse even to fill out an anonymous questionnaire, the results of which might very well have direct effects on their lives within the university? And why does the report not speak to the inevitable skewing in the essentially positive results most likely caused by having so few surveys completed by the population under study?

Clearly the flow of liberal rhetoric currently surrounding various issues of inclusiveness and diversity is not sufficient to allow more faculty with disguisable risk factors to speak up or come out. One lesbian at a liberal arts college in the Midwest put it this way:

> Increased sensitivity to discrimination and harassment? WORDS but little ACTION compared to race issues or Jewish issues for example. About 12 years ago, after several years of requesting, I got my partner's name listed by mine in the college directory as spouses generally are. [There is] tension in Multi-cultural Development as this office was established and a building was dedicated

to supporting such students whereas lesbians and gays were excluded for not having or being a "culture." Presently I have few supporters in the administration.

This faculty member may have even less administrative support than she calculates. Allowing historically marginalized groups to bicker among themselves over meager resources has long been a tactic for subverting genuine institutional change. An administration truly committed to opening up a campus to the range of students and faculty/staff personnel would act to prevent the spread of such divisive and wasteful accusations and distrust.

On questionnaires and in follow-up narratives, faculty I surveyed repeatedly commented on the absence of atmospheric or substantive changes to back up the rhetoric to be found in policy statements. The result is that on most college and university campuses in 1994, more gay and lesbian faculty members remain closeted than are open or out about sexual identity. Sorrier yet is the reported perception that even being out to colleagues on the faculty and staff or with some of one's students does not insure equitable or humane treatment from one's institution. As is often the case, change at the level of individuals is more easily achieved than systemic alterations in the structures of organizations and mindsets within them.

Benign Neglect

Gay and lesbian faculty too seldom feel actively supported by their administrations. Untested tolerance is common on many campuses. But such tolerance does not warm the atmosphere; acceptance and appreciation do that. The following incident occurred in the life of a professor of English and creative writing, 23 of whose 33 years in the academy have been at a southern state college. His narrative is all too representative of the situation for many faculty who participated in this study:

> In the fall of 1990 I went to the men's room in the other wing of this building—where the Education Department is housed—and I saw this on the wall: HUNTING SEASON OPENED TODAY— NOW IS YOUR CHANCE TO SHOOT A FAGGOT! I phoned Housekeeping and they washed it off. My thought was, "When I want something like this dealt with, I call Housekeeping!" That

bothered me. Supposing it had read: NOW IS YOUR CHANCE TO SHOOT A KIKE? or NOW IS YOUR CHANCE TO SHOOT A NIGGER? or NOW IS YOUR CHANCE TO SHOOT A WOMAN? Something could have been done. There are people I could call who are trained to deal with threats against Jews, Blacks, and women. But when I encounter graffiti which advocates the murder of gay men, I call Housekeeping. The college has done nothing on this issue. I have been here 19 years and have heard not one single word on this issue. But I'm a gay man. It's me they want to kill. So I tried! I said to other members of the English department, "Please! Address this issue in your classes!" A woman had been given $4,000 to bring in speakers for her multi-cultural class. I asked her if gay and lesbian issues were to be dealt with and she said no. I said I wanted to speak on this issue. She said the money for speakers had been spent. I said I would speak for free. She turned her back on me. But the truth is, it isn't up to someone else to address this issue. It is up to me. I may have been born to do this. I can't do it from the closet. So I am coming out to you today.

These comments were part of a speech the gay man delivered at a professional growth and development program presented by the English, foreign language, and journalism departments at his college. Obviously the hate speech scrawled on the men's room wall galvanized this professor to take radical action. A major realization for him was that as long as he remained closeted to his immediate colleagues, he was useless to himself in trying to erase the attitudes that produce such threatening and disgusting hate speech. He also began to grasp how intransigent some of our otherwise well-meaning colleagues can be on the issue of sexual diversity. How many times have lesbian and gay academics listened to faculty members and administrators tick off the categories of diversity to which they are firmly committed—categories that almost never include the words "gay, lesbian, bisexual, and transgender."

In addition to needing more active support, faculty also need to trust that administrators will stand with them under pressure. I myself and many of those responding to my survey are unable to rest in such assurance. A lesbian professor of women's studies for 16 years, currently teaching at a public state college on the East Coast, reports that key administrators, including the dean of her academic unit, have shown general support for a controversial course she teaches entitled "Lesbian Issues." It seems that many parents have been "horrified" by their daughters' taking this course, though none has so far openly complained. Reflecting about potential support if such complaints were filed, the professor remarks as follows:

> The dean of my unit is prepared to back the course up 100%. I am doubtful about her superiors, however. Some of my lesbian colleagues (both closeted and uncloseted) think that the "support" I've outlined here is very thin indeed—I suspect they're right. Given any sustained *public* attack, I wouldn't anticipate continued support from top administrators. The supportive dean I speak of, who is openly very pro-faculty in general, could lose her job. So could I.

Whether or not support would continue for this professor and her course is not the most important element behind this narrative. Rather, faculty members' suspicion that it would not continue is the crux. Undoubtedly these faculty members have years of history of tepid backing or indeed of outright discrimination that mitigates against any simple assurance about their top level administration.

Members of groups historically marginalized, trivialized, and scorned are worn down by unforthcoming institutions. The academy remains by and large just such an institution, notwithstanding official documents proclaiming the end of discrimination on the basis of sexual orientation. This unforthcoming mode and mood on campuses prevent more lesbian and gay faculty members from being intellectually and pedagogically engaged in the production and transmission of gay and lesbian knowledge. It also impacts directly our willingness to be public with administrators about our lives. If I am afraid to tell an administrator the truth, I will certainly think long and hard before revealing myself even to good colleagues. I will have to make case by case decisions about everyone with whom I come into contact, expending far too much energy in judging my contexts for their relative safety to my person.

In my own case, faculty and staff colleagues have either cemented their associations with and trust of me because I am able to declare myself, or they have confirmed their distaste for me and my ideas based on knowing what they guessed. In far more cases than not, my coming out to such individuals has been met by an equal candor and personal sharing on their parts, as well as by some lively intellectual exchanges.

The overwhelming majority of students either admire my honesty or work through what qualms they have inherited from the culture to arrive at least at a laissez-faire attitude toward my "lifestyle" as long as I do not judge them for theirs. A few find that lifestyle repugnant if not immoral, preferring the old days during which lesbian and gay faculty hid our identities, living entirely separate and private lives from our heterosexual colleagues. This level of persistent prejudice stems from homophobic responses that are at least theoretically amenable to education and change.

Simultaneously with all this personal success, however, the institution's structures remain firmly in place. As with other oppressive systems in the United States, heterosexism blocks change in academic policy and climate even more than do unexamined attitudes about "homosexual behavior."

During my 30 years at the University of Minnesota, I can count on one hand the instances in which an administrator has shown interest in my lesbian research or pedagogical concerns. For a few years in the 1980s, we had a president who himself belonged to a group historically discriminated against. He understood irrational prejudice and was eager to erase the more subtle vestiges of it on campus. It was he who pushed through (in record time according to academic clocks) the inclusion of "sexual orientation" in the University's anti-discrimination statement. He also was able to discuss lesbian and gay issues without stumbling over words or flushing with embarrassment at the interjection of such issues into everyday academic discourse. When he left office, top-level comprehension left with him. Since then, we have made some progress and we have been able to get our president's attention, but only when the data have become unavoidably conclusive. There has been virtually no initiative from central administrators.

If I stand in front of a vice president or college dean and tell him or her just how the University's heterosexist policies hurt or offend me and render me invisible, that person is often able to hear me. Several such encounters have even shown me that administrators can be moved to compassion and anger over the inequity of matters. At the end of each such exchange, the person to whom I have been speaking (always at far greater emotional expense than I expect) promises to make something different happen. Things remain essentially the same. I am left with the nagging suspicion that, once we are no longer in the same room, I and my concerns cease to exist.

Let me give two concrete examples. The first involves a financial inequity referred to earlier in this book. A lesbian who has been on the faculty almost as long as I have and I had a long visit with one of our senior vice presidents, trying to explain how unfair it would be for our partners of many years to have to pay huge sums to the federal government if we died suddenly. The administrator agreed that the current practice is grossly unfair but said he could not solve a problem initiated at the federal level. We proposed that the University take out short-term insurance to cover the amounts our partners would have to pay out upon our death—an idea that would solve our sense of employment discrimination while costing the University very small yearly payments.

The University has not done this. Furthermore, rather than seizing this opportunity to act affirmatively toward two faithful employees with an acknowledged grievance, the senior vice president joked that we had better be sure we wanted to marry, since then we would have to pay a special marriage tax. Had we considered that? Stunned, I replied: "No, but I can tell you one thing. If I could choose between such a tax and continuing to work under circumstances as brutally unfair as these, I'd gladly pay the tax. Not only would doing so allow my partner to keep the money that is hers, but it would acknowledge that our relationship is legally and morally the same as yours with your wife." There was no reply, and the blatant inequity still stands.

I know that not all gay men and lesbians seek such solutions, often because they are fundamentally out of sympathy with the institution of marriage. Similarly, some heterosexuals refuse to engage in a wedding ceremony out of a moral rejection of an institution that has historically hobbled both parties while severely limiting the scope and development of women. I respect such positions and share much of the analysis of the institution of marriage; but from a purely pragmatic and economic perspective, I want my committed relationship to be treated the same as anyone else's.

My second example of administrators' failure to keep us in mind turns around visibility on campus. When the President's Select

Committee on Gay, Lesbian, Bisexual, Transgender Concerns concluded its investigation into climate issues, it made five programmatic recommendations considered crucial to improving the campus environment. One of these—the easiest—was to make the
wording on all official documents and forms inclusive of the gay,
lesbian, bisexual, transgender community at the University. This
recommendation went up the governance ladder and was accepted
at every stage, including our Board of Regents. While we all understood that some of the recommendations would take a long time to
implement, I expected to see new categories and language quite
soon.

However, this was not the case. Early in the fall of 1994, all faculty had to complete a medical insurance form. Imagine my surprise and disappointment when I opened the form only to find
the same tired categories of relationships—"married, divorced,
single, separated." For the last 16 years, I have been baffled by a
question that most likely seems totally innocuous to most heterosexuals. (Some heterosexual feminists, who do not define themselves in relation to being married, also object to these stunting
and short-sighted categories and have worked to make such forms
more inclusive.)

Faced with this question, I continually feel emotionally torn.
Do I lie and say "single" when I am so clearly joined to my partner?
Do I lie and say "married" when no institution in this country rec-
ognizes our commitment legally or morally? Of late, I have been
crossing out "married" and writing "committed relationship," or
"partnered" when there is no room for the longer phrase. In addition, I often make a note to the intended recipient of the form in
question, calling his or her attention to the sexist and heterosexist
cast of their document.

On the evening in question, however, I simply felt depressed
and hopeless, the way any of us feels when we finally grasp just
how tiny we are in relation to the monolithic and unyielding institutions governing our lives and behaviors. I decided to write the senior vice president mentioned in the first example, hoping he
would remember how he had felt for those few moments while my
lesbian colleague and I were sitting in his office. Rather than make
a political argument or fume at the cruel opacity of the place, I told
him exactly how I felt as I sat at my typewriter on the third floor of

my home late at night. I used words like "sad," "despairing," and "hopeless"—not the usual vocabulary in such exchanges. But giving a local habitation and a name to institutional neglect seems crucial to erasing gay and lesbian invisibility. To my surprise, I received a response within days, in which he said he was so sorry I had had to go through that humiliating process again. Shortly thereafter, I had a similarly apologetic note from the head of employee benefits, assuring me that she would get the forms corrected. One of her comments is germane to a larger consideration as lesbian and gay faculty attempt to win more acceptance on our campuses. She lamented the irony of the situation, telling me how long she had spent designing a special packet for gay and lesbian faculty who elect to register a domestic partner claim, only to realize that she had not even thought to examine "regular" forms sent to everyone on the faculty.

Her process demonstrates my theory about the distinction between homophobia and heterosexism. This woman was not personally homophobic and could accommodate sexual diversity as long as it was clearly separate from the mainstream audience for her forms. This progressive stance made her a welcome ally to those of us trying to obtain equity in the fringe benefits program at the university. But her unexamined assumptions about the world, i.e., that it is heterosexual, remained intact because they were unexamined. These albeit unconscious assumptions kept her from seeing gay and lesbian faculty as simply part of the bigger picture. We were somehow "irregular" or outside the mainstream of university employees, not a subset of that population. In my correspondence with her, I thanked her for her good intentions and careful work to prepare a special packet for us even as I pointed out ways we remain invisible in her considerations.

On my own campus, as well as on the campuses of the majority of respondents in this study, neglect persists at the top. Only a handful of faculty in my study report having presidents or other top-level administrators who take active leadership roles in eradicating campus prejudice and discrimination against their lesbian and gay students, faculty, and staff. Most attribute change to vocal members of the academic community who exert steady and noisy pressure on such administrators:

Sexual identity was included in the university's non-discrimination statement 7 years ago; today, the university extends full benefits to partners. Some well-known instances of malicious and/or violent harrassment intervened, which may have affected the administration. But chiefly, the large, broadly based faculty/staff organization, that pressed for a benefits policy actively and persistently, helped change matters. Then the university's support of a Lesbian and Gay Studies Workshop has mattered greatly. It has brought some older, previously closeted faculty at least partly "out."

Activists on 2 or 3 of our 4 campuses brought a lesbian-gay non-discrimination clause to the campus/university table. My own experience of having a homophobic death threat from a disgruntled student became an occasion for me and my allies to argue for more rational measures like such a clause, and helped move it forward on *our* campus.

While a few respondents feel a lack of support at all levels of their campuses, most find students or fellow faculty to be significantly more positive than administrators about acknowledging and valuing a spectrum of sexual identities. This does not bode well for institutional change, since it will inevitably be top-level administrators who are able to effect a pervasive warming of campus climates. Several follow-up commentaries point to this alarming disparity between faculty support and administrative neglect or downright hostility. A gay professor who has been at a California state university for 28 years reports the following:

> The institution, largely through the efforts of some faculty and staff, has become more supportive. Faculty response (and that of the academic senate) was uniformly strong in opposition to a homophobic stance taken by the president.

A lesbian professor who has spent the last 11 of her 20 years in teaching working at a research university in southern California concludes this way:

> Given that the president refused to endorse statements supporting domestic partner benefits passed by the faculty senate, it seems that "institutionalized" awareness of the gay and lesbian presence on campus has increased and that overall, the majority of the faculty are supportive of lesbian and gay issues. . . . I'm not

certain if I would say that there have been significant advances in lesbian and gay tolerance in the academy.

This woman's assessment makes a fundamental and discouraging distinction between support from one's colleagues and an institutional willingness to accord lesbian and gay faculty something as fundamental as the same employment rights as their heterosexual colleagues.

Outright Hostility

My data reveal 31.9% of respondents to my questionnaire listed "administrators" as a major source of campus hostility. So large a figure and percentage, in 1994, is cause for serious concern for any lesbian or gay faculty advising younger scholars about coming out on the job. The figure also suggests far less institutional progress than might have been expected by pioneers like Louie Crew, who studied English department chairs in the mid-1970s. Results of that early study, published in 1978, shocked many of us who read or heard them. The opening sentences of that study set the scene:

> Even to research the status of gay persons is viewed as subversive by many in this country. The following comments come not from the minds of the usual riffraff, but from the graffitic imagination of persons distinguished by being chairpersons of departments of English in colleges and universities across the United States, writing with anonymity in the margins of a questionnaire:
>
>
>
> "Gay Persons"—do you mean queers?
> This is the damndest thing I have ever seen!
> Returned with DISGUST!
> God forbid!
> Tell me, Louie, are you a daisy?
> Your questionnaire has been posted on our department
> bulletin board and has been treated as a joke.
>
>

Crew titled his study "Before Emancipation: Gay Persons as Viewed by Chairpersons in English." Eager as always to assist others, he recently sent me some material germane to my project. On a post-it note attached to the first page, he had penned the following: "Are you able to report 'post-emancipation'? I hope so." As with other criteria for improvement discussed here, one's conclusions finally depend less upon reported data than upon whether one considers the glass half empty or half full.

The score for administrators, however, is low if I consider the position of any one of those faculty members in the 31.9% of this study's respondent pool currently coping with substantial hostility from administrative officers who exercise enormous and crucial influence over academics' daily lives and research agendas. One of these faculty members puts it this way:

> Two presidents back . . . I was already the open public gadfly for gay students, staff, and faculty. Whenever that president and I met face-to-face, he could not look me in the eye or address me by name. No one ever heard him say the word homosexual, gay, or lesbian during his entire 15-year term as president. The year after he left, we added "sexual orientation" to the anti-discrimination policy but faculty mostly stay in the closet.

Fifteen years of destructive silence cannot be erased by inclusion of a two-word phrase in a generalized document.

A second faculty member points out the contradiction between official declarations and university policy:

> I haven't seen any changes in university policy. The university decided to welcome army recruiters to campus despite their discriminatory policy [which includes sexual orientation in a list of protected groups]. This led to quite a bit of debate, but no change in atmosphere. Student Affairs has a committee on intolerance which found most intolerance to be directed to gays and lesbians. Little has been done to stop this.

A final reflection will clarify how slow the pace of institutional change can be, as a professor with 28 years at a midwestern graduate/research university observes:

> At least now everything is much more above-board than it used to be. Homosexuality is a *speakable* subject. Things are better than they were 27 years ago, but there is still a *long* way to go!

In the remainder of this chapter, I want to trace the paths traveled by a variety of institutions as they have met or sidestepped the reality of employing lesbian and gay faculty members.

Gradual Improvement

Most surveys reflect a policy of gradualism on the part of administrations. Here is a sampling of comments. A faculty member teaching in the Southwest said, "Institutional attitudes have had little change towards anything gay since I've been here. This area is a hotbed of religious fundamentalism—not likely to change. Very provincial attitudes prevail; lots of distrust towards change or education in general." A professor at a university in the Northeast said, "some slight improvement, though virtually all LGB faculty are in the closet. Sources are hard to pin down but ROTC was given permanent status in 1994 in contradiction to the university's policy [against discrimination based on sexual orientation]." A recently retired professor with almost half a century in academe said, "[There's a] liberal faculty now and administration. But in the 1950s there was witch-hunting. Outing would have cost jobs until the late 1960s at least. It is the 60s which provided the change. Students pioneered, youth culture made the difference; administrators had other worries [than who was gay or lesbian]."

Finally, this icy reflection from a faculty member teaching in the South:

> [There has been a] modicum of improvement in the institutional culture/climate over the last 20 years. For example, at least it is now *universally recognized that there are lesbian and gay faculty, students, administrators and staff on campus.* Individual academic departments have gone so far as to make their lesbian and gay colleagues feel OK about *bringing their partners to social functions.* The student code was amended to guarantee lesbian and gay students the right to be *free from discrimination in grading,* etc. [emphasis mine]. Probably the most significant external force was the decision of the state supreme court declaring our consensual sodomy statute unconstitutional.

Reading this last comment was upsetting. What does it mean to the human spirit that a person of intelligence and professional training should be grateful that he and others like him are acknowledged as existing or should be pleased to be able to bring a loved one to a party? And what effect does it have on the learning environment for the lesbian and gay students who are supposed to rejoice that someone can assure them that they will not receive a poor grade for being who they are? Yet progress for lesbians and gays within higher education is measured in terms of miniature gestures such as these. It is precisely this shriveling of expectations that follows upon institutional prejudice that I find so maddening and so flawed. Colleges and universities boast that they are places where people are allowed and even encouraged to develop their full potential. That is hardly the case in locations where intelligent adults can be brought to the point of thanking administrators for acknowledging their existence on campus.

This culturally produced, lowered threshhold is a theme in many follow-up narratives I received. A physics professor on the East Coast with 28 years in the academy reflected that his university as a whole had "become very gay positive over the past 10 years. The fraternities no longer get away with homophobic remarks or hanging gays in effigy." Since I can detect no note of irony or sarcasm in this remark, I can only conclude that the absence of effigies on fraternity lawns counts as a genuine gain over past conditions. But before I can lament how deprived such a position is, I recall how moved I myself have been if my dean remembers to say "partner" rather than "spouse" or "husband" when referring to the man with whom she chooses to make her life. Or I think of my own remarks, made to some of my impatient colleagues, insisting that it *is* positive progress that our partners may use the university library and join the recreational sports facility. What my colleagues quite rightly want is full health benefits for their domestic partners; like the colleague quoted above, I sometimes grasp at straws.

Diminished expectations are the focus of comments made by a lesbian professor of linguistics who has taught for 27 years, working at a state university in the Southwest. She spoke of her administration's singular ability to ignore the issue of gay/lesbian faculty for many years. Finally, a few years ago, the university president, whom she believed to be "unusually insensitive to women's issues," behaved surprisingly. When told of the existence of gays on campus, he "asked a few questions, was astonished to discover that lesbians and gays felt there was a problem, and appointed a task-force on sexual orientation to look into [the matter]." A non-discrimination policy resulted.

The startle reaction in this account is quite familiar. Since I generally expect nothing or worse from administrators, getting a small but positive response from one of them can be a cause for celebration. I remember early feminist humor which pointed out that women often thanked men for doing things or being ways they simply took for granted in dealings with their women friends. If I lower my expectations too much I allow those with power over my life to continue to dole out rhetorical crumbs at minimal cost to them or the system they serve.

Other narrative accounts of gradual improvement leave a more positive impression. A lesbian who has spent the last 12 of her 26 years teaching in the South considers her school to be moving in the right direction:

> My current institution certainly has changed, although there appear still to be pockets of hostility in some areas that don't directly impact me. Suspected gays/lesbians were routinely in danger of losing their jobs when I came here in 1982. Now we have an official advisory committee to the president on sexual orientation issues, a number of "out" faculty members and administrators, and little overt hostility. The number of gay/lesbian faculty who remain closeted leads me to think, however, that many fear departmental colleagues' reactions.

When considering strategies for long-range success, two factors found in this account are paramount: an ongoing committee reporting directly to the institution's president, and the presence of lesbian and gay administrators on campus who will be receptive to whatever recommendations may be generated by such committees.

A gay professor with 28 years of teaching in the Northeast (field unknown) writes as follows:

> Before I arrived, a professor in my department had been terminated (not given tenure) for being gay. That is unthinkable now. Although grudingly, the university now supports a (part-time) advisor to glb students; and partnership benefits. It will not, however, countenance sexual diversity in its 'vision statement' or [allow] an alumni group [to be] officially recognized.

A similar conclusion is reached by a lesbian historian with 30 years experience in the academy: "While covert hostility among conservative faculty is very present, overt oppression and discrimination is not rampant. The university has just initiated gay partner benefits." A gay professor of English at a midwestern research university recalls that when he began his career in his present job, 37 years ago, he was threatened with dismissal over his sexual identity, and told he could not be tenured even though he had just been promoted to assistant professor on grounds of good research and teaching skills. This professor believes the 1960s brought change, lessening the prejudice against gays. His conclusion is at least partially hopeful:

> One could not be fired today here just for being gay. Although this institution is comparatively enlightened (as compared with fundamentalist colleges in the area), there are still parts of the university that keep faculty and students in the closet, especially the business school.

Offering further positive evidence of change, a professor with 32 years of teaching at a university in the northeast recounts this story:

> The academic year 1959–60 was my first as well as the first of an individual about whom some male students complained. I first heard about the man's departure when colleagues in my department wondered if he had been arbitrarily dismissed without due process. My understanding of the case is that the man gave gifts to male students. They then informed administrative officials, who talked with him and persuaded him to resign. He was in the discipline of education. An announcement was made via the president's weekly newsletter that he was "sick" and had returned to his home.
>
> A second instance [in which the administration tried to force a faculty member to leave] was [around] 1962–63. The man this time was in the discipline of art. He also joined the faculty the same year as did I. He was arrested with several others at a local "tea room." [In English gay parlance, "tea room" became the name for a place where one could meet other men.] His name was listed in the newspaper, along with others. As I understand it, he was asked to resign, but refused. The institution could not insist because the case went to court and he was given "probation before verdict," therefore not found guilty, so there were no legal grounds for dismissal. He retired in 1986 or 1987. (In this case, I already knew he was gay and also knew another [of the men] arrested. That person committed suicide about two weeks after the arrest; he was not totally in academe, but did teach part-time in another institution, where his wife was a faculty member.)

Several aspects of this story warrant further scrutiny. First there is the difference between the two cases: in the first instance, the faculty member seems to have violated a boundary that properly obtains in faculty and student relationships; the second seems much more clearly a case of police harassment of a group of adult men for being in the wrong place at the wrong time. This story also illustrates the equally terrible consequences of closets and of random harassment—the man who committed suicide was unable to cope with blatantly public disclosure of his (bi)sexual orientation, while the faculty member who resigned was living so closeted a life that not even his gay colleague knew of his sexual orientation. Neither of these paths is recommendable.

While some of the change in these two narratives may have stemmed from the second man's having the courts on his side, the difference between a faculty member who went quietly when confronted and one who stood his ground and forced the institution to decide how to proceed may also spring from the latter's understanding that he was doing nothing about which to feel ashamed.

In each case, comparative gains must be measured against depressingly punitive standards. Yet this fact only serves to reinforce the depth of fear and hatred in which lesbian and gay faculty members can be and have been held by their supposedly rational and certainly well-educated colleagues. Gradual change has a way of blunting the edges of protest, just as Skinnerian experimental psychologists discovered that intermittent reinforcement would keep a rat returning to the mechanism that delivers shock longer than any other simulus-reinforcement pattern. I and many of my colleagues with long-time service records in the field of higher education stay essentially loyal to institutions that often grudgingly dispense acceptance and positive valuation of us. I stay put and keep pushing the administration at my university because I know that were I a senior partner in a law firm or a senior surgeon at a hospital or a senior financial analyst in a brokerage house, my closet could not be opened without risk of losing everything. Perhaps administrations recognize this predicament in which a sizeable portion of their faculty are caught—even if at a subconscious level—and exploit their relative advantage. If so, their benign neglect or sporadic support is craven and cynical in the extreme.

Be that as it may, none of the faculty participants in this study begrudges even the smallest show of progress on the parts of their campus leaders. In fact, some posit that the problem may lie at least partially within ourselves as well as in the flawed and capricious systems in which we try to teach and conduct research. An assistant dean at a prestigious southern university recounts an exchange he had with "a fundamentalist professor in the department of which I am now chair." The colleague "was exercised by the interest shown by students in sexual orientation questions. When I reminded him that I was gay, it changed his whole attitude to both myself and his gay students. He became more sensitive and friendly. *It was the fact that I was not 'ashamed' of myself which helped him not be ashamed to acknowledge my existence*" [emphasis mine].

Additionally, a lesbian English professor with 24 years at a midwestern community college has clearly thought long and cogently about the matrix within which progress resides:

> While there was opposition about seven years ago for our student Lesbian/Gay group to form, the group has now become a part of the school. There are two groups I would identify as hostile on campus: the religious people with conservative beliefs, and young immature males, or immature males [of any age]. But I can now speak openly in faculty groups about the gay/lesbian club without being followed by stony silence. Some faculty are supportive to me privately about the group. Administration perks up when any mention of sexual harassment is presented, although they often feel helpless to solve some of the problems. Last, but not least, the gay and lesbian teachers who were not out at the college are still not out, and not likely to be. Old habits die hard. Overall, there is system-wide and administrative support where there was once none, but the personal turmoil is still there.

The following narrative of relative acceptance by one's institution also involves the faculty member's own attitude as much as it does the administration's. After 22 years on the West Coast, a lesbian professor of foreign languages reflects that her college had no antidiscrimination policy when she arrived in 1972, but it does now. The addition is seen not so much as a change in the institution but rather among the faculty who made the policy:

I have felt comfortable here as a lesbian, but I have rocked no
boats, made no waves, and done what was expected of me. My
tenure and promotion decisions were made with no problems.
But my sexuality was not an issue because I never made it one.
Until recently, I wasn't willing to even talk about my partner with
any faculty other than my closest one or two friends. I think
other faculty would respond differently to these questions than I.
For example, a friend of mine is planning to bring suit against the
college because of her negative tenure decision. She is a lesbian
who does research on lesbian issues. Some members of the
tenure committee were homophobic, others were not. The committee vote was 3-3. Since my primary research was not about
lesbians, I may have escaped such demonstrations of hostility. On
the other hand, the existence of homophobic faculty on a tenure
committee does not indicate that the institution is homophobic.

The implicit linkage of retributive or punitive professional action
and overt lesbian (or gay) research is telling, as is the final comment separating homophobic individuals from homophobic institutions. This lesbian professor does not hold whoever appointed
the college's tenure committee responsible for seating on so crucial a body persons incapable of a fair assessment of all potential
candidates for promotion. I have to wonder if she would be equally
sanguine if that same administrator had appointed known racists
to so powerful a position over the lives and futures of faculty of
color.

I find myself writing letters fairly often to deans and central administrators, chastizing them for committee rosters which ignore
or fly in the face of stated university policies which pledge not to
discriminate against faculty, students, or staff. An appointed committee is a reflection of the institution, not of the people who serve
on it. Therefore I hold the institution responsible for the composition of such bodies. Persons empowered to set up tenure committees must weigh the naming of prospective appointees in the light
of official campus policy. If a person is known to be homophobic,
he or she has no place on such a pivotal academic committee.

The other salient point raised in this narrative concerns dif-
ferential institutional responses to lesbian and gay faculty who insist on being active voices for atmospheric and policy changes.
Faculty respondents have recounted numerous stories in which

administrators have taken dim views of gay and lesbian activists on the faculty, giving them much less slack than is granted to their counterparts in the student body. This practice is inhibiting and divisive. Punishing activists constitutes a major detriment to a campus' becoming someplace where more faculty will feel safe or comfortable enough to declare our sexual identity. Furthermore, it makes for destructive and extremely painful conflict between nonactivist and activist faculty. As I noted earlier, liberal academics have virtually no trouble with their colleagues' *being* gay or lesbian. They are much less sanguine about those who insist on *working as* lesbians or gay men. These two unfortunate spinoffs allow institutions to continue to ignore the needs and concerns of many of their most senior and creative faculty.

Perhaps the clearest statement of this phenomenon comes from a lesbian who spent 7 years as an assistant professor at the same large midwestern research university where she has served subsequently as an associate dean for 14 years: "The more out I became in my department (physical education), the more a threat I was. I had a 14-2 positive vote for tenure in my department, but my chair (a closet lesbian) did not support me and I did not get tenure."

A slightly more subtle case substantiates the presence of this kind of punitive behavior. A lesbian professor of education with 17 years at a state university in the southwest speaks to the destructive internalizing of homophobic attitudes by lesbian and gay faculty:

> When I first began at the university, the lesbians warned me to stay in the closet with them. When I bolted, they never forgave me—it was 'irresponsible' [to them]. Now some of them are in positions of leadership in the university but have not helped particularly with increasing awareness or changing attitudes. (Fighting for domestic partner benefits was made easier by strong support from queer and straight faculty, and by the fact that our president had added the wording in his affirmative action statement when coming to the university several years ago.)

This respondent confirms what many of us know; i.e., that once a culturally marginalized individual takes negative messages from the broader society into his or her value system, that society can go about its business without giving much further thought to the outsider. We in the marginalized groups will guard the status quo for the mainstream, often being forced to seek recognition and reward from the very people who distrust, fear, and hate us rather than being able to align with those similar to us. This lesbian academic had the support of other lesbians on campus as long as her choices mirrored their own. Once she stepped out of the group, her logical comrades chose to turn against her. I understand this dynamic since it is so like what happened in my own case, as discussed previously. Of course I felt confused and abandoned by my support group. More importantly, I comprehended that the "winners" were neither they nor I but rather administrators and faculty who hope never to have to change on account of a visible presence of gays and lesbians in their midst.

An ancillary point raised in this narrative concerns what happens when closeted lesbians and gays achieve leadership positions in academia. The respondent has found their holding such positions of little assistance in the continuing struggle for acceptance of lesbians and gays as employees with the same rights as all others within the university. This professor also makes a distinction between lesbian and queer faculty when speaking of the sources of campus support:

> Lesbian faculty are those who are queer but don't necessarily identify or particiapte in queer politics. Queers are those who identify, participate, and are political, and have an identity which incorporates relationship with, in our case, gay men. I am a queer, and when I threatened to sue the university to include domestic partners in our benefit package, this insured that I would stay out and in the front lines. I got secret support and some condemnation from (gay and) lesbian faculty who are in the closet or barely out, but more outspoken support from queers, as well as many straights.

A final theme articulated almost in passing is that of the crucial difference it makes if a president takes initiative on gay and lesbian issues without having to be proded at every turn. In this narrator's case, a new president simply added wording to official policy so as to protect gay and lesbian faculty from arbitrary discrimination. Such a person can make a profound contribution to improving the campus atmosphere, as further attested to in this statement from a lesbian professor of music. In her 20 years in the profession, she has experienced severe harassment for years, even-

tually going into therapy to deal with the negative effects such harassment was having on her ability to function as a productive academic:

> I stopped trying to continue my research into women and music.
> . . . I enjoy academia and teaching, and I value research, but I put
> all my energy into a professional world outside of the academy
> where I am recognized for my competence even though I am a
> lesbian. The [college's] new president (a woman) and a new acad-
> emic dean appear to be supportive of diversity and gay issues.
> Previous administrators sought out ways to persecute and harass
> lesbians in particular. I had to hire a civil rights attorney to inter-
> rupt the harassment even after I was tenured.

The pervasive sense of being devalued is eloquently expressed
in the following two narratives. The first comes from a lesbian professor working the last 11 of her 20 years at a liberal arts college in
the northwest:

> There is a school policy not to discriminate—but I don't know
> that all my courage and imagination in being an open lesbian
> *counts* at all on the positive side, as something the school benefits
> from having. I do know that the affirmative action officer was un-
> hearing when I tried to make the case to her that I added some-
> thing to the school in the way of diversity.

The second is recounted by a gay professor who has taught at a
four-year liberal arts university for 27 years:

> Last spring the GLB group decided to have an all-campus Hal-
> loween dance. The opposition from the administration stag-
> gered me. I expected benign neglect. I got grief from the Dean of
> Students from Day 1. Career student personnel workers were
> embarrassed to see me. Only after I did a couple of TV inter-
> views and a political science faculty member pointed out that
> the university's position could lead to our being on the wrong
> end of a First Amendment law suit did the active, overt opposi-
> tion disappear. The "out" students got hurt in that it set back
> their self-acceptance. We lost several from the school. I wrote
> the director of enrollment management last fall mentioning I
> knew personally of 4 GLB students not returning in January and
> never heard back from him. Today's newspaper laments 10 black
> students' not returning. My conclusion is GLB students are
> "throw away" kids here. I resent being devalued after 27 years

because of sexual orientation. "They" aren't going to spoil my professional life as a college prof!!

My own case is painfully similar in that my collegiate curriculum committee refuses to recognize courses in lesbian or gay studies as fulfilling its cultural diversity graduation requirement. Furthermore, because of their silence on the subject, administrators leave me convinced that they only suffer my presence and that they secretly wish I would pursue some more mainstream line of research and teaching. If that assessment is inaccurate, I am not to blame. Three decades of silence do not suggest active interest or institutional valuing. Nor are they erased by such positive gestures as awarding me a highly competitive sabbatical supplement to write this book.

In addition to feeling devalued as productive scholars and leaders within our academic communities, too many lesbian and gay faculty are still harassed for being who we are. Such harassment affects faculty differentially. The lesbian and gay academics who are the most damaged by such policies are, understandably, those of us who have been part of the academy the longest. Existing within our colleges and universities for so long as invisible men and women, we are naturally inclined to experience elation at the slightest sign of improvement. This renders us emotionally vulnerable to incremental changes in the direction of toleration and minimal recognition. In my case, I must work constantly to avoid two unproductive consequences of extended bad treatment by a long and sad procession of departmental, collegiate, and central administrators: I must not be overly grateful for small signs of human or humane responses to me and my work; I must not be unncessarily demanding of younger colleagues just because academic life is more accepting of their sexual identities than it was for so many years of mine.

Passive Acceptance

For a variety of reasons, many administrations currently set a tone of polite but passive acceptance or toleration of their lesbian and gay faculty members who force the issue of their existence by coming and staying out. Such passivity is certainly preferable to overt

162

hostility and repression. But many long-term faculty, having made the momentous decision to break out of our own silences, believe we deserve more from the institutions we have served so long and well. We yearn to be seen as valuable additions to our campuses precisely because of our diversity; we want engaged conversations about our research with administrators in our departments and colleges; we even imagine that it is not too much to ask to hear language reflecting our lives and concerns coming from the mouths of our presidents and provosts.

When trying to assess what prevents most administrators from filling any of these modest dreams, I run up against older understandings of the role of education within society. From my readings of Dewey, Gramsci, Freire, Coles, and other communitarian educators, I know that all schools—from kindergartens through postdoctoral programs—exist at the pleasure of the larger society and are therefore expected to perform certain missions for that society. If such schools are publicly funded, their capacity to be inclusive depends upon the parameters of what is acceptable to state legislatures and their often politically determined oversight boards. If such schools are privately funded, their capacity to be inclusive depends upon the parameters of what is acceptable to donors and alumni. In either scenario, addressing lesbian and gay issues, be they job-related, pedagogical, research-centered, or personal, will most likely run into numerous and vexing obstacles before enjoying even partial satisfaction.

Some concerned faculty feel this reality as an absolute barrier to their own advancement within the upper levels of administration at their schools. One such person, currently an assistant dean at a university in the South, lives in an historic area of his university where many senior administrators, often devout Christians, live. The dean reports as follows:

> They have tended to avoid me as being an embarrassment. I was a priest for many years and on being interviewed by the press, I stated my new-found philosophical position in no uncertain terms, including what I thought of religious arrogance. This has, to some extent, inhibited my personal associations and perhaps advancement, while at the same time enriching my life with colleagues who think as I do. I believe sexual orientation will remain a "frontier" hazard for some years to come, possibly an entire generation.

163

The phrase "frontier hazard" seems graphically accurate for the position too many publicly open lesbian and gay faculty occupy. Relatively few of us would choose to inhabit so dangerous a site, but the alternative of remaining closeted—to ourselves in some instances, to our colleagues and students often, and most certainly to administrators who wield considerable power over our intellectual and financial welfare—becomes untenable.

External Pressures

The politics of funding for higher education play a major role in institutional responses to campus lesbian and gay populations. Boards of trustees, individual and corporate donors, regents, legislators, and governors often manifest blatantly negative reactions to policies designed to recognize gays and lesbians as equal members of the academic community. In the face of such external pressure, most presidents recede from any previously pledged or vaguely contemplated support.

This phenomenon figures in several narratives I collected. A professor with 15 years at a midwestern research university identified the two sources of hostility on her campus as "religious right speakers and campus proselytizers" and "high administration, i.e. board of trustees, who are afraid the state will find out we have some gay faculty!" Considering how the situation has or has not changed during her time there, she finds her campus "not embracing but tolerant," though the state which supports it is conservative. The result of such tension is an administration made easily anxious about "anything *officially* in support of gay or lesbian rights":

> People try very hard to ignore the problem or deny the existence of gays or lesbians. A straight colleague once commented that "there may be one or two homosexuals here [university of 35,000+), but I sure don't know any." I told her she did!

In a similar vein, this faculty member in psychology has taught 8 of her 18 years at a research university in Oregon:

> In the state elections in 1993 and 1994 we battled legislation which would have permitted discrimination against gays/lesbians. Thus, there has been much open discussion on our campus about this

issue. My academic unit has taken a clear stand against these measures. The university declined to do so.

Another professor upon his arrival to take a responsible administrative position at a prestigious university in the South recalled being told by closeted gay faculty, that if he intended to be an activist he had "better return to California." Instead, he began encouraging a few colleagues to come out. In turn, that small group first proposed the addition of sexual orientation to the nondiscrimination policy in the college of Arts and Sciences. The measure passed by an overwhelming vote at a crowded faculty meeting; "only the closeted faculty voted against it." The faculty went on to form a lesbian, gay, bisexual faculty and *staff* association which, after 3 years, boasts a membership of more than 50 people, including tenured and non-tenured faculty and an increasing number of staff and administrators. This story affirms the power of organization and alliance-building. Unfortunately, the state's governor officially prohibits domestic partnership benefits on grounds that they would undermine "family values."

This same man listed closeted lesbian and gay faculty, elderly faculty, and the governor and state senate as major sources of overt hostility on his campus. He also recalled a president's stating at a meeting in 1989 with the Lesbian/Gay Student Union that the reason the trustees would not include sexual orientation in the hiring policies was that "you can't change attitudes." Despite this dauntingly fatalistic and anti-educational stance, the institution's policy was changed the next year. The atmosphere is "very accepting" presently, though the gay professor points to "religious fundamentalists among the faculty who remain intransigent."

A lesbian with 17 years at a midwestern university recounted an exemplary story of official neglect. Because the university does not recognize her relationship, her partner cannot be covered by her health insurance plan. After some talk of approving a domestic partner recently, the Board of Trustees voted it down, though the faculty senate approved the plan. This professor reports "virtually NO support for gay and lesbian faculty or student concerns" by the Board of Trustees, citing the following incident as a glaring example:

Last year funding [at the campus budget level] was approved for the establishment of a Gay and Lesbian Student Center. When the press found out, there were several state representatives who had a fit. They supposedly objected to state funds being used to support a specific minority group. But when it was pointed out that the state funds already support the Black Student Center and the Hispanic Student Center and the Women's Center, they found other objections. Finally, the center was funded through private funds and the name was changed so that it no longer includes the words "gay" or "lesbian." It is so innocuous that I can't remember what it IS called. When legislators (a few but very vocal) objected even to private funding, the Board of Trustees backed off again.

This faculty member finds the same kind of stubborn refusal to acknowledge difference in connection with a domestic partner policy. Preliminary steps were taken by the university: a study of the financial implications of such a policy found, as usual, that the impact would be minimal; a package was worked out including rules about who would qualify and how the policy would be implemented. Once again, the faculty senate passed the measure, and the president sent it to the Board. Once again, the trustees voted it down in response to pressure from the (same few but vocal) state legislators:

There are several "really out" faculty here who are not in any danger of losing their jobs or not getting raises they deserve or anything overt. I don't think you would get fired here just for being gay. But people, including some administrators, just never THINK about the possibility that everyone is not heterosexual.

Prejudicial responses from individuals and groups outside the university environment continue to exert heavy influences on which policies administrators are willing to defend. One of the more disheartening aspects of this narrative is the repeated reference to only a "few" legislators who are nonetheless able to prolong a cruel unfairness toward a portion of the university community. How can so few people, even if vocal, have so large a say in academic policy? Why do others not stand and refute such objections? Is the vocal minority truly so powerful or do they give voice to attitudes quietly held by a majority of their fellow legislators? Do they even articulate some of the most deeply ingrained prejudices of the university's own leadership?

A particularly troublesome source of external pressure is the federal government through its ROTC programs. Several survey respondents referred to the flagrant disregard for stated policies forbidding discrimination based on sexual orientation caused by universities' allowing ROTC programs to remain in place. Additionally, some campuses with such policies also allow the military on campus to recruit when their own position on "homosexuality" continues to be repressive.

I recently received the following notice on one of my lesbian-gay networks:

> About two weeks ago [on March 21, 1995], the University Senate here at Columbia was given the option to pass a bill that would require ALL recruiters (who use the Center for Career Services) to abide by the University's non-discrimination policy. This bill was presented in an attempt to stop the military (who discriminate against people based on sexual orientation) from recruiting on campus. At stake: $14 million of DOD grants. The Senate refused to pass the bill because they did not want to lose this money! The Senate essentially told the Department of Defense that they can dictate University policy AND discriminate in violation of our policies for a fraction of a percent of the University's operating budget! The matter is further complicated by a bill pending in the U.S. Congress which would deny ALL federal funding to schools who don't allow the military to recruit on campus. In Columbia's case, this could cost us $300 million if we were to bar recruiters.

Virtually all universities faced with such a threat would renege on liberal positions toward gay and lesbian members of their community. The academy is not a freestanding institution. More and more colleges and universities are increasing their financial dependence on outside funders. Such funders often hold fierce prejudices against lesbians and gays, and yet they are rapidly assuming the power to disrupt, threaten, and compromise any fragile gains we may have made over years of struggle.

A Moment in History

Since the first modest efforts to offer courses exploring homosexuality in a positive or neutral light, prejudice and fear of reprisal have discouraged individual faculty and slowed the pace of change at the curricular level in serious ways. In the interests of history, I want to reproduce a shortened version of an archival essay written by Louis Crompton, a pioneer in the field of gay and lesbian studies. The course about which he writes was among the two or three "firsts" in the United States. Responses to it at the legislative level remain models of homophobic censorship 25 years later.

To the best of my knowledge, the first undergraduate course on homosexuality in America was offered at Berkeley in the spring of 1970. Another appeared at the University of Illinois in Edwardsville in the fall of that year. I am not aware that either received much publicity or caused political controversy. A course I introduced at the University of Nebraska-Lincoln the same fall was not so lucky. Though staunchly defended by the university administration, it was in the news for several months, and came under a strong attack by a senator who sought to institute a ban on any discussion of homosexuality in state college classes.

The idea for such a course came to me at a conference on student life in May, 1969—a month before Stonewall. In a speech on university policy, Vice-Chancellor Merk Hobson suggested that the university sponsor interdisciplinary courses on social problems. The Vice-Chancellor was the soberest of engineers, hardly to be suspected of any radical proclivities. I'm sure the issue of homosexuality was far from his mind, but I thought it would make a fine topic. I conceived the course as focusing on civil liberties issues, but I thought the material would be especially useful for social workers, counselors, clinical psychologists, and other members of the helping professions, including clergy. The sociology and anthropology departments immediately agreed to co-sponsor the course, as did my department, English. The department of Psychology was not willing to authorize credit but the idea received strong support from a senior professor, James Cole.

I also sought and received agreement to participate from faculty and staff in the Graduate School of Social Work, Teachers College, the University's Psychological Clinic, the Nebraska Psychiatric Institute, the classics and political science departments, the College of Law, and the University Counseling Center. Later, guest lecturers were added, including a former police chief from Bloomington who had worked with the Kinsey Institute of Indiana University, an officer in the off-campus Naval Reserve, and two members of the Phoenix Society of Kansas City, a homosexual civil rights organization, and the nearest openly gay men I could find at that time.

I was very surprised at the general willingness of faculty to cooperate. President Joseph Soshnik and Dean of Faculties Peter

Magrath, were immediately supportive, suggesting that we might minimize political criticism if the direction of the course was placed under a "troika" of me, James Cole, and a psychiatrist in the University Student Health Center. While I did not accept the official view of the APA as to the pathological nature of homosexuality, I agreed to the arrangement which I realized was designed to protect me (and the university) from attack.

Why did I suggest the course? From 1964, I had close contact during summer months with homosexual civil rights groups in San Francisco and had come to realize how many crippling sanctions American society maintained against homosexuals. Most (but by no means all) of these disciminatory practices have since been abolished, but in 1970 very few educated people even knew they existed. My perhaps naive hope was that if decent people understood the depths of prejudice implied by these official positions, and were exposed to reasoned discussion of them, they would come to question them.

What caused the attacks on the course? To begin with, the objections of one regent, Richard Herman of Omaha, alerted the public to the fact the course was being offered, since his protests received ample coverage in a press account of a meeting in which the regents finally agreed to approve the offering. (The publicity helped enrollment—34 students registered representing a broad range of disciplines.) One faculty member known to me—Philip Crowl of the history department—had opposed the course during approval hearings, presumably because I had strongly attacked military policy on homosexuals before the campus ROTC committee, which he chaired. Later, at a faculty dining table where he was once seated next to me, he volunteered that the course would not have faced difficulties if I'd stuck to literary matters and avoided raising other issues.

A few weeks after the course began, a state senator chose to make it a political issue. The legislator who took this stand was Senator Terry Carpenter. I can only speculate as to what motivated his attack. In the spring of 1970 the shooting of students at Kent State had inspired a wave of campus protests against the war in Viet Nam. The senator was particularly antagonistic to the anti-war movement and sought to show his displeasure by campaigning against the incumbent regents. He supported Dr. Robert Prokop, who made my course on "Homophile Studies" an issue in seeking a seat on the Board of Regents. To help Prokop, Carpenter scheduled public hearings on the course a few days before the election.

169

In 1969 the legislature had passed a harsh new criminal law pertaining to "sexual psychopaths." Both the courts and the attorney general found it unconstitutional. Hearings were scheduled for a week before elections, and were to cover a range of issues including the sexual psychopath law, pornography, and homosexuality in prisons. Carpenter announced that he wanted, in addition, to "get specific reasons why the University feels it should have a course on homosexuals." A week before the hearings, Prokop declared "A subject like this should not be an elective course for students unless they are studying in the medical field."

It was generally held that the university counsel could have gotten the hearings quashed by the courts on grounds that they were an unconstitutional abuse of legislative powers. However, it was felt that such action would be politically unwise, since it might have suggested that the university had something to hide. As a result, a large number of people spent a full day in the Omaha Federal Courthouse being grilled by Carpenter and another senator. The most dramatic confrontation involved Dean Magrath. A week or so before the hearings, Carpenter had asked him for a list of students enrolled in the course. When Carpenter demanded angrily at the hearing that he get the list, Magrath adamantly and courageously refused, pointing out that university policy made students' course registrations confidential.

At the hearing on October 29, Regent Greenberg, whose seat Dr. Prokop was seeking, opined that homosexuality was an "emotional cancer" and a "scourge on humanity"; he declared that the course would not attempt to promote homosexuality or indoctrinate students. Carpenter struck an alarmist note by remarking that "A nationwide movement is under way to make abnormal forms of behavior acceptable." Prokop, pointedly invited to testify, said that in medical school he had received only 15 minutes of training on homosexuality, implying that this was ample.

The campus paper provided a candid account of the hearings. It described Carpenter as "thundering": "This course will not have a long life if I have my way. The Board of Regents will rue the day they ever thought of it." It reported him as saying, "I am completely without knowledge in this matter. I have had no contact with homosexuals. I would think that all these instructors ought to go out and try it if they're going to teach it."

Carpenter shared the interrogator's role with Henry Pederson of Ohama, chair of the Legislative Health Committee, who

170

remarked "For a long time it was understood that a queer was a queer was a queer. Do you need a 40-hour course to be told that there are nice literary queers as well as dirty queers? I hope this course teaches that homosexuality is abnormal conduct and should be avoided." When Professor James Cole sought to talk about theories of homosexuality from a professional psychologist's point of view, Carpenter impatiently interrupted him, asking for the "nitty-gritty." "What's it like?" "How many positions are there?" Finally, the campus paper praised the dignity and restraint of the course's defenders: "The administrators, regents, and instructors who were called to testify performed admirably despite all the harassment and abuse. Standing center ring in Carpenter's private circus, they let the clown trap himself in a web of contradictions, malice and nonsense."

The course was not without its defenders in the press. Regent Edward Schwartzkopf of Lincoln, not up for re-election, took the public stand that courses of this sort were highly desirable. Strong letters of support appeared in the local press, including one co-signed by two ministers who had taken the course. Dean Magrath made a thoughtful and eloquent public speech defending the course on educational and philosophical grounds. But none of these efforts stemmed the tide of popular disapproval.

True to his threat, Carpenter introduced a bill that would have made it illegal to discuss homosexuality in any state university classroom. By a parliamentary maneuver, the bill was called up for a vote in the spring of 1971 by legislators who opposed it. It was defeated. But the homophile course was not repeated. I felt I could not ask faculty to face more harassment. Moreover, it so happened that in 1970 the university had no course in human sexuality in general. This seemed anomalous, and Professor Cole decided he was interested in giving one. For more than a decade I participated in this course, teaching the material on homosexuality. I also taught a course on homosexuality in literature in the English department from 1973 until my retirement in 1988, without any further repercussions.

The experiment had the mixed result of persuading a few academics to take a serious professional interest in the subject, while scaring others off. In my case, I determined that for the rest of my academic career, I would do no new research or writing that did not deal with historical, literary, or legal aspects of homosexuality. Since my retirement, younger colleagues in the English department have continued to teach the course in "Sex

Roles in Literature," adapting it to these very different times and to the much higher level of gay and lesbian consciousness that now exists on campus. Attacks by conservative regents, faculty, and students on what they perceive to be the university's (very modest) support for gay rights are common, but they now focus on other issues than the right to teach.

The sheer fact that, in 1994, legislators at all levels are still introducing bills to prohibit open discussion of gay and lesbian issues in public schools and to deny federal funding to colleges and universities which "advocate" (i.e., mention) homosexuality make this particular piece of "history" as relevant today as it was in 1970 when it occurred. I am grateful to Professor Crompton for making his archival essay available to me for inclusion in this study (Crompton, 1994).

Prods for Change

When considering how institutional change comes about, my questionnaires show two primary gadflies: faculty and student groups who lobby long and loudly from the bottom; presidents (or similarly central administrators) who instigate change from the top. In the words of a gay professor with 27 years of teaching at a state university in the midwest, "It's night and day here since 1966! The single most dramatic change involves the president's formation of the Commission on Gay/Lesbian Issues, which lent gay/lesbian issues a legitimacy and a visibility. That really was an extraordinary stroke—it truly transformed the ambiance." The significant aspect of this commission, different from most described by respondents, is its initiation by a chief administrator without having been pressured to do so by lesbian and gay faculty, staff, and students.

In another case, the same lesbian professor has watched her landscape change dramatically over the 26 years she has been in the academy:

> For years, how they treated me was the sole indicator since I was the only out gay [faculty member]. I only got tenure after a huge political battle in 1973. Then years later my promotion [to full professor] was turned down and I only got it a year ago, years after all my peers—at least those who were publishing [as I was].

> Now suddenly SEVEN other faculty are out and we have a program listed in the catalogue!

As the "only one," the professor made very painful progress in her own career; as part of a group, she is currently enjoying a lively and productive environment.

Faculty on campuses without at least one of these agential components find themselves mired in custom and habit—the institution's and their own. Some faculty are painfully aware that they and their gay and lesbian associates are too quiet, leaving whatever impetus for change there may be to students. As one such person mused, "I don't think there's been enough push from the faculty/staff. The students push but they're only temporary—we who've been here longer and will (hopefully) be here longer are in a better position to work with the administration to address these issues." This professor understands that in most cases no single gay or lesbian academic can hope to effect broad change. Either the individual eventually exhausts him or herself, or the institution simply rolls over them as it lumbers along preserving the status quo. But banding together can mean that faculty and staff will have a chance to be heard and heeded. The situation described in the narrative that follows is representative of what is possible when faculty members are able to organize:

> [Our campus] has become more open as more people come out. Once we began to be able to identify and talk to one another openly, it became obvious that we have many lesbian and gay faculty members (and of course students), and that if we work together, we can create courses in lesbian and gay literature, psychology, etc. which students will take. Numbers rule here, so if we can get 50 students to take a course, the administration is delighted to have us offer it and capture those 50 bodies. Students are pressing for more visibility, more courses. Part of it I attribute simply to us being a particularly open campus where we LIKE one another.

This professor who has been part of the academy for 22 years is benefitting from the strength that can come from cooperation and friendly respect. But she also knows that such reinforcements cannot exist on a campus where the majority of gay and lesbian faculty still feel it necessary or preferable to remain closeted.

A tricky aspect involved in nurturing cooperative bonding and support stems from the years of training most academics have received in guarding our theories and practices from all competition. Gay and lesbian faculty members must struggle against such conditioning if we hope ever to coalesce in the face of administrative hostility, ignorance, and apathy. Furthermore, many of us may need to come to grips with our own academic classism regarding staff colleagues. Otherwise we may find ourselves so small an enclave as to be rendered ineffectual against institutional inertia and resistance. Some of my best allies are women and men who hold staff positions with long service records to the university. These people seldom labor under any professionally blunted illusions about whose world it is they inhabit as employees.

Roadblocks to Change

Among the roadblocks to acceptance and change I identified and discussed in the course of this study are: being a faculty member at an historically same-sex college; teaching at religious colleges or universities; becoming comfortable creatures of habit; qualifying for certain campus top honors; seeking to incorporate courses in lesbian and gay studies. The remainder of this chapter focuses on these obstacles.

Same-Sex Colleges

Several faculty taking part in this study have worked for many years at all women's or all men's colleges. They tell compelling stories about trying to make their way in such a climate as gay and especially as lesbian faculty members. A professor of women's studies with 34 years at a prestigious college in the East reports that "the fears of alumnae support and new admissions have been extreme, even though our president has been very supportive and will not accept homophobic alum's objections." When pressed to recount particulars in connection with this assertion, the respondent told a heartening story. She recalls that before about 1980, when some academic feminists began to come out of the closet and align themselves with women's studies, no one spoke of lesbianism. If she used the word, "there was a silence and a refusal to think it was other than someone's private affair."

As increasing public support for lesbian students and for her has evolved, this professor has periodically spoken with her president and public relations staff about the issue, attempting to set their minds at rest by pointing out that lesbians are everywhere, in every occupation, and that many are actually out. Support from non-lesbian women faculty has also increased, a fact which the respondent believes has made a real difference in overall campus climate for lesbians.

Perhaps the most positive aspect of this narrative is found in the respondent's reflections about leadership:

> The president has consistently and with elegance supported the students' and faculty/staff's right to be whoever they are and the best that they can be. When confronted by threats from alumnae to withdraw support, she has responded with a reiteration of the college's commitment to inclusivity and justice for all. She has tried to treat lesbianism as a non-issue. Although she has made no direct speeches for gay liberation, she has created a college-wide committee to advise her on gay, lesbian, and bisexual issues to the end of making the college a safe and productive place for everyone.
>
> As for alumnae objections, some find lesbianism a sin or a perversion—usually religious-based people; some find lesbianism problematic at best and think that the college should discourage women from being lesbians and certainly not allow the public expression of lesbian existence; some find any discussion of lesbianism or mention of it dangerous to the college. Then some believe women will be discouraged from coming to a women's college because they (or their peers or parents) view women together as "unnatural," "abnormal," border-line "deviants."

The conviction on the part of some alumnae that prospective students and/or those around them view women together as somehow aberrant warrants comment. I must point out the collosal irony of having graduates from such an institution voicing such fears. Do they consider themselves to be "abnormal, deviant, or unnatural" because they attended this excellent college when they were young?

A gay faculty member with 22 years in the classics department at another women's college in the East reflects as follows:

> No one was out when I started in 1972. The senior colleague in my department was a vehement homophobe (closet case). Colleagues

within the preceding decade had been fired for being gay. The admission of women in 1978 shook things up. After out lesbians arrived, most of the gays came out. But this is a fairly liberal state.

Finally, a lesbian professor of political science for 23 years at yet a third prestigious eastern college observes the following:

> As a liberal arts college for women, this institution has often been labelled or targeted as "too lesbian." During my first years here [the early 1970s], the response was mostly denial and repression by the administration—trying to keep lesbians quiet and unseen. More recently, partly as a result of more of us coming out and speaking up, and partly as a result of a more sympathetic president, the college has been addressing those fears and the lesbian-baiting somewhat more directly. More and more lesbian faculty feel comfortable being out. This process has involved the college's extending its benefit programs to include same-sex domestic partners of employees.

Undoubtedly, lesbian and gay faculty working in same-sex colleges corresponding to their own sex still must cope with historical denial and anxiety on the parts of colleagues and administrators, as well as some students, parents, and alumni. Just as surely, the model for improving such debilitating circumstances will involve open discussion of such feelings within the broader context of personal homophobia and cultural heterosexism.

Religious Schools

Fourteen percent of the 270 respondents counted in the quantitative data pool for this book listed religious conservatives as the primary source of hostility on their campuses. It stands to reason, then, that faculty teaching in colleges and universities with overt religious affiliations would continue to feel massive pressure to keep their sexual orientation private and hidden.

I was provided with an entirely contemporary scenario centering on the difficulties of being open about sexual variation at such schools. In the fall of 1994, Notre Dame University denied official recognition to a gay and lesbian student group. For the past nine years, this group had met on campus without difficulty but also without being classified as a legitimate student organization. A resolution seeking such recognition was brought to the administration by the president of the student body and chair of the Campus

Life Council which oversees all student activities and associations. By refusing to grant official recognition, the administration denied the group's members access to meeting space on campus and to other modest forms of support granted to student groups.

News of this action spread rapidly through the various bulletin boards for lesbian and gay academics and activists. When I read the announcement of this decision, I decided to do what was requested, i.e., write the president of Notre Dame with copies to his vice president for student affairs and the campus newspaper. My letter must have been printed because I received a long and serious response from a male student, assuring me that he and virtually all other students agreed wholeheartedly with the policies of the university and with the policies of the church with which it is affiliated. He spoke of having no malice towards "homosexuals on campus"—indeed, he offered to pray for them (and me in absentia) in hopes that we might see the error of our ways. After contemplating whether to answer this letter, I decided to remain silent. The depth of feeling behind the words written to me, a total stranger living far from campus, suggested that no amount of counter-argument on my part was going to alter the author's beliefs.

A few weeks later, I received institutional responses. One was from the president's legal counsel, informing me that the president had read my letter and asked his vice president for student affairs to respond more fully. The other response, from that vice president, was a longer letter with an enclosure which was her public apologia to the campus at large. Her personal letter was respectful and politic, ending by saying that even after I had read her official response, I might well see matters through a different lens from her own. She hoped, however, that I would at least understand more fully the broader context within which the single decision had been made.

The aspect of the open letter that most alarmed me was this: the woman who composed it firmly believes that the institution's refusal to grant recognition to the Gays and Lesbians at Notre Dame/Saint Mary's College (GLND/SMC) in no way reflects "a desire on our part to disavow our gay and lesbian students as integral and valued members of the Notre Dame community." Rather the quarrel is focused on the tenor and actions of THIS group of such students. It seems that the administration has a "long-standing dispute with GLND/SMC" over its position about sexuality. Notre Dame University, consistent with church teachings, "has an explicit policy that expresses our belief that a genuine and complete expression of love through sexual union requires a commitment to a total living and sharing together of a man and woman in marriage. . . . Consistent with the moral teachings of the Catholic Church, Notre Dame explicitly calls all students—whatever their sexual orientation—to chastity."

Against this backdrop, the institution judged in 1992 (when GLND/SMC also petitioned unsuccessfully for official recognition) that the application materials did not meet these moral standards. Their official argument was as follows:

> Taken as a whole, the application materials were cast in a framework that expressed a value-neutral approach toward a variety of ways in which gays and lesbians may live out their orientation. At another point in the application materials, GLND/SMC stated its belief that Notre Dame has a [sic] unique opportunity to influence young gays and lesbians by steering them in the direction of stable, monogamous relationships. Neither of these approaches, however, is consistent with official church teaching.

The obvious double bind in which such "teaching" places lesbian and gay students means that in essence there is no way such men and women can ever qualify as having a committed relationship. If they do not advocate monogamous bonds, they are denied legitimacy because they are not truly committed; if they do advocate monogamous bonds, they continue to fall short because they are not, nor can they ever be "a man and a woman."

The open letter lists several measures that Notre Dame is contemplating in its efforts to reach out to its gay and lesbian students. However, no mention is ever made of the existence of counterparts on the faculty or staff. Reading it could leave someone with the impression that there simply are no such individuals in positions of responsibility at this institution. Surely such an anamoly does not exist, but in such an environment, why would any faculty members or university staff personnel risk coming out to colleagues and students, teaching courses or conducting research having to do gay or lesbian issues?

The faculty as a whole, however, have taken a public stand in opposition to the administration. One day after the publication in the campus newspaper of the open letter by the Vice President of Student Affairs, the Faculty Senate adopted by a vote of 30-3 (with four abstentions) a resolution calling for the formal recognition of GLND/SMC. This action means that every representative body on the Notre Dame campus (the undergraduate Student Senate, the Graduate Student Council, the Hall Presidents' Council, the Graduate Theological Union, the Campus Life Council, the Faculty Senate) has opposed the institutional position on this issue.

One lesson to draw from this incident is that by utilizing electronic media to inform people across the country of an attempt to marginalize a student group on the basis of sexual orientation, the action could not proceed unnoticed. People like me who wrote protesting this action may never lay eyes on the persons directly involved. But we came forward to establish solidarity with them, and this special long-distance community response helped keep the issue before the university administration. The institution felt compelled to try to justify its actions to those who wrote. It may well be that such public support from outside the walls of Notre Dame may have strengthened the faculty's resolve to take a stand on behalf of fairness and human rights.

Some church-affiliated schools are making honest attempts to change their attitudes and policies toward their lesbian and gay citizens. A faculty member with 15 years at such a location on the West Coast reflects as follows:

> I work for a conservative Christian university. The president, however, is very supportive as are several faculty and staff members. Because the church is not generally supportive of gays the wheels of progress turn slowly. But they are turning. I think [the school] has become more tolerant. We have had a very out student the last few years. The school had an official presence at the AIDS walk this year and displayed an AIDS quilt in the library. These things would not have happened a few years ago.

Similarly a lesbian professor with 29 years working in the South at an institution with an anti-discriminatory policy in place gladly affirms that her school does not openly discourage gay/lesbian student groups. In fact, the students are quite open about their sexual preference now. Additionally, younger and more recently appointed faculty are quite positive about being "out," even if sometimes intolerant of older faculty who have chosen not to make "an issue" of their sexual orientation. This respondent is herself over 60 and so feels part of that "older" group of faculty. Her final comment bears serious consideration by any of us working in relatively more enlightened locations in the country: "Consider regional differences, i.e., the South is still the Bible belt, as well as the fact that [her school] runs under the auspices of the church with which it is affiliated."

The generational emphasis found in this last story will not easily vanish. Institutions truly desirous of assisting faculty members between the ages of 45 and 65 in efforts to integrate their personal and academic lives will need to make special overtures and give special assurances. Most gay and lesbian faculty who fall into this age group rightly refrained from declaring our sexual identities during the early years in the academy for reasons referred to in this and previous chapters. We had to find some way to "handle" the expedient disjunction forced upon many of us by a society unwilling to inform itself about gay and lesbian history and culture, hence able to remain ignorant and prejudiced against us.

To expect such faculty suddenly to exit decades-old closets is naive and unproductive. One professor of English with 33 years of academic service, 28 of which have been at a four-year liberal arts college in the Midwest, argues as follows:

> Despite the published [anti-discriminatory] statement, there are more closeted gay and lesbian faculty here than those of us who are out. I suspect that owes to lingering anxiety about tenure and promotion decisions and to a long history of being in the closet. After years of practice at passing, it's often less traumatic to keep doing it. Faculty feel more comfortable avoiding the controversy and loss of esteem that they fear may follow coming out. I respect their decision even though I sometimes try to convince them to give students and colleagues the chance to accept them.

At my own university, no administrators have ever tried to discuss the changing climate with older, more established faculty members who may be lesbian or gay. None in the 304 returned questionnaires mentions any such institutional efforts, though well over half refer to the significant group of still-closeted colleagues. Many such references also mention hostility and opposition coming from such people. Like the respondent above, I do not blame such colleagues; rather I hold the institutions responsible for their continuing complicity in the preservation of silence. It is to their advantage to act this way, since encouraging their more senior faculty to come out might mean significantly more pressure for equitable treatment. Such faculty might well agitate to be chosen for leadership positions currently denied us.

A geologist with 17 years at a university in the Southwest remarks that he remained closeted for the first 8 years (time to secure tenure) and then came out slowly. Now he is the only openly gay faculty member on his faculty senate:

> I believe that my movement upward into an administrative position such as department head or associate dean is blocked permanently because I am gay. This is a conservative university, and while they tolerate and sometimes even support my openness, they would never go so far as to appoint me to such positions. They would get too much flak from alumni.

I share this man's perceptions. At the University of Minnesota, there are 20 coveted faculty awards called Regents Professorships. These are reserved for faculty with truly extraordinary accomplishments in at least one of the three merit arenas of scholarship, teaching, and service. I have published five books and numerous substantial articles, won four different teaching awards, and held virtually every committee assignment possible on the campus as well as many leadership positions at the regional and national level. My nomination for a Regents Professorship has been turned down several times in favor of white men with, in several cases, no better records than my own. I am convinced that a major deterrent to my receiving this honor lies in my open lesbian stance and the resultant research emphasis. The committee who selects such nominees, the president who has to take such names to the Board of Regents, and that group of overseers of my university, are simply unable to "see" my achievements in and of themselves. It saddens and tires me to contemplate yet one more discrimination suit against my administration (I have had to sue three times over salary and promotion issues), but once my publications currently in the pipeline are in print, that is what I will need to do. And this time, it will be on the basis of sexual orientation in addition to gender. To force one's institution to treat one fairly blunts any positive outcome that may finally come about. So if such litigation should become necessary and should be successful, it will greatly reduce the joy I might have felt over the well-deserved honor.

Curricular Reform

Very few of my respondents report having gay or lesbian studies programs at their institutions. Many more faculty speak of small clusters of courses, usually taught under the rubrics of women's or cultural studies, English, history, psychology, and anthropology. Faculty recount having taught such a course once or perhaps twice or of planning to do so in the near future or before they retire.

It seems clear from these scattered data that efforts to systematize curricular reform to be more inclusive of lesbian and gay history and culture meet with cool response in most instances. At the University of Minnesota, talk of a coherent program in gay and lesbian studies has not progressed very far among our faculty. This delay stems at least in part from internal struggles along sexist and classist lines. Some lesbians maintain that our angle of analysis is gender rather than sexuality, while others take the reverse position. Those in the former group tend to join forces with heterosexual feminist colleagues. We also note with dismay that many of our gay colleagues are ignorant about major scholars and creative voices coming from the lesbian world, while we tend to know about comparable gay figures. Such inequities mitigate against easy intellectual cooperation. It is much easier to bond with gay colleagues around work equity issues and other general concerns of visibility and recognition than it is to plan for meaningfully inclusive curricular programs.

Aside from such complexities, however, our institutions certainly are not eager to meet us half way once faculty are able to organize along curricular lines. A lesbian professor of psychology at a graduate university in the mid-Atlantic region speaks about the superficial changes at her university. In 1985 a sexual orientation clause was added to their union contract. In 1993 a center for lesbian and gay students was opened. But the reality of students' lives has not changed:

> Lesbian and gay students I have worked with and had in classes still face incredible homophobia in their other classes. For example, a woman who teaches feminist theory begins by saying "We

will not discuss lesbians because they are different." Another student described a class meeting in which the two straight female professors gave a whole lecture on how lesbians destroyed the women's movement, looking at her the whole time because she was the obvious out dyke in the room. She felt abused, but since she was young and new to graduate school, she really didn't have the information to counter them.

In addition to this personal harassment of students, few courses incorporate lesbian and gay material unless they are specifically "about" such topics. This professor firmly believes the existence of the Center for Lesbian and Gay Students was an outgrowth of the AIDs movement coupled with the general rise in activism around the country. These winds of change are not enough, however, and she concludes by pointing out that "the majority of lesbian and gay faculty, despite the sexual orientation clause in our contracts and despite their having tenure, are not out still."

The colleagial disrespect and the slighting of gay and lesbian subject matter reported in this narrative are possible in large part because no institutional voice has spoken out in favor of such inclusiveness. Faculty feel no external incentive or pressure to alter their heterosexist approaches and will not unless people like chairs, deans, and upper level administrators make it clear that they expect their faculties to rethink all relevant courses along the criterion of sexuality in much the same manner as they have used to rethink unexamined but ubiquitous racist and sexist biases. Only then will we begin to see more course titles and programmatic clusterings which focus on gay and lesbian subject matter.

The importance of such curricular inclusion cannot be overstated. Because classes are at the heart of any educational institution's life, failure to teach courses about lesbian and gay subject matter cannot be offset by any amount of tolerance from administrations about allowing student groups to meet or hold social or even political meetings on campus. A professor of classics for the past 22 years at an eastern college historically all-male until the 1980s speaks eloquently about the centrality of such courses in any long-term improvements of life on campus for students. This professor gave a talk in April 1995 as part of his college's first gay/lesbian/bisexual alumni-student mentoring weekend. Finding this event one of the most salutory moves on the college's part on behalf of its lesbian, gay, and bisexual student population, he was shocked by what followed:

> In the wee hours of the following night, some male students were harassed in a dorm room after an l/g/b dance by a band of drunken males (jocks and frat members). The language and gestures were assaultive, but Security arrived quickly. The subsequent Gay Awareness Week included a large outpouring of support from the whole community. One of the points in my speech, i.e. the comfortable positions that out faculty enjoy, together with the high state of evolution of g/l studies classes does NOT translate to equal ease or the same proportion of outness for students) was confirmed.

The professor goes on to consider the fact that a largely closeted student body showed up in great numbers after this unfortunate incident:

> In the open meetings for students after the homophobic incident, I was impressed by how much difference lesbian and gay studies classes had made. The students were remarkably more sophisticated, forthright, yet also temperate than they would have been ten years ago. The student community is largely shaped, stabilized, given its identity by the l/g studies courses. Though the official l/g/b association seems destined to keep shifting, almost going out of business, coming back again, the class offerings give the basis of some sort of community for students.

This thoughtful account of how an institution might best serve the needs of its gay, lesbian, and bisexual student body can serve as both goad and model for administrators currently debating such issues on their own campuses.

Genuinely Supportive Institutions

Though at times I began to believe there were no truly supportive colleges or universities, several success stories did emerge. In follow-up narratives, faculty were able to describe not only what their campuses were like but, in some cases, why they may be as positive as they are.

A social work professor who has spent 11 of her 16 years at a midwestern research university reported that in the past few years, gay and lesbian issues have become visible at her university in a positive way relative to most other comparable institutions:

> I feel fortunate to be at a place where this has happened and find it very affirming. I expect there may be a backlash, but I believe this university, surrounded by this community, will continue to be on the forefront of g/l (and other social justice) issues. I think this is primarily due to the willingness of g/l people to be out and verbal, to push and do the work it takes to make [change] happen here.

In spite of these congratulatory words, this professor states elsewhere that she feels largely unappreciated for being a voice for diversity at her institution. At one point, she comments that she is still waiting for her dean to tell her how much her research into gay/lesbian issues lends to the University's reputation.

A professor at a graduate university on the West Coast has a different analysis of how change has occurred. Her institution has over 10 years instituted a domestic partner policy that is one of the best in the country. But she is clear that her campus was never "bad" on the subject of lesbian or gay faculty, even when she arrived:

> When I was interviewed in 1981, I was very delicately yet sympathetically informed by my chair about opportunities/networks for lesbian/gay faculty. I'm one of the lucky ones. Undoubtedly a large element in the relative tolerance/support I experience at my university is due to: a) geography (proximity to San Francisco); and b) the early onset of the AIDS epidemic among faculty, staff, and students. As early as 1983, as the deaths began to mount, a new openness and sympathy for all gay people at the university began to make itself felt as a "humanizing" and *institutional* desire to mitigate the suffering of those affected.

This professor attributes her institution's support to people's responses to AIDS in their midst. While such a response is preferable to hostile intolerance, I cannot help but regret that such positive attitudes must attend upon horrible losses to the gay and lesbian community. I also regret that once again in Western history, sympathy from the dominant society is based on its response to what it can only see as an "illness," in this case equated primarily with gay men.

Finally, a professor of English for 27 years at a research university in the South finds a more personal cause for changes on his campus:

> Since I've been here, watching a small-town college of 3,000 students in 1969 become the state's second largest residence university (14,000 students), I've seen a great deal of change. Largely due to my good fortune and persistent effort to make the school a gay-positive place, we now are becoming known for our openness to gay faculty. One positive person, supported by a loving partner for 19 years, can make a difference. I should add that my partner's becoming [a high level administrator] a few years ago has doubled our strength as examples to the campus.

These narratives, and others like them in this study, denote the central role to be played by administrative leaders in any genuine progress for lesbian and gay faculty members. Even such advocacy does not insure rapid change; at most institutions, presidents must answer to others who hold both power and the purse strings. But not having it definitely insures the virtual absence of change. Seeing no models at the top, other administrators who wield tremendous power over the lives and futures of faculty members have no institutional impetus to create environments in which lesbians and gay men will feel respected or safe enough to discuss their sexual identity. Having no institutional goals before them, administrators and faculty alike will merely drift along as they have always been, forcing those within their midst who do not fit the assumed definitions of human choice and behavior to remain in closets.

After reading hundreds of accounts of the consequences of lukewarm or absent support from various levels of administrators around the country, I hold such men and women directly responsible for the preservation of academic closet culture. Since that culture not only stifles those within it but at times clearly punishes those who step out of it, the effects of neglect and inertia are severe and wasteful indeed. It is time for all university and college administrators to educate themselves about their gay and lesbian faculty colleagues and then to make conscious and active moves to warm the climate of their campuses.

As final proof of this urgency, let me quote a professor of computer science with 24 years at a graduate research university:

I think there are two real tragedies [connected with being gay or lesbian]: 1) I see old, lesbigay faculty who retire still in the closet. One lesbian couple still "pretends" after 25 years even though they are the only ones who don't talk about it; 2) The *massive* lack of sympathy by most straight colleagues, to the AIDS conflagration, or any real understanding of the need for repealing sodomy statutes, etc. They just don't care.

Words like these should be sufficient to motivate administrators at all levels to work actively to improve their campus climate for lesbian and gay faculty.

CHAPTER 6

"Is There a Metanarrative in the House?"

Having reported the many opinions and choices in relation to being lesbian or gay in the academy, I want to step back and reflect on the story these stories tell. At the beginning of this project, I had a few preconceptions of what I would find. Many of those have been altered if not wiped out by the realities of our lives as teachers, artists, advisors, colleagues, scholars, and members of campus communities. For instance, I believed I would find more concrete change in attitudes and policies than has been the case; I thought many fully closeted faculty would respond, welcoming an opportunity to air their grievances anonymously; I was sure that most faculty who have chosen to come out to colleagues would be out to students and in classes as well; I dared hope that, as some faculty made public the relationships between their sexual identities and their research and teaching, they would be joined by older, more private colleagues. In a word, I wanted to find a better world than the one into which I walked thirty years ago.

In many ways, I did find a better world. The words and issues surrounding our lives are in the air on college and university campuses; many administrations have added "sexual orientation" to their anti-discrimination statements; increasingly, students and younger gay and lesbian faculty are agitating for greater visibility as human beings and as a group worthy of research studies and learning opportunities. Happily, I found a few campuses where the atmosphere is genuinely lesbian-gay friendly. All these signs of progress are encouraging and deserving of at least guarded celebration.

But in far too many cases, faculty, staff, and students continue to experience hostility, ignorance, trivialization, and hateful prejudice, all of which reinforce an atmosphere of fear in which the need for invisibility lingers like fog.

Gradualism

One of the clearest story lines woven into countless questionnaires and follow-up narratives included here concerns what I call gradualism. One person after another has told of the often painfully slow path on which she or he set out, ending in many instances at a destination unimaginable at the outset. A few of the most poignant of these unfoldings suggest that perhaps none of us is ever truly or entirely static.

The following story comes from a gay professor of philosophy, teaching for 25 years at a midwestern state university:

> I started teaching here in 1969. Two years later I married a woman I met here, following the general social plan that "when you settle down. . . ." About six years into it, things were not going well and we separated. In the process of deciding what to do about that relationship, I realized I needed to figure out what the attractions I had felt toward other men (and had not acted on) meant. That resulted in my falling in love with a man, coming out, and realizing that the marriage could not continue.
>
> After I came out (1977–1978), I became very involved in developing a support system for gay and lesbian people in this area. My volunteer activities took up all my spare time, making research virtually impossible. Furthermore the school has a primary teaching mission. I did manage every other year to give a paper at the state philosophical society. I have done two three-year stints as chair and that too made it difficult to do any research.
>
> In 1988 I joined a fledgling organization, Society for Lesbian and Gay Philosophers. I soon became an officer. The man responsible for arranging programs at the American Philosophical Association conventions invited me to comment on a paper on outing. That same man got me to do a paper myself on outing for the next APA meeting. I wrote a paper which I first gave at a department colloquium, then at the state philosophical society, and

then at the national caucus session. Subsequently I submitted it for a volume being prepared on "Gay Ethics." It was accepted and was finally released in November 1994.

The success of that venture led me to decide to give more emphasis to research the later part of my career (this is my 26th year of teaching). I've started on a project I'm calling "The Moral Dimensions of Passing." Thinking about the closet and its evils when I was working on the outing paper got me started on this. It is not just about the closet for gays and lesbians but about other varieties of passing as well—people pretending to be something they are not, generally in contexts of oppression. I got released time last spring to work on this and submitted the final version for consideration for the main program of the APA meeting in the spring of 1995. It was accepted. I am continuing work in the area and envision it becoming a much longer paper or even several papers.

So at this stage of my career, I find myself getting more involved in research, anxious to give it a higher priority. Teaching and volunteer activity and activism resulted in my not having the opportunity to get more involved in research earlier. . . . The combination of my own coming out, being a gay person of integrity working for change in an oppressive society, and the opportunity to use my philosophical skills and training to do scholarly work on issues of importance is what has resulted in my decision to devote more energy to research.

This [research] is connected to my activism, too. It is a way of working for change through scholarship, influencing thinking and ideas over the long run. It affords some personal rewards, too, in terms of experiencing a fulfillment, that one tends not to get from activist activities. I think that being encouraged by the man who first invited me to comment on a paper was important. We all need contexts that invite work on gay and lesbian projects.

As for reception, I have found my colleagues to be very supportive. I've gotten excellent feedback when I've done departmental colloquia. I've routinely sent in items relating to work I'm doing on gay topics for listing in the "notes and news" section of the school's faculty-staff newsletter. I have hopes that some of my gay and lesbian colleagues will think about working on g/l topics themselves. However, some of them seem so deeply mired in the closet that I'm not sure how much hope there is of that.

Before commenting on this narrative, I want to present an account sent me somewhat later by the same professor, detailing the effect his being out on campus has had on his life in the larger community. The mayor of his city, referred to by the gay professor as "a wonderful man," had issued a proclamation for Gay Pride Week in June 1984. The city commission staged a debate on this proclamation at the same time as people were raising an issue about a women's health organization which performed abortions. Because of the expected attendance to hear discussion of these two controversial issues, the commission meeting was moved to the civic auditorium. The philosophy professor reported this:

> Over 500 attended. Many people were negative about the proclamation; some were positive. I gave testimony. The commission voted to rescind the mayor's proclamation, but the mayor announced he would reissue it. The next week I was heading for a writing workshop on travel writing. I was looking forward to some time away from gay/lesbian activism but when I arrived in the city where the workshop was to be held, I learned that its city council would be considering whether to overturn their mayor's veto of a council decision to include sexual orientation in their human rights ordinance. A friend asked me to attend and testify since most of the gay and lesbian people living there were afraid to speak up.
>
> Given what I'd just been through, that was about the last thing I wanted to do. However, I went and signed up to speak out of duty. Waiting my turn, I listened to what was mostly fairly boring testimony about what the Bible says. A minister got up and told the council that on these matters he was, as a man of God, their superior. He went on to say that he favored the death penalty for homosexuality. We were jolted out of our boredom.
>
> I spoke soon after him, saying: "I'm shocked to hear that someone would want me, as a gay person, to be executed, on religious grounds." From behind me I heard jeers and some people yelling "Amen" and "Go back where you came from." I was stunned, and found myself barely able to speak (which doesn't happen often). But I finished. When I left city hall, I found myself fearful, looking over my shoulder. The next day I read the local paper and nearly choked on my sandwich when I found my experience reported in detail in an AP story.

The man decided to write about his experience in his workshop, getting shock and support from other members and encouragement from the teacher to do something further with the writing. He converted it into an opinion piece, sent it to the newspaper published in his state's largest city, and received a call telling him it would be printed. The year was 1984, about four years after this professor had first come out to any of his colleagues in the department. However, he was not publicly out at his university, which had no anti-discrimination policy at the time:

> The newspaper's policy was to indicate profession along with name. I had a little worry that some administrators might not like my using my university affiliation in the article. I also thought some anti-gay people might hassle the president. I wondered with colleagues if I should alert the president, but my chair suggested that I not do that. He said by doing so I would be suggesting that I thought there might be something wrong in what I was doing. I let the matter alone.
>
> I did get some hostile mail, but there was no adverse reaction from the administration. The president received no complaints. As a matter of fact, we found out later, indirectly, that he had some pride that the philosophy department had two people involved in activism (me in gay/lesbian matters; the other [person] in animal rights issues) and that he had not gotten any complaints about lack of objectivity in our teaching. (It would have been nice if he told us that!)
>
> For those of us who are gay or lesbian, particularly in situations where we're not covered by a law or policy, we inevitably have to worry about how much we'll stick our neck out, and whether that will come back to haunt us. I had decided by that point that out of integrity I was not going to let that sort of worry significantly interfere with my activism. But it is an emotionally exhausting process, a worry most of our [heterosexual] colleagues don't have.

As a postscript to this remarkable account of evolutionary growth, here is an update I received while revising this manuscript concerning this professor's presentation at the national conference of his professional association:

> My paper at the APA meeting went well. The audience wasn't huge but my work was well-received, and we had a very good discussion. Several people asked for copies. I intend to work more on the issue this summer. In the past when I went to APA meetings, I found them stimulating in terms of being able to attend

various sessions and hear papers in areas I'm interested in, as well as areas I know little about. This time I felt much less an "outsider," envying those who seemed to be in situations that enabled them to engage in more research-oriented scholarly activity than my situation allowed. I felt like a "participant."

The lessons and models in this story are clear:

- All of us with entree into academia need to consider drawing in colleagues not currently part of that scene. The acknowledged impetus for so much that has unfolded for this professor came from a more publicly placed colleague's invitation to do something low key, e.g., respond to someone else's paper. Having gotten his toe in the water, the professor has slowly but surely moved into deeper, more satisfying seas.

- Never assume it is too late for a colleague or for oneself to begin coming out professionally. Literally hundreds of faculty across this country are thinking thoughts and brewing theories all the time which proceed from or are influenced by their perspective as lesbians or gays. Nobody knows exactly what is needed to turn such private, fragmentary ruminations into coherent research projects and course designs. But remaining open to clues and signals of readiness seems well worth the effort.

- Being out to oneself and to a few academic associates seems to be one necessary condition for further growth. As long as this man was married and closeted, no overtures could possibly be made to him by interested colleagues. Once he was willing to undertake exploration of his own emotional and sexual patterns and then brave enough to make the changes suggested by what he found, he became visible and potentially available for such invitations like the one he received from his mentor.

- One person who is clear enough about his or her own identity can make a significant difference in their academic communities as well as in a broader social context. Deciding not to collude in the irrational prejudices against lesbians and gays by remaining silent can liberate and empower the person making that decision, and it can alter the way our campuses and communities do business.

The converse is equally true, as seen in this brief but moving self-analysis by a retired lesbian professor of anthropology who had spent 23 of her 30 years teaching at a liberal arts college which upgraded to a state university on the West Coast. Though she assured me that "I cannot think of a class I've taught without self-identification that would have been aided by my doing so," she reported the following:

> Being gay, combined with the upbringing I had, has made me timid and perfectionist and for many years shy about stepping into the arena of scholarship. My fear of homophobia was inseparable from a general fear of disapproval. This has meant that I have never mobilized my capacities for scholarship, and have had to spend my life at a second rate campus with heavy workload. *I had great potential but was crippled by lack of self-esteem, flowing in part from self-denigration as gay.* On the other hand, once I accepted my identity more fully (thanks in good part to therapy), I gradually began to do research on gay and gender topics, which has been most satisfying both intellectually and in the contact with gay peers it has provided. This has led to active involvement in gay academic politics, a matter of great pride and satisfaction [emphasis mine].

Though I have read these words several times, I continue to feel a sharp poignancy, followed closely by anger at the waste to herself and the academic community occasioned by this woman's having grown up and come to her sexual identity in a culture which denied her information and acceptance. Her reflection also highlights the unavoidable connection between an academic's self-esteem or self-respect on one hand and his or her ability to pursue intellectual and scholarly interests on the other. This lesbian anthropologist never fooled herself, even when she was unable to focus her considerable energies on her research potential. She also understands the satisfaction that has come to her from finally being able to engage her intellect and spirit in the work for which she was always so admirably suited. She assigns credit for the change exactly where it belongs—to her own decision to seek help from therapy, not to any alteration in her university's or the society's crippling attitudes toward lesbian or gay people.

Cost of Maintaining the Status Quo

As I contemplate the stories behind this book, I still feel astounded that universities and colleges seem content to lose scholarship and research rather than institute and support efforts to make the working environment more open and accepting of sexual diversity among their faculties. Given the parallel fact that many of these institutions have publicly stated missions involving the pursuit and dissemination of new knowledge, upon which they depend in large measure for their funding support, this short-sightedness is a reminder of the destructive power of prejudice. Such attitudes, if left unexamined or unchallenged, can even hinder universities and colleges from realizing some of their own sincerely held goals and desires.

In the face of such unyielding prejudices, change clearly depends upon lesbian and gay faculty members' willingness to work for it and demand it from colleagues and administrators who remain in far too many instances politely passive at best and coolly unforthcoming at worst. I believe such a structure is unfairly skewed toward vulnerable individuals who cannot be expected to swim against such a relentless tide. Many of us will remain closeted—to ourselves in some cases and certainly to those with the power to derail our careers and besmirch our lives. This melancholy conclusion is reinforced by stories like the following, reported by a professor of romance languages with 16 years of teaching in the Midwest.

> The apparent reluctance to test support for gay people is part of the general reticence seemingly characteristic of people in this part of the country. Some perceive this as negative: people are reserved to the point of blandness and timidity; others might say that it is a function of the desire simply to leave people alone and not interfere in their business. The fact remains that civic and campus communities are fundamentally conservative, with great emphasis on consensus. There is an evenness to life here which can be appealing, a kind of idyllic quality; noisiness and unseemly behavior are not part of the scene. To come out strongly on social justice issues is rare. Taking risks, stirring the waters, engaging fully, accepting a life of surprises—none of this is valued. For gay people, this means a kind of live-and-let-live approach. So, while this is not the worst of situations, neither is it especially hopeful, since there seems to be little evolution or progress. The refusal to engage poses a formidable obstacle; it's like trying to move a cemetery. I believe there is support on campus, but it is of the passive kind: violence or open discrimination will not be tolerated. If by support you mean encouragement, however, then we have a long road ahead. If you mean

196

acceptance of diversity which goes beyond the harmlessly odd, no time soon.

Unfortunately, this kind of polite toleration is not geographically specific, as the narrator seems to believe. Respondents from all over the country report similar climates, underscoring just how oppressive this kind of inertia can be. Faculty make clear that virtually no change can occur in terms of professors' deciding to incorporate their gayness or lesbianism into their professional and pedagogical lives. Rather, most of us will work to convince ourselves that a safe location, even in the kind of "cemetery" alluded to by the professor above, is preferable to possibilities of danger and loss in the open air. The price of such closeting is too high both for the individuals who must choose it and the institutions that tacitly expect us to do so.

The following story from a professor of Spanish further illustrates my point. Though he began his teaching career in the Midwest, he soon moved to a research university in the South, where he has been for 11 years. In his narrative commentary, he raised and answered a question I can only wish I had asked in my original questionnaire: How has being in academia affected personal lives?

When I came to [the southern university], I was in a long-distance relationship with someone who was not an academic. Within two weeks after getting tenure we broke up, since he felt that, once I had completed my goal, I could then quit and follow him to his new job in the southwest. . . . The point I am trying to make is that being gay in academia often means the sacrifice of a personal life. When I turned down a job in the midwest [the alternative to the southern location], I knew I was sacrificing an urban setting with a lot of gays for a rural school in the "bible belt." I made the decision for professional (and climatological) reasons, and that decision meant that I would probably never have a long-term relationship. I think a lot of gays and lesbians are forced to make that type of decision, since most universities and colleges are not in progressive, urban locations; they are in small, rural communities, where the pressures to remain in the closet are very great. Most of the gay and lesbian people I know here are not in long-term relationships, nor do they have any prospect for one. I have known several men who entered into "convenience" marriages, to facilitate tenure and promotion. This is as sad as not having any relationship at all, since it is based on social convention rather than emotional/psychological needs. The saddest part of this kind of situation is that researchers can rarely get reliable information from this area of gay life.

Finding a suitable life partner in a small town context can be difficult for heterosexual academics, but at least such individuals have the blessing of their immediate environs to set about doing so. Such women and men also have access to similarly inclined colleagues. For the gay or lesbian academic, however, matters are bleak indeed. The towns about which this respondent speaks are not likely to be places where it is easy or commonplace to be out. If the college or university community does not foster an atmosphere in which one can be public about sexual identities that lie outside the majority position, people are cut off from each other.

It is within these contexts that lesbians and gay men stifle their best impulses, first on a personal level but eventually on a pedagogical and research level as well. Such environments give rise to acts of denial, falsity, and desperation on the part of many such faculty. I believe that institutions which lose opportunities to create friendly climates for all their faculty run the risk of colluding in inappropriate behaviors towards students. If an adult is prohibited, by such potent forces as fear of social sanction or loss of one's very livelihood, that person may eventually turn to the powerless in order to meet basic human needs quite taken for granted by heterosexual colleagues.

Repressive environments also breed bitterness. A professor and dean who has spent 10 of his 15 years in academia at a large, prestigious southern university, sent me the following story:

We have [on our faculty] a singularly frightened professor who was once seemingly liberal, was apparently caught cruising the campus, and was the subject of an outing which he then denied. He later cast the only dissenting vote against the inclusion of sexual orientation in the anti-discrimination faculty hiring clause and later publicly attacked an attempt by the law school to deny access to recruiting firms without sexual orientation in their hiring practices. In my view, such desperate attempts to protect ourselves even at the cost of rejecting our own are similar to those made by Jewish kapos in the camps, and are to be taken as evidence not so much of cowardice as of the extent of the problem for which we are not to blame. Infuriating though widespread internalized homophobia is, I know from my own experience how easily the oppressed mind will deny facts.

Some readers may find the comparison to the structure of concentration camps too severe, but the man who made it clearly is struggling to find a sufficiently graphic allusion to impress upon those who guard the camp(use)s and all of us who work within them just how destructive it can be to force someone to deny his or her very identity. This respondent names with clarity the true source of the problem—it resides not in his frightened colleague, but in the system that refuses that person legitimacy.

When I first began collecting data and making notes for this book, I struggled with the question of legitimacy. Initially, I thought it had to do with the fact that I was undertaking an ethnographic study when I am a literary critic, not an anthropologist. As the writing went along, however, I found that I had to take long breaks from the growing manuscript. These "time-outs" allowed me to recognize the much more significant level at which I felt illegitimate. Working with scores of stories of painful years in closets, of lost research and scholarship, and of constant isolation from the social world of our departments, I felt again the debilitating sense of not belonging. Pariah status was attached to me because of whom I loved and wanted to share my life with. Root legitimacy is what I call this need to be able to see oneself mirrored in the society to which one gives one's allegiances and energies. Without this fundamental validation, most of us will not thrive, no matter how hard we try to adapt and adjust to the systems that hire but do not accept us.

What is required of all lesbian and gay academics is patience with individual colleagues who are not able to make the decisions we would prefer about public acclamation of sexual identity. We must resist individualistic explanations for such decisions, going deeper in our analyses to comprehend the systems which exact denial as a precondition for admission, systems which disguise this demand in the coin of the academy's realm—research grants, tenure and promotion, offers of administratively powerful positions, validation of teaching goals and practices. If those of us fortunate enough to work in more neutral or genuinely accepting locations can extend our imaginations enough to let us be nonjudgmental of our colleagues, we may be able to build a strong enough base of support on our campuses and across the country to force more presidents, deans, and department chairs/heads to change policy if not attitudes. Then we all win.

Models

Throughout this book, I have recounted stories from campuses where coming out is perceived by many faculty to be a dangerous decision. Now I want to showcase one campus at which faculty from across several disciplines report working in truly positive climates for gays and lesbians. I do this because I believe other institutions can take lessons from the case study.

A liberal arts college located in California, this institution emerged from my study as one of the most supportive campuses in the country. A professor of social sciences who has worked there for 24 years had this to say:

> We could not [have succeeded] in making the changes that have been made without administrative support. These include exclusion of ROTC, domestic partner benefits, a redesigned annual charity campaign to eliminate an automatic United Way monopoly because of the Boy Scout issue, the creation of The Closet (a student-staffed space for gay, lesbian, bi students), introduction of gay courses in the curriculum. The administration has generally received support from trustees for pro-gay policies, but it has also taken flak from alums who objected to the ROTC exclusion. They have a balancing act to perform, and that means that everything we want as gays and lesbians is not approved immediately or automatically. That's understandable, but the progress has been steady, under two administrations.

I am struck by how much latitude this gay professor is able to give his administrative leaders. His ability to accept that some changes will be gradual signals a fundamental level of trust that someone at the top is taking an active role in moving the items affecting the lives of lesbian and gay faculty as rapidly as possible toward realization. In my own case, and in the cases of the majority of respondents to my questionnaire, no such trust exists. In its absence, we tend to feel frustrated and angry at the slow pace of change on our campuses, with an underlying belief that our administrators do not give our issues a thought unless some of us are in their offices demanding to know why more is not happening.

I am also struck by this institution's rare success in acting in accordance with policy in the crucial matter of an ROTC program. Any campus espousing nondiscrimination on the basis of sexual orientation which allows the continued presence of a program which blatantly violates such a policy sends a message to faculty, staff, and students that its rhetoric is precisely and only that.

Faculty from several disciplines, in their accounts of life on campus, speak positively about active support for research on the part of top administrators: As one of them notes

> I send copies of my writings on gay sex and AIDS to the deans and president and often get complimentary and supportive handwritten replies. The Research Committee, administered by a dean, has given me financial assistance for gay research when there was no place off-campus to find grant support.

Once again, the proactive and personal elements in this account make all the difference to the faculty member involved. As I said earlier, in the 30 years I have been at the University of Minnesota, I can count on one hand the number of times any administrator at any level has spoken to me about my published lesbian research.

When I queried this professor more closely about what he thought made his campus different from most, he sent me the following list, which I offer in its entirety as a possible blueprint which might well be copied by other institutions wishing to improve the climate:

1. Almost every department in the college has an "out" gay/lesbian on its faculty; in many cases, these are people who were not out when hired, i.e. more senior people like myself who came out to themselves—and the world—later. One faculty member directs [a community-based gay male] chorus and brings that group to campus for concerts. To my knowledge he has not had problems with the administration. He was chair of the music department.

2. For almost a decade, at the faculty-trustee retreats, held every two years, domestic partners/lovers of gay and lesbian faculty have been invited on the same basis as spouses of heteros. In actual fact, many glb faculty don't take advantage of this, but some of us

do, even to the point of same-sex dancing at the retreat's Saturday night dance. Some bemused statements by trustees occur, but in general there's no overt homophobia.

3. The faculty is relatively liberal, but except for the gay and lesbian members, I'm not sure they are on the whole more accepting of us than the administration. It's not too long ago that I had to call a colleague on his homophobia on a committee. (He's come around since because he discovered that his straight son's best friend and a longtime friend of the family is gay). My own department chair was not overly joyed to discover my sexual orientation; since then a family member has come out and he has become extremely supportive of gay rights issues. He says his attendance at a same-sex wedding was the most impressive event in his own life.

4. The institution has a good deal of faculty involvement in administration.

5. Incident: When my lover wanted to open a bank account, I discovered that the credit union the college uses did not extend that privilege to domestic partners. I called them and they said they could do nothing about it, it was in their constitution which is approved by the government. I made one phone call to an econ professor who's been here as long as I have and who is a major figure in that credit union. He said he'd look into it. Later he phoned to say it would require a change in the by-laws and government approval, but he'd see what could be done. The credit union ended up within weeks getting their charter modified and obtaining federal regulator approval of the change.

6. Miscellaneous factors which help us: A solid Women's Studies program which is successful and respected; an ideology that says we train the best without regard to matters other than intelligence, character, etc. We have an admissions policy, one of the few in the country at this point, of accepting anyone who meets the entrance requirements without regard to financial ability to pay. (Maybe it also helps that we are a rather well-endowed school and don't live as close to the edge as some other institutions who must therefore be more careful about alienating some of their constituencies.)

As I study this list, two themes stand out: The campus has integrated its lesbian and gay faculty into the fabric of its programs and structures, not demanding silence or secrecy in exchange for acceptance or reward; gay and lesbian faculty perceive their environment as sufficiently open and friendly to allow them to be public in large numbers about their sexual identity, creating thereby a critical mass which makes it virtually impossible for them to be marginalized.

If these two truths seem circular, an example of the proverbial chicken-egg dilemma, I intend that impression. From many years of working in a far more closed and unwelcoming environment, I can speak to the difficulty most faculty on such a campus have with coming out. Because most remain partially or completely closeted, we are isolated from information and power within the institution, allowing it to continue drifting in its passive neglect of us and our issues.

When summing up his feelings about working at this institution, one long-term gay professor had this to say:

> [The school] is a rather liberal institution, and it has a history of defending intellectual freedom. During the McCarthy era when loyalty oaths were the fad and when the state universities were obediently adhering to the requirement that faculty sign oaths, the president categorically refused to allow a loyalty oath. His was a rather isolated voice in academia at a time when most meekly obeyed. Our successes are due primarily to an "out" faculty of at least 15% of the total faculty. Gays and lesbians have been important leaders on campus, winning quite regularly "best teacher" awards, staffing committees, and so forth. Gay and lesbian faculty have been hardworking members of the community and their contributions are well known. This gives clout. We have [out] gays and lesbians in important administrative positions as well.

Certainly it is the case that many of us work at colleges and universities where gay and lesbian faculty members come to hold important administrative positions. But this can be an ambiguous situation if the person in such a position is closeted from his or her administrative peers. Once again, the key in the model case seems to be the fact that such administrators are public about their sexual identities. Given their own comfort (or at least determination) with being open about their personal lives, they then can offer genuine and palpable support to faculty with whom they work.

The retired professor emphasized that not all gay and lesbian faculty members at his college would see things as positively as he. Furthermore, he enumerated instances of what he termed "subtle forms of discrimination" that have existed even within such a generally supportive context. I offer some of the latter, to round out his narrative and to make clear how difficult it is to avoid tension if one happens to fall outside the socially prescribed behavior patterns.

> There have been incidents of homophobia experienced by students, which I do not want to downplay. But students are also aware that they have plenty of faculty support. An exercise I use in my human sexuality class, to demonstrate how many gay/ lesbian faculty we have, is to ask students to list departments in which they know there is at least one g/l/b faculty member; and to list departments with none. Students are quite aware as evidenced by their accurate listing of departments with and without a g/l/b member. . . .
>
> When I applied to live as a faculty resident in the dorm, they disallowed it, never admitting that it was because I was a gay man; but in fact, that was the reason. They subsequently eliminated the faculty residence program to avoid just this problem of having to accept queer faculty for those positions. They have once more reinstated the program. Ironically, if they were worried that a gay man might "molest" or harass students or be ineffective, the year before they abolished the program, the spouse of a female faculty member, living in the dorm, did get involved with a student and it was a big scandal.

The last paragraph of this man's follow-up narrative reads as follows:

> This very day, the President of the college sends my secretary and me a letter about our work, which I quote in its entirety. "I enclose a copy of a wonderful letter I have received concerning *The AIDS Bibliography.* Congratulations to both of you. It would be hard to think of a more important contribution any of us could make to the well-being of our fellow men and women."

It is impossible to generalize from this institution to other campuses, each of which has an unique culture and a set of unique pressures. The institution's history in relation to its lesbian and gay citizens cannot be equated to that at such institutions as Ohio State University, Harvard University, the University of Michigan or Minnesota, or even other California schools such as Berkeley or San Diego State University. This campus is a private undergraduate college with a faculty-student ratio of 1 to 10. Approximately half its funding comes from tuition, the rest from endowment income; and, as a professor pointed out, they are among the very few institutions in the country to maintain an admissions policy based solely on ability.

However, what can be generalized are such universally desired conditions as an actively supportive and celebratory administration which in turn prompts large numbers of gay and lesbian faculty to feel valued and secure enough to come out. Given this context, change will follow in the multiple formats determined by particular university or college settings.

The Future

A professor of history, who, for most of his 15 years, has taught in the Northeast, summarizes his life as follows:

> When I went off to graduate school years ago, I assumed that I was straight and that I would spend my professional career teaching and researching straight material. By the time I landed my first job, I realized that I was gay and that I was interested not only in the traditional scholarship in my field, but also in more innovative subjects and approaches. Until I came out to colleagues and in the classroom, I felt alienated from much of my academic work. I am now active in a variety of professional organizations, teach a variety of courses, and publish about a variety of subjects. It is a matter of considerable importance to me that my identity as a gay person and my interest in gay issues are part of all of these. Being "out" has had the effect of making me feel more personally invested in all my academic work. I do not think of myself first or only as a gay/lesbian studies scholar/teacher, but adding that role to my repertoire has resolved the tension I used to feel between my personal and professional selves.

This simple but profound articulation asserts the absolute connection between comfort with self-identity and a successful academic life. In doing so, it points the way toward the future in higher education.

All the stories offered so generously for inclusion in this study leave me even more convinced than I am from my own unhappy past and productive present that any academic whose environment does not provide for open expression of the relationships between sexual identity and professional development is being short-changed by his or her institution. Whether a lesbian or gay professor decides to come out on campus is not the point; what matters is the presumption that doing so will not involve overt or covert retribution. This is what all of us working at colleges and universities deserve in our futures.

No longer can leaders on college and university campuses in the United States debate *whether* such an atmosphere increases faculty members' contributions to the academic world. So all that such leaders can do as they move into a new century is decide *if* they are willing to act positively and consistently to warm their climate in the face of pronounced homophobic impulses originating in their own communities as well as from outside the boundaries of their campuses.

The narratives found throughout this book share at least one fundamental theme: Most faculty will not risk coming out unless and until their presidents, deans, chairs, and colleagues show them through direct word and deed that these actions will be not only tolerated but valued and even celebrated. The gains are enormous and thrilling. I want to close with three narratives that consider what it can mean when faculty feel empowered to work openly as gays or lesbians.

The first story comes from a professor of romance languages whose tenure in the academy spans 36 years, all but 1 of which have been at a prestigious eastern university:

> One day in class, during the recent winter in which I was at last coming out (at age 60!), the text was one of Beaudelaire's lesbian poems. I heard myself commenting with more passion than usual on its sexual aspect and noted with amusement that I was addressing myself most directly to the two males in class whom I had identified to myself as gay. While I frequently experience moments of particularly passionate engagement with the text at hand, what was new here was the combination of a gay text subject and gay-identified students. It was a curiously exhilirating experience. . . . Now, almost two years later, I still don't know exactly how to interpret that day's event, but I think that probably I was and still am excited about the possibility of having still more ways available to transmit enthusiasm to students about the way literary texts can deal directly with the conduct of our daily lives and the way in which we understand our deepest feelings. (Let

me add that I was private about my own sexual identity and that I think I was right to be: students tend to be embarrassed by personal revelations from older professors, and my judgment is that more students would have been unnecessarily distracted by any statement from me that I was gay than would have been helped by it.)

In a course I have taught several times, both before and after coming out, I note that now I try to identify for myself the lesbian and gay students and make sure they understand what in the texts we read is particularly applicable to their personal situation. I suppose what is happening is that I am now trying to add a "Gay Studies" aspect to my teaching in standard departmental courses.

I recently received a letter from a former colleague who knew I was gay, it turns out, long before I came out. He told me that I had always been very helpful to younger gay colleagues, and I was pleased to know that that was true. I don't think I am yet truly helpful to lesbian colleagues, but being openly gay seems to extend collegiality's reach.

I have begun research on the writings of a major contemporary gay writer [in my field] who is just beginning to come under the academic spotlight; I expect to devote a significant portion of my teaching and writing to his works during the few years remaining [before retirement].

I find this senior professor's commentary inspiring. His eagerness to become ever more available to younger colleagues marks him as an extraordinary model to all of us who have moved into the ranks of the most experienced in our departments and professional organizations.

A second account comes from a man who began his career teaching comparative literature at a prestigious eastern university. After 12 years there, he took an administrative position at a research university in the West. After four years as an administrator, he has definite ideas about the observed differences it can make to have someone fill a leadership position as a fully out gay man:

> I find that as a full professor, white, with very, very tony credentials, I can use being openly gay as a way to penetrate, even perforate what would otherwise be a totally "privileged" position. I don't mean to say I don't have privilege. But I can perform differently and selectively deflate that privilege. (In that "selectivity" lies yet another privilege, but that's another topic.) This can

help build bridges to a variety of other groups, and open "gaps" in the discourse, particularly in seminars or graduate classes, which I think are conducive to inviting student involvement and advancement.

[Being openly gay] disrupts some sexual politics that I have observed going on, (even being the object of), with some [under-achieving] women graduate advisees. Over the years I have frustrated what must have become a trained habit, trained or en-grained because some men not only like it but reward it in terms of grades. I don't. I've gotten some students very mad at me when they get their first B or C with a comment that I expected better. Some of these students years later thank me for calling them on their anti-intellectual performance and getting them to perform to their potential.

An area that could be applicable well beyond the university is that of being an administrator. By not fitting into the cookie-cutter mold, a gay administrator may have a greater quotient of empathy. I certainly have to listen carefully to nuances, and I can often see around corners—I'm used to picking up on clues. This works in many areas, but obviously in issues of sexual politics. I have had women come to me with concerns about sexual harassment and I daresay my responses are different (I wouldn't say better, but certainly different) from those of a non-gay male. I may not do everything right, but at the very least my participation in discussions breaks down a rigid set of binary oppositions.

Another area that goes with the administrator job is that of supervising secretarial staff, which remain largely female. In a situation where a straight white male is supervising a female secretary (whether white or of color), the power dynamics are all running in one direction. However, not only does being openly gay reduce any threat of sexual aggression by the supervisor against a female staff person, it starts to break down the oppressiveness of an entirely one-sided power dynamic. I believe the testimony I've had from several secretaries in two very different institutions that I am the "best boss" they have ever had has something to do with my being openly gay. I add to this the fact that I have observed several other gay men who are outstanding administrators—and hold positions much loftier than I do. The queer deans, as it were. Two that I can think of are as good as they get, and are widely recognized as such. I'm quite convinced that some of their own power, and their ability to interact with people in a flexible way, comes from being gay in a world where few of us [deans] are, and even fewer are open about it.

In sum, when you're out, you're at once saying "I'm vulnerable," "I can empathize"—but also "I'm honest," "I'm very confident, even gutsy," indeed, "I'm willing to put my butt on the line for what I believe in."

A final and sadder note: When some nastiness is coming down through the department or the administration—standard academic politics—and I'm in danger of getting over-cathected, I think about friends who are dead or dying. Whatever matter is going wrong in the university doesn't seem very important any longer.

The excitement this administrator feels at his ability to disrupt some of the most destructive heterosexual power dynamics within the academy hinges on his firm commitment to airing and using his gayness as a political tool. He offers his own experience as a possible template for other gay or lesbian administrators to adapt to their own circumstances, dispelling concerns that most of us probably harbor that such openness about so controversial an aspect of our lives might bring us down professionally. His case has been quite the opposite and his geographical location in a western state is not automatically progressive or accepting.

The third account is told by a professor of Spanish with 15 years of service, most of which have been at a state university in the South. It reminds me that we seldom fool the people with whom we work:

Although I knew I was "different" from the time I was 4 or 5, I was in total denial until I was almost 28 about my sexual orientation. I got my first teaching job when I had just turned 28 (in Kansas). I had both wonderful and horrible experiences there when I came out to people. There was one undergraduate student who is still very dear to me, who came over to my house with a friend who was having boyfriend problems. In the course of the evening, she just said "Well, I wanted ____ to talk to you because she thinks her boyfriend is gay, and since you are I thought you could help her." I was dumbfounded! After a couple of gasps for air, I managed to stutter "How did you know?" She just started laughing hysterically, and finally said, "Well, it's because you never hit on me, and virtually every single male professor I've ever had has hit on me, so I figured you must be gay." That to me was a revelation.

209

This professor then recounts a long and painful story of his decision to come out to a woman colleague with whom he became quite good friends. Over time, he gradually realized that she did not want him to tell anyone else on campus about his sexual orientation. Furthermore, he recognized that while he was allowing colleagues to assume that their many hours together signaled an affair, she found that same rumor comforting proof that she could still be attractive to someone twenty years her junior. Only after much awkwardness and pain was the professor able to disentangle himself from this relationship made possible in large part because he was out only to her.

In his concluding remarks, he returns to the subject of working with students:

> After I decided [recently] to work opening with the [gay and lesbian] caucus, I sent an e-mail message to a woman who is doing her thesis with me, telling her about the Caucus and its importance to me, and about the potential repercussions [working with] it might have. I also told her that if she were concerned about what consequences her working with me might have on her future, she could choose someone else to direct and I would understand. I got back the most wonderful message from her, and we have become even closer as a result. So, my own experiences, both bad and good, have finally made me realize that out is better than in, and certainly better than selectively out.

This professor, separated from me by sex, age, and field, would nonetheless recognize his own situation as analogous to my own. His decision to come all the way out of his closet before any more unpleasantness could occur has obviously been met by positive responses from some of his students. Elsewhere in his survey, however, he rails against the administration and the state government upon which that administration depends for financial support for their cowardice and adamancy in the face of faculty, staff, and students who desperately need support.

Yet social psychologists affirm what most of us know: Those profiting from things as they are seldom support or adopt change enthusiastically; they resist out of a well-founded fear that such change will unseat or at least destabilize them and their associates. Given this axiomatic state of affairs, lesbian and gay faculty must never expect colleagues and administrators to embrace our desire for visibility and equity. Such goals will not only cost such individuals economically; they will force them to confront some of their bedrock definitions of social groupings and human interactions. Most important, within North American academies, visibility and equity for gay and lesbian faculty members will alter inevitably and drastically the landscape of research and teaching on our campuses, at our professional meetings, and in the journals and books published in our fields.

Why should faculty and administrators meet the growing demands of their lesbian and gay colleagues? Because not to do so is to give the lie to the very foundation stones upon which higher education in this country is laid; not to do so is to enable the continuance of a system that silences women and men of enormous potential and genius; not to do so reinforces the least noble aspects of those who refuse to recognize and value us; not to do so allows everyone—heterosexual as well as gay or lesbian—to hide and to stagnate, conditions hardly desirable for the furtherance of knowledge and understanding.

As I was sending the manuscript for this book to the publisher, I received e-mail from a lesbian/gay network, Channel Q, informing me that "Nation's top *business schools* embrace gay professors, students, applicants" [emphasis mine]. And a mathematic professor e-mails me his thrilling news:

> A small but distinctive event on January 6, 1995, at the San Francisco AMS-MAA [the national professional association for mathematics teachers and researchers] meetings was a reception for lesbian, gay, and bisexual mathematicians and their friends. Nearly 100 persons, both men and women, attended the reception at a restaurant near the headquarters hotel.

After our conversation at a conference, a legal scholar whose tenure at her university is too short to qualify her for inclusion in my study writes me the following call to arms:

> In legal academia it is especially important to integrate one's sexuality and politics with one's professional work, given the tremendous flux in the law at this point with regard to lesbians, gay men, bisexuals and transgendered persons. I might go so far as to say that any legal academic who is *not* so engaged is shirking the responsibilities that flow from their considerable privileges.

211

A few months ago, an academic librarian shared with me his life-time project of buying up books, initiated in 1961 when he copied the bibliography at the end of Donald W. Cory's *The Homosexual in America* (1951) and began his endless rounds of bookstores throughout the country. Now, three decades later, this devoted ac-quirer has a private collection consisting of about 2,500 hardback books and 1,500 paperbacks, all of which he will donate before his own impending retirement.

A classics professor tells me in a telephone interview that his university has been given $200,000 to encourage gay studies. His president has asked him, as one of the most visible gay faculty on campus, to work with the development office to write a proposal to utilize the monies. This man, who loves teaching classical philol-ogy, muses with a mixture of delight and dismay in his voice: "If we get a gay/lesbian studies program, I may have to run it and not do Latin grammar."

These snapshots in turn cause me to reflect on my immediate situation in comparison to how I was 31 years ago when I first em-barked on an academic career. I am about to teach a graduate sem-inar on the poetry of Emily Dickinson and some of her woman contemporaries where I will be able to assert without qualms the deeply homoerotic strain in much of this poetry. The editor of an encyclopedia of lesbianism has asked me to write several entries including one on the relationship between alcoholism and closets. An associate vice president at my university, with whom I am friends, told me in an offhand way that her favorite finalist for a top-level administrative post is an "out lesbian." And I recently joked to a heterosexual colleague who had scheduled a meeting in a remodeled building whose room number was duplicated in the original structure. In the new scheme "204" is a bright seminar room. "What is this—you're trying to have us meet in a restroom—that's what *I'm* supposed to be up to." She laughed as easily and loudly as I did.

However, matters clearly are not settled on our campuses or even within our own ranks. Ensuring the futures of all of us will re-quire an adroitness for which few of us have received preparation. We will have to listen to and respect voices across generations, classes, races, disciplines, methodologies, and the broader political spectrum. Those of us who have been in the academy the longest will have to retell our war stories to younger colleagues all too ready to believe "that was then and this is now." Those of us who are convinced that out is the safest place to be will have to have patience and genuine acceptance of our peers who do not share that perspective. Those of us new to the academic world will have to assimilate history without losing heart and passion for the openness we know we deserve. Those of us who remain closeted will have to suppress our fears of "guilt-by-association" so that we can extend at least silent support to our colleagues who insist on being public about their sexual identities.

Beyond these individual stretches, all lesbian and gay academics are called upon to occupy a difficult place, especially in North American culture. We are asked to inhabit a middle ground between exhiliration and watchfulness, between the beginnings of ease and the necessity for alertness, between appropriate gratitude to colleagues and administrators who are working to improve our environments and continued pressure on such people to do even more. If we can manage this political and emotional balancing act, the academy will never be able to go back to the dismal and cruel state scores of people like me found in 1964.

UNIVERSITY of MINNESOTA

Twin Cities Campus

Department of English	207 Lind Hall
College of Liberal Arts	207 Church Street S.E.
	Minneapolis, MN 55455-0134
	612-625-3363
	Fax: 612-624-8228

You are invited to be in a research study focusing on the institutional climate for gay and lesbian faculty who have taught at North American universities and colleges for at least fifteen years. You were selected as a possible participant because of your research and teaching interests, because a colleague thought you might be interested, or because you responded to an announcement about this project.

The purpose of this research is to get a broad picture of conditions on campuses across the country and to include narrative accounts from a diverse population. If you agree to be in this study, you are asked to: complete the enclosed questionnaire; indicate your willingness to engage in a follow-up interview. The questionnaire should take about 30 minutes of your time. While there are no direct benefits to participation, you can help make this book reflective of a cross section of the gay and lesbian faculty population in this country.

Questionnaires will be stored through June of 1995 in a locked file in my office at the University. Only my Research Assistant and I will have access to them. Data will be reported anonymously. In June of 1995, all records of this research will be destroyed. Your decision to participate is purely voluntary; returning the questionnaire constitutes implied consent to take part in this project.

My telephone number is (612) 824-9433; my e-mail address is mcnar001@maroon.tc.umn.edu. If you'd like to receive a report of the results of this research, please include a self-addressed stamped envelope. Please return the questionnaire by November 30, 1994.

Sincerely yours,

Toni. McNaron

Toni A.H. McNaron
Professor, English and Women's Studies

215

Questionnaire for Lesbians and Gays in Academe

Thank you in advance for taking time to respond to the following questions. Results from this questionnaire will be worked into a book I'm completing entitled *Not So Gay Studies: A Lesbian Looks at Academe, 1964–1994.* My goal is to trace the relationship between institutional change (or lack thereof) and the lives of lesbian and gay faculty who have been in the profession at least 15 years. My own 30 years at the University of Minnesota will provide a narrative center, but I'm very eager to write an ethnographic rather than autobiographical study. I need your help to do that. I also want to enlist your help in distributing this questionnaire to colleagues and friends, since I cannot possibly know even a small fraction of the relevant population. If you do not want to copy the questionnaire, let me know how many you could use and I'll mail them to you. As you work through this questionnaire, please consider whether you'd be willing to participate in a follow-up interview. Direct quotations from faculty around the country will strengthen the book. If not, I will of course value your anonymous responses. Again, thank you for returning this questionnaire as soon as possible.

Toni A.H. McNaron, Professor

1. Type of institution at which you work:
   _____ graduate/research university   _____ 4-year liberal arts college
   _____ community or junior college   _____ other (specify)
2. State or region in which you have done most of your teaching:

3. Number of years you've worked at current institution: _____
4. Total number of years you've taught in higher education: _____
5. Rank _____ Age _____ Female____ Male____
6. Ethnic identification_____ Class background_____
7. To what extent are you "out" at your institution:
   Not at all _____   To the campus at large   _____
   To individual faculty _____   To department head or chair _____
   To students in classes _____ To students out of classes   _____
   To administration outside department _____
        Has this condition changed over time? _____ If so, please specify.

8. Are you "out" in settings away from campus? If so, please specify.

9. Does your institution have any of the following:

Anti-discriminatory policy statement	Yes ____	No ____
Space for lesbian/gay students to meet	Yes ____	No ____
Student support groups	Yes ____	No ____
Faculty/staff support services	Yes ____	No ____
Courses in lesbian and/or gay studies	Yes ____	No ____
A gay and/or lesbian studies program	Yes ____	No ____
An office of gay/lesbian concerns	Yes ____	No ____
Other support services	Yes ____	No ____
(please specify) _____		

10. Please list the main sources of support and hostility which you identify on your campus.

    Support:

    Hostility:

11. Has being gay or lesbian had an impact on your teaching and/or research? If so, please describe in some detail.

12. During your tenure at your institution(s), has the institution changed its attitude in regards to lesbian and gay issues? If so, in what ways? If no, why? Please identify internal and external forces involved.

13. Additional comments you would like to make on this subject

---

If you are willing to participate in a follow-up telephone or e-mail interview, please provide the following information:

Name _____

Telephone number _____ E-mail address _____

(My e-mail address is mcnar001@maroon.tc.umn.edu; I'd enjoy hearing from you as I move ahead on this timely project.)

Please return to: Toni McNaron, English Department, 207 Church St. S.E., Mpls., MN 55455

Institutional Responses to Lesbian and Gay Faculty and Students

About a month ago, I wrote asking for your participation in an ethnographic study concerning gay and lesbian faculty in higher education over the past two decades. Thank you for being willing to assist me in this important project. Below you will find a relatively brief questionnaire which I am asking you to complete. Feel free to involve other colleagues in order to give the fullest response possible. Please return your questionnaire to me at the address below <u>BY DECEMBER 1, 1994.</u>

1. At what kind of institution do you work?
   - _____ 4-year liberal arts college
   - _____ large research university
   - _____ community or junior college
   - _____ vocational/technical college
   - _____ other

2. In what state or section of the country is your institution located?

3. Which of the following does your campus offer to lesbian and gay faculty/staff/students?
   - _____ inclusion in your anti-discrimination statement
   - _____ a gay and lesbian studies program
   - _____ counseling services for lesbian and gay students
   - _____ courses on gay and lesbian subjects
   - _____ extension of fringe benefits to
     - _____ lesbian and gay faculty
     - _____ lesbian and gay students
     - _____ lesbian and gay staff
   - _____ recognized student organizations
   - _____ space for student meetings and activities
   - _____ faculty and staff support groups
   - _____ faculty who are public about their gay or lesbian identity
   - _____ other

4. Have any of the following examples of hate speech or action occurred on your campus in the last 5 years?
   - _____ anti-gay or lesbian graffiti in restrooms
   - _____ anti-gay or lesbian graffiti on buildings
   - _____ notices of gay or lesbian activities defaced or stolen
   - _____ demeaning name-calling directed at lesbian or gay students, faculty, or staff
   - _____ homophobic remarks or jokes made by faculty in class or elsewhere
   - _____ physical assaults or threats made on gay or lesbian students
   - _____ physical assaults or threats made on gay or lesbian faculty
   - _____ physical assaults or threats made on gay or lesbian staff
   - _____ other

5. If you checked any of the above, please comment briefly on whatever responses were made by your institution.

6. Have you had a faculty member come to you about discrimination on the basis of sexual orientation? If yes, please describe the complaint or charge and your institution's response.

7. What is the position of your institution's top level administrators concerning lesbian and gay faculty, students, and staff issues?

8. What changes, if any, have occurred on your campus in relation to gay and lesbian issues over the past 10 years? Who precipitated such change or where did it come from?

9. Please make whatever other comments you would like to on any aspect of life on your campus as it pertains to lesbian and gay employees or students.

THANK YOU FOR YOUR TIME AND ATTENTION. Your responses will make my study significantly more valid and will, in particular, make it more relevant to college and university administrators.

In order to secure responses from a broad crosssection of lesbian and gay faculty, I made my project known to as wide a network of such academics as possible. With the help of Carolyn Law, my research assistant, I did the following.

- I sent letters to personal friends, asking for their own participation and for names/addresses of colleagues in their field or at their institution who might be interested in participating.
- I sent somewhat longer more formal letters with similar requests to all faculty to whom such friends referred me.
- I contacted 33 professional associations or organizations, asking them to publicize my project in any manner consistent with their policy on such matters.
- My research assistant wrote 38 newsletters, magazines, and journals in the field of gay or lesbian studies asking for a posting of the study in their next issue.
- My research assistant posted an announcement about the project on 8 extensive electronic bulletin boards or networks, again asking interested faculty to contact me via e-mail or regular mail.
- My research assistant searched tables of contents of recent scholarly works in lesbian, gay, or queer studies and sent requests for names and participation to authors who seemed qualified in terms of years in the profession.
- My research assistant attended the Third Annual Conference of Lesbian, Gay, Bisexual Faculty at the University of Iowa, where she distributed 85 questionnaires.
- I placed notices of the project in such widely circulated publications as *The Chronicle of Higher Education* and *lingua franca*.

These strategies yielded more than 500 volunteers, to each of whom was sent a questionnaire and cover letter explaining the project and my process for protecting anonymity (see Appendix A). This latter point was crucial, since for many faculty the very real danger of having their identities discovered could have been a serious deterrent or a source of unnecessary worry. In this connection, several public lesbian and gay faculty queried themselves and me about how to elicit participation from faculty still to some degree or other in the closet. We all agreed that "outing" was antithetical to our definition of ethical behavior. For my part, I have relied on the judgment of colleagues in the contexts of their local academic communities to gauge the wisdom or kindness of handing out questionnaires. I have made every effort to respect every-one's right to privacy, and am deeply endebted to colleagues across the country who have acted similarly.

Even before I began conducting follow-up interviews, I realized that this project was assuming an importance to lesbian and gay history far beyond my original conception. As the first question-naires were logged and, out of excitement and anticipation, I began glancing at the narrative portions, I knew it would be alto-gether wasteful to destroy such precious data as I had promised to do in my initial cover letter.

After much internal debate, I discussed this issue with a les-bian lawyer who was appalled that I would even contemplate doing away with such invaluable records of gay and lesbian lives. Consequently I made a decision to write all those faculty who had identified themselves on their questionnaires, tell them what a treasure trove they had created, and ask permission to preserve re-sponses while detaching names. Of the 304 respondents who were informed of this change in plans, 260 agreed. I will not include in the archival collection questionnaires returned anonymously, since I have had no way to secure their permission. I am currently investigating a number of local and national repositories so that these data might be used by other interested researchers. Given the size of the pool, I assume there will be gay and lesbian social scientists who may want to take a look. Anyone interested in pur-suing such a topic may contact me until such time as the question-naires are more permanently housed.

Questionnaire and Follow-up: Design and Circulation

Over a period of 8 months, 865 questionnaires were distributed to gay and lesbian faculty from virtually every state in the U.S. Of that total number, 304 (approximately 35 percent) were returned. However, in order to have time to register and compute re-sponses, I had to close the pool upon which quantitative report-ings would be based on February 1, 1995. This means that all the quantitative reportings which follow are based on a pool of 276 respondents.

I sent follow-up questions to everyone who indicated a willing-ness to provide additional information. For follow-up interviews, I offered two options: faculty could speak with me by telephone; faculty could e-mail or surface mail their written responses to me. In both cases, the same set of questions was sent to people in order to allow time to reflect on their answers. Since I was asking faculty to discuss memories from several years back and at times of uncomfortable or even painful moments in their lives, providing preparation time seemed both courteous and wise. The quality of responses, both by telephone and written, reflects the correctness of this decision.

Not only were follow-up interview data thoughtful and specific; they were moving, infuriating, occasionally funny, and always full of generous efforts to reconstruct bygone incidents as faithfully and coherently as possible. The power of this book has one of its primary sources in the words of colleagues from across the country. My decision to quote extensively from faculty narratives became mandatory as I sifted through the extraordinary documentation of ways in which working as a gay or lesbian academic has impacted personal, pedagogical, and scholarly or intellectual development, for better and for worse.

I chose a representative sampling of 25 faculty in terms of sex, geographical location, disciplinary interests, and years in the profession with whom I proposed to conduct half-hour, taped telephone interviews. I actually spoke with 20 of those people. I then sent requests for written follow-ups to 141 respondents, asking them to respond to the same bank of questions as those used with the telephone sample.

The questions were grouped within the three major categories I planned to write about: pedagogical concerns; relationships with colleagues; research/intellectual development. The questions asked people to recall situations in the classroom and within the faculty structures of their departments where it seemed to matter significantly that they were lesbian or gay. For those who had taught both closeted and out, comparative situations were to be discussed. Additionally, they were asked to comment on at least one way in which being gay or lesbian had contributed positively and negatively to their research or intellectual and professional development. Finally, each follow-up candidate was invited to share a significant moment in their academic life where the impact of being lesbian or gay had figured, but which fell outside the parameters of my questions. I have incorporated material from 100 of those narratives.

As a supplement to the narrative histories and conclusions to be drawn from the questionnaires, I want to present and comment upon some relevant demographics. Given my training as a literary critic, however, my knowledge of data analysis is rudimentary. What follows therefore is descriptive in nature.

Population

By States

I asked respondents to tell me the region or state in which they teach so that I could know whether there were regional distinctions in terms of institutional attitudes toward lesbian and gay faculty. The breakdown by states reflects a genuine crosssection of United States geography. Faculty from 47 states and the District of Columbia contributed to this study. The only states not represented are Mississippi, Louisiana, and Montana.

As for the numerical distribution, I found the following: California made up 29 of the respondents; New York, 25; Minnesota, 18; Massachusetts and Ohio, 14 each; Oregon, 12; Illinois, 9; Missouri, Pennsylvania, Washington, and Wisconsin, 8 each; North Carolina, 7; Connecticut, 6; Florida, Indiana, and Michigan, 5 each; Georgia, Iowa, Maryland, Maine, and Virginia, 4 each; Colorado, Hawaii, New Jersey, Oklahoma, and Texas, 3 each; Alabama, Arkansas, Arizona, Kansas, Kentucky, Nebraska, New Mexico, and Rhode Island, 2 each; and Alaska, the District of Columbia, Delaware, Idaho, North Dakota, New Hampshire, Nevada, South Carolina, South Dakota, Tennessee, Utah, Vermont, West Virginia, and Wyoming, 1 each.

By Regions

By grouping the states into regions, I was able to determine that responses were scattered liberally over most parts of the country. Only the Great Plains region and the Southwest seemed somewhat underrepresented. A simple breakdown reveals the following:

New England (Maine, Vermont, New Hampshire, Massachusetts, New York, New Jersey, Connecticut, Rhode Island) provided 21.3

percent of all women and 23.8 percent of all men participating in the study.

The South (Florida, Georgia, Alabama, Mississippi, Louisiana, Texas, Arkansas, Tennessee, North Carolina, South Carolina, Kentucky, West Virginia) provided 7.6 percent of all women and 13.4 percent of all men responding.

Mid-Atlantic states (Virginia, District of Columbia, Maryland, Delaware, Pennsylvania) provided 7.6 percent of all women and 7.1 percent of all men responding.

The Midwest (Ohio, Indiana, Illinois, Missouri, Iowa, Minnesota, Wisconsin, Michigan) provided 32.0 percent of all women and 25.3 percent of all men responding. The Plains States (North and South Dakota, Nebraska, Kansas, Oklahoma, Montana) provided 1.5 percent of all women and 2.3 percent of all men responding.

The Northwest (Alaska, Washington, Oregon, Idaho) provided 10.6 percent of all women and 7.9 percent of all men responding, while the Southwest (New Mexico, Arizona, Colorado, Utah) provided 1.5 percent of all women and 1.5 percent of all men responding. Finally, the West (California, Nevada, Wyoming, Hawaii) provided 12.2 percent of all women and 12.6 percent of all men responding.

I attribute the fact that the highest percentage of returns came from the Midwest to my own location there. My personal network of colleagues logically is most fully developed in my own geographical locale.

Tenure in the Profession

I was most curious as to the distribution of respondents in terms of years in the profession. The majority of faculty completing my questionnaire fall within the range of 20 to 30 years (123 respondents, or 46.3 percent of the total). Those who had been in the profession between 15 and 20 years numbered 65 or 24.4 percent of the total.

The relatively small numbers of persons with more than 30 years in the academy (36 or 12.9 percent of the total) suggests one of two hypotheses. Perhaps longterm personal accommodations, including the decision to remain closeted within their home institutions, make it less likely that members of this group would choose to participate in so open a study. Or perhaps environments even more unfriendly than present-day campuses discouraged more people from entering or drove more out of the academy. Given the narratives that inform my thinking on this point, I lean toward the former explanation. Additionally, campuses have always been, relatively speaking, more congenial spaces for lesbians and gay men than have most other professional arenas in the United States.

Professorial Rank

Slightly more than half the responses to my questionnaire (137) came from faculty at the full professor rank, while 80 associate and 14 assistant professors returned a questionnaire. This skewing toward those senior in rank is encouraging because it reflects an identification with gay and lesbian issues on the parts of women and men with the longest tenures at their institutions. Such people in many cases already provide leadership in a broad band of campus activities; they have the respect of many colleagues. To find that significant numbers of these same individuals are working for greater recognition and acceptance of lesbian and gay faculty, staff, and students suggests the profound level of change that has occurred since people like me entered the profession some thirty years ago. (Given my requirement of at least 15 years in the profession, the number of assistant professors was understandably small. Additionally, 6 emeritus professors and 8 instructors filled out questionnaires.)

Since many of these same full professors report in follow-ups that they still encounter distinct hostility from various quarters of their campuses, their willingness to advocate on behalf of the intellectual and social well-being of themselves and their colleagues fills me with respect. That respect is the greater perhaps because in my own case, there never were faculty more senior than I who led the way at the University of Minnesota. I can only hope that younger academic gays and lesbians register an awareness of and appreciation for such leadership and persistence on the parts of those with long service records.

Cross-Tabulations of Data

As a lesbian feminist, my alliances have long been with other women rather than with men, even those who are gay. When I began this project, I worried that my pool would be skewed toward lesbians. Therefore, the final sex distribution delights me in its balance. The breakdown between male and female respondents is almost exactly half and half (136 women and 127 men, or 51.1 and 47.7 percent respectively).

Because of this balance, I want to present some data cross-tabulated by sex. The most glaring discrepancy turns about the interrelationship between gender and length of time in the profession. Beginning with a comfortable majority in the group with 15 to 19 years (60 to 40 percent female to male) and the category with 20 to 24 years (53.5 to 46.5 percent female to male), lesbians begin losing ground after 25 years of service. We then become a tiny fraction in the two divisions registering longest service, constituting only 30.8 percent of the group with 25 to 29 years of service and 23.1 percent of the group with 30 to 34 years. There are no lesbians at all in the group registering 35 years or longer in the academy.

The breakpoint year is 1969, a year that falls squarely within a period of more generous funding for academic hirings, during which tremendous social pressure was exerted to open up many white male preserves. Newly activated affirmative action programs for women and minorities were burgeoning well into the 1970s, so no wonder the demographics change drastically on either side of that pivotal moment. Lesbians, like many privileged white heterosexual women, benefitted from the general social upheaval of the time.

The groups that did not benefit in terms of being hired and retained by colleges and universities were American minorities. Of the 304 questionnaires returned, 213 were completed by white gays and lesbians. When I made my initial decision to canvas faculty with at least 15 years at an institution of higher learning, I feared I would be reporting on an overwhelmingly white population. Given the blatant racism at the very core of higher education's standards and practices, the total population of minority faculty with that much tenure will surely be minuscule. If the history of politically motivated homophobia within most minority communities is filtered into the picture, the likelihood that gay and lesbian members of such communities who have made their way into a college or university will come out remains slim at best. The self-identified African American (2), Hispanic or Latino (6), American Indian (3), Asian or Pacific Islander (2), and Jewish (25) faculty may even represent a higher percentage of the total possible number of such respondents than do the 213 white faculty members participating in this project. I hope these shockingly low numbers have swelled since 1969 and that a study of lesbian and gay faculty with fifteen years or less in the academy would reflect that increase.

Seven Degrees of Outness

When I initially designed the questionnaire for my project, I thought to structure a question around the various permutations of being out that might obtain for participants. My categories were these: Out not at all; Out to individual faculty; Out to students in classes; Out to students out of classes; Out to a department head or chair; Out to administrators outside the department; Out to the campus at large. My hypothesis was that most faculty would be out to colleagues and students outside classes, while relatively smaller percentages would occupy the other categories.

Descriptive data from the questionnaires reveal quite a different story. Of the 276 respondents figured into these statistics, only two are not out at all, while 184 report being out to their campuses at large. Only 146 (56.4 percent) are out to their department chair or head, and 137 (52.9 percent) are out to higher level administrators, even though 89 percent of the institutions represented by respondents to this study have antidiscrimination statements in place. In Chapter 5, I present excerpts from commentaries to explain this unsettling paradox. Rhetorical statements promising not to discriminate against gays and lesbians are not sufficient in and of themselves to create an atmosphere in which large numbers of such faculty feel secure enough to make their sexual identities known to persons holding power over them and their careers.

Finally, when assessing degrees of outness on campuses for the faculty involved in this study, a marked difference exists in the numbers of faculty who are out to students in class versus those who are out to students outside the classroom. Only 37.1 percent of the respondents say they are out to students in their classrooms, while 54.8 percent are open about their sexual identity to students outside formal classroom settings.

Campus Climate

One of the most revealing sections of the original questionnaire focused on perceived sources of support and hostility. While responses concerning support fell into a few predictable categories and were generally brief, people spoke often at length about their clear sense of who and what stands in the way of achieving hospitable and open campuses.

Individual faculty colleagues or administrative friends figure most prominently among sources of support. Groups of sympathetic students, not always gay or lesbian themselves, also make a significant contribution to how a given faculty member feels about speaking openly about issues of identity. In many cases, a single high level administrator is listed as being all-important in determining campus climate. Similarly, one open faculty member has often made a significant difference.

As more than one respondent pointed out, however, this "single savior" phenomenon is dangerously idiosyncratic and subject to change. Such a circumstance may not facilitate longterm decisions such as coming out prior to having tenure or daring to publish on gay or lesbian topics. This situation is graphically illustrated in the following response from a professor with 27 years on the same campus:

> My first five years, our president was quietly concerned. From 1969–73, great progress was being made in America for gays and lesbians. Our campus group was recognized and funded but without open support from the president. He was a nice guy who did not get in the way. Our next president, 1974–87, was a loser. He never could even say the word homosexual. He denied me a promotion, which I felt was done in spite, because of my gay visibility. Our next president, 1988–93, was an active and vocal supporter. He let the campus community know in no uncertain terms that lesbians and gays were members of this university. Great strides forward. One of his first honorary doctorates went to an 80-year-old gay in our support group. Our newest president (1994) seems to be supportive but we have not had a "test" yet. He

immediately endorsed the Task Force to End Homophobia. He attended a meeting soon after arriving, said he supported our goals and objectives, and wished us luck.

This detailed account is unnerving because of the absolute dependence of lesbian and gay faculty, staff, and students on the personal stance of a single individual. I am reminded of the North American South during slavery days when the fate of literally thousands of African slaves hung on the thin thread of whether their particular plantation master took a brutal or relatively kinder approach. No systemwide change can be forthcoming in so uncertain and fluctuating an environment. This account also demonstrates the necessity of institutional policies as a more permanent avenue to recognition and protection of minority members of academic communities.

Other sources of support mentioned include campus newspapers willing to report stories and editorially support gay and lesbian student activities. In several instances, all involving small liberal arts colleges, survey respondents speak of a strong traditional tolerance of differences among the campus' citizenry. This tradition fosters at least an appearance of acceptance of gays and lesbians. However, several faculty from such campuses assert that most of their colleagues truly want to be more tolerant and hence are willing to listen to lesbian and gay concerns, inform themselves somewhat about gay and lesbian history and culture, and actively work for curricular and policy reform.

More than one respondent listed campus librarians willing to order relevant books as being pivotal. Given the recent flowering of publications by and about gays and lesbians, such people become increasingly important if faculty are to offer courses and conduct their own research, and if students are to have access to appropriate intellectual resources.

Similarly many respondents included equal opportunity employment (EEO) officers (or similar personnel) who advocate for the inclusion of lesbians and gays in the category of faculty, staff, and students who are vulnerable to sexual harassment. These faculty are convinced that making sexual orientation a grievable category goes a long way toward safeguarding persons and careers.

Here again, a campus will need to do more than employ sympathetic EEO officers; formal and unequivocal statements and programs protecting the rights of community members on the basis of sexual orientation will have to be put into place before most faculty members will be comfortable enough to come out.

Bibliography

Anderson, Margaret. "Report on the Campus Climate Survey," University of Delaware, April 22, 1994.

Bergman, David. "The Gay and Lesbian Presence in American Literature," *Newsletter*, Heath Anthology of American Literature (Fall 1993, Number X): 5–7.

Christensen, Craig W. "The Trivial Concerns of the Invisible Minority," Association of American Law Schools Plenary Session, San Francisco, January 6, 1990.

Cohen, Jean L. "Strategy or Identity: New Theoretical Paradigms and Contemporary Social Movements," *Social Research* 52 (1995): 663–716.

Collins, Patricia Hill. *Black Feminist Thought: Knowledge, Consciousness, and the Politics of Empowerment.* Boston: Unwin Hyman, 1990.

Committee on Women Historians. "Report on the Lesbian and Gay Historians Survey," *Perspectives* (April 1993): 13–15.

Cory, Donald. *The Homosexual in America.* New York: Greenberg, 1951.

Crew, Louie. "Before Emancipation: Gay Persons as Viewed by Chairpersons in English." In *The Gay Academic,* edited by Louie Crew, 3–48. Palm Springs, CA: ETC Publications, 1978.

Crew, Louie, and Karen Keener. "Homophobia in the Academy: A Report of the Committee on Gay/Lesbian Concerns," *College English* (43.7, 1981): 682–689.

Crompton, Louis. "Politics and Education in Nebraska in 1970," Lincoln: University of Nebraska Archives, 1994.

D'Emilio, John. *Making Trouble: Essays on Gay History, Politics, and the Universities.* New York: Routledge, 1992.

Diamant, Louis, ed. *Homosexual Issues in the Workplace.* Washington, D.C.: Taylor & Francis, 1993.

Friskopp, Annette, and Sharon Silverstein. *Straight Jobs, Gay Lives.* New York: Simon and Schuster, 1995.

Gilgun, John. "Sustaining the Spirit," Professional Growth and Development Series, Missouri Western State College, St. Joseph, Missouri, April 11, 1991.

Kaplan, Claire. "Women in the Academy: An Interview with Charlotte Patterson," *In Other Words: A Publication of the University of Virginia Women's Center,* Charlottesville, Virginia: May 1993, 3 & 10.

Knopp, Lawrence. "Social Theory, Social Movements, and Public Policy: Recent Accomplishments of the Gay and Lesbian Movements in Minneapolis, Minnesota." *International Journal of Urban and Regional Research* 11 (1987): 243–261.

Levine, Martin P., and Robin Leonard. "Discrimination Against Lesbians in the Work Force," *Signs* 9 (1984): 700–710.

O'Hara, Patricia A. "An Open Letter in Response to the Campus Life Council Resolution Calling for Recognition of GLND/SMC," University of Notre Dame, Spring 1995.

Phelan, Shane. *Identity Politics: Lesbian Feminism and the Limits of Community*. Philadelphia: Temple University Press, 1989.

Plummer, Ken. "Speaking Its Name: Inventing Lesbian and Gay Studies." In *Modern Homosexualities: Fragments of Lesbian and Gay Experience*, edited by Ken Plummer. New York: Routledge, 1992.

Quality of Life Survey. "Campus Climate for Lesbian, Gay, Bisexual People on Campus." Gainesville: University of Florida, 1993–1994.

Rich, Adrienne. "Compulsory Heterosexuality and Lesbian Existence," *Signs: Journal of Women in Culture and Society*, 5(4) (1980): 631–660.

Savin-Williams, Ritch C. "Personal Reflections on Coming Out, Prejudice, and Homophobia in the Academic Workplace." In *Homosexual Issues in the Workplace*, edited by Louis Diamant, 225–241. Washington, D.C.: Taylor & Francis, 1993.

Schneider, Beth E. "Coming Out at Work: Bridging the Private/Public Gap," *Work and Occupations* 13 (1986): 463–487.

Sherrill, Kenneth. "Presentation of Findings of the Committee on the Status of Lesbians and Gays in the Profession," American Political Science Association Conference, New York, 1994.

Taylor, Verta and Nicole C. Raeburn. "Identity Politics as High-Risk Activism: Career Consequences for Lesbian, Gay and Bisexual Sociologists." *Social Problems* 42 (1995): 252–273.

Winfield, Liz, and Susan Spielman. *Straight Talk About Gays in the Workplace: Creating an Inclusive, Productive Environment for Everyone in Your Organization*. AMACOM (American Management Association), 1995.

Woods, James. *The Corporate Closet: The Professional Lives of Gay Men in America*. New York: Free Press, 1993.